Little
Saint

Little Saint

Hannah Green

RANDOM HOUSE
NEW YORK

Library of Congress Cataloging-in-Publication Data

Green, Hannah.
Little Saint : / by Hannah Green.
p.   cm.
ISBN 0-394-56595-9
1. Foy, Saint, ca. 290–303.   2. Christian child saints—
France—Conques Biography.   3. Conques (Aveyron,
France)—Religious life and customs.   4. France—
Religious life and customs.   I. Title.
BX4700.F37G74   2000
270.1'092—dc21
[B]   99-23023

Random House website address: www.atrandom.com
*Printed in the United States of America
on acid-free paper*

24689753

FIRST EDITION

*Photograph on title page: Rue Charlemagne,
Conques. Photograph by Bill Barrette.
Line drawing: John Wesley*

Book design by Carole Lowenstein

For Jack

———

Golden Spark, Little Saint:
My Book of the
Hours of Sainte Foy

Black darkness covered   with clouds God's body
That radiant splendour   Shadow went forth.

      —*The Dream of the Rood*

Contents

List of Photographs

All photographs by Bill Barrette

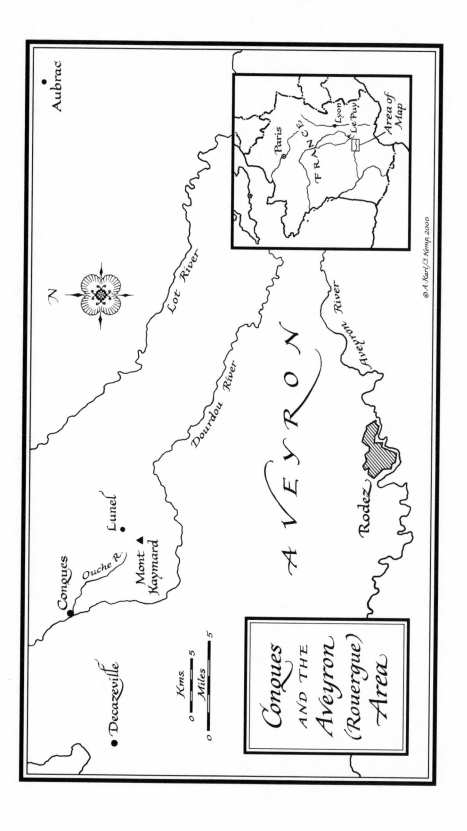

Aubrac

N

Lot River

Conques

Ouche R.

Lunel

Mont
Kaymard

Decazeville

Dourdou River

A V E Y R O N

Aveyron River

Rodez

Paris

F R A N C E

Lyon

Le Puy

Area of
Map

© A. Karl/J. Kemp, 2000

Kms.   5
0

Miles   5
0

Conques
AND THE
Aveyron
(Rouergue)
Area

Author's Note

The time is in the continuous present of a June day. It is 1979, although certain passages apply to 1978 or to other moments and centuries, at Conques, France, where, "the present lasts so short a time there is no count nor memory of it, while the past, both the near and distant, wells up at every moment into the consciousness of the living, whose lives proceed onward, close to the mysterious presence."

She is the sacred center. Around her the wheel of the story with its thousand starry spokes spins. It might begin at any time, from the hour when she was born at Agen in December of the year 290 to the hour of her martyr-death less than thirteen years later, and at as many shining points as there are gemstones on her statue or silver nails in arabesques on the coffer that holds her body's bones; but the story opens now in the mountains of the Rouergue, here at Conques, where, since 866 her bones have been enshrined and guarded.

We came first as travelers, Jack and I, in the springtime of 1975, to have our hearts caught unaware—Jack a painter, a Californian by birth, I a writer, an Ohioan from an old Swedenborgian and Episcopalian background, a stranger to saints; and yet I was given through Sainte Foy, in this remote and ancient place of pilgrimage, the gift of seeing into that zone which has been held sacred since the beginning of human consciousness.

I

Morning: Descent into the Treasure

On the far side of the cloister in the long, chapel-like room called the Treasure, she sits on her throne—a small stiff gold figure robed in gold and covered with jewels and crowned with a golden diadem.

Up the hill, Jack stands tall beside the fountain behind the little house we have rented for the summer. Here we are once again after several returns, here we are in the month of June 1979, not yet St. John's Day. Jack is about to mend his bicycle tire. This afternoon we are going to Lunel.

The springwater flows forth through the mouth of a mask deep in a niche in the stone embankment of the hillside and splashes into the round basin below. Sunlight quivers on the surface of the water, and dapples of watery sunshine fly like lunar moths on the stones of the niche above, and across the mottled face of the mask, which resembles the grimacing head that guards the church from the outer wall of the tribune on the north, high above the western entrance. The bells ring for eleven o'clock.

Sunbrowned and strong, Jack takes the inner tube in his competent hands, good hands, and plunges it into the water.

"*Ah, mais il est beau! Il est fin! Il est un bon garçon!*" old Madame Benoit was saying this morning, smiling her smile of infinite sweetness, her eyes as blue as the sky, her face and her hair as white as the clouds. I was in her tiny apartment in the old convent for a few minutes to pick up a book she wanted to lend me. "I am not afraid of death," she said quietly. "I have my faith." And she lifted her right hand in a gesture like a bird flying off, a gesture so perfect that I could see as she did it how her soul would fly out of the window and up, and she would go down there—*là bas*—to the cemetery below the church. She waved her hand in that direction. "I have my reservation," she said with a mixture of pride and humor.

Sometimes she speaks triumphantly: "I will go on the cloak of the Virgin," she says.

Just now I remember to tell Jack. "Madame Benoit was saying earlier this morning, 'Oh, but he is handsome, he is fine, he is a good boy. Everyone agrees!'" Jack laughs, pleased. He will be fifty in November. But Madame Benoit is ninety-one.

Ninety-one! *"Quatre-vingt-onze!"*

"Quatre-vingt-onze et un demi," said my friend Rosalie, correcting me, nodding her head tenderly up and down. (Not in Madame Benoit's presence.)

> *La Rosalie de bon matin*
> *S'en va t'au jardin*
> *Pour y culir la brioulete*
> *La belle fleur . . .*
>
> One fine morning Rosalie
> Goes out to her garden
> To cut the brioulete,
> That pretty flower

So sings Madame Benoit, who sings, who sings, who has a song for every occasion, and who, ninety-one and a half, and tiny and plump and limber as a rag doll in her soft clothes, her soft shoes, goes with her cane up and down the steep streets of Conques with a swiftness and agility so remarkable that someone—I could not make out who she was talking about, but someone, another woman—had gotten very excited and somewhat angry, declaring she was on this account *"Pas normale."* *"Pas normale!"* she repeated, echoing her friend's anger, and laughing.

The other day when Madame Benoit was walking with her cousin Madame Fabre, from whom we rent our house, out the Rue du Château, beyond the old Porte du Foumouze with its Romanesque fountain and, a little farther on, the lacy iron cross that rises above an ancient stone Virgin, now beheaded, there, Madame Fabre told us, Madame Benoit tripped and fell down on her knees in a mud puddle. Madame Fabre lifted her hands to her face to show us how aghast she'd been. But in that very moment, Madame Benoit turned her head and looked up. "I am doing the Stations of the Cross," she said.

Madame Benoit is a *force*. I am moved by her and drawn to her. It

makes me feel warm to sit near her. Her breath smells of strawberry jam. Sometimes she says, like a litany, in her low, intimate
voice, "Sainte Foy, holy martyr who died for Christ, Sainte Foy pro-
tects us here at Conques," and she smiles her smile of pride.

And besides she has a memory that goes back further than her
ninety-one years, straight back through her mother and her grandmother and her great-grandmother, so she can tell you, for instance, the story of the great complot of 1791 when the people of
Conques saved the statue of Sainte Foy and the rest of the golden
Treasure from the soldiers who were coming to confiscate it. "Oh,
there was a terrible storm that night," she says. "There was thunder
and lightning and the rain fell in torrents, the streets turned into
rushing rivers and veritable cascades. No one dared to go out . . ."

The bells ring eleven a second time. It is their way. To the south,
a quarter of a mile off and up in the sun-green afternoon, the
wooden cross at the high outermost point of the gorge of the
Ouche stands tall and thin and slightly askew against the sky. Above
us bees hum in the wisteria that grows over the fence along the
wall. Below us the stone roofs glint in the sunlight.

Les lauzes they call these stones cut from the schist rock and laid like
slates in a scalloped pattern as beautiful as shining fish scales across
the steep roofs of Conques. The schist stones are blue-gray with a
sheen of silver (mica) or rose-beige with gleams of gold (mica), and
the dark lichens and mosses have grown over them, as they have
over the craggy rocks that jut forth from the mountainsides here
and rise up like castle ruins in the chasms. Cut in irregular slabs and
laid on their sides and bound and covered with the pinkish mortar
and stucco made from the red sand of the Dourdou, these are the
stones from which the houses of Conques are built.

Carrying my notebook and pencil in my tiny deerskin Indian
bag, I descend in among them, down through the roses, down the
stairs that form the street—*la ruelle*—that runs past our house, and
down through the narrow stone streets below. From above, from
their kitchens half-shuttered against the noon heat, come the happy
voices of the Conquois finishing their lunches.

The Place de l'Église is still empty. And it is silent except for the hoarse whistling screeches of the dark swifts soaring, wheeling, darting into and out from the ancient yellowed walls of the basilica; and the splashing of the Plô—the spring whose virtues were already praised in the twelfth-century *Guide for the Pilgrim to Saint James of Compostelle*. Sainte Foy of Conques had become a major stop along the Via Podiensis, the route of Notre Dame du Puy, one of the four pilgrim routes that led across France toward that far Finisterre, end of the earth to the west, beyond the Pyrenees, where, toward the end of the eighth century, the body of Saint James was discovered by the hermit Pelayo beneath an ancient shrine on a thickly wooded hill over which a great star hovered.

"The Burgundians and the Teutons who go to Saint James by the Via Podiensis must go to venerate the relics of Sainte Foy, virgin and martyr," writes the author of the *Guide* (traditionally thought to be Aymery Picaud); and he tells us the manner of her martyr-death at Agen and that of the blessed Caprais, bishop of the town, whom she inspired. "Finally," he writes, "the very precious body of the blessed Faith, virgin and martyr, was entombed with honor in a valley called, in the common speech, Conques (Conquas), and over her sepulcher was built a beautiful basilica, where for the glory of God, even up to our own day, the Rule of Saint Benedict is observed with the greatest care; many graces are granted to those who come to venerate the relics of Sainte Foy, both to those who come in good health and to the sick; in front of the doors of the church there flows forth a most excellent source whose virtues are more admirable than anyone can say. Her fête is celebrated on the sixth of October."

When we first came here, in 1975, we came from the south, from Provence, where we had been staying that winter in a house in the olive groves of the wild white stone Alpilles. It was our first year abroad together and Jack and I had fallen in love with Provence, with the country around us as far as Les Baux and Glanum and St. Rémy and Avignon, as far as Arles and the Camargue and Les Saintes Maries de la Mer at the edge of the sea. It was a kind of rapturous pagan love that extended outward to become a delight in all of France and the desire to see and learn all we could.

Yet an image of Sainte Foy, gleaned almost by chance from a conversation among friends standing on the red Kirghiz rug in front of our fire one winter evening in the house on the Route du Destet, had caught my imagination, and I felt we must go to Conques to see her. It was as if I felt her to be a beloved sacred doll I had lost a long time before. I had not seen a photograph, but somehow—stiff and gold and encrusted with jewels—she began to burn like a garnet with her own light in the night of my mind. There was something in my image of her that was deeper, older, more secret to me, more central, than the joyous openness of my love for Provence and its mystique.

I read what little I could find about her in our green Michelin *Guide to the Auvergne,* and in Muirhead's *Blue Guide to the South of France* (1926), given to us in New York by older writer friends, who had lived in France in the twenties, among the Surrealists, as we in the seventies sailed off on our fellowship year; but had I learned more in advance, I still would not have been prepared.

Coming here we had crossed the Cevennes and stopped at Albi for two nights along the way, and the smooth and sinuous red-brick fortress cathedral at Albi was still strong in my mind when we arrived in Conques late that April afternoon.

All day, as we drove northeast across the high rolling green plains from Albi to Rodez, it was sunny, but twenty-five miles north of

Rodez, suddenly, after St. Cyprien, we entered the stone gorges of the Dourdou and after several miles began to climb the steep ascent to Conques. It had been raining shortly before we arrived. The streets were wet. The slate-stone roofs glistened with water. The air felt clean, like mountain air, and when we opened the casement windows of our room in the Hôtel Sainte Foy and looked out onto the steep roof across the narrow street, and up to the yellow stone church looming silent above it, I thought we had arrived in heaven.

I was in a trance of joy as we rushed out, for it was nearly six by then, to see the statue of Sainte Foy before closing time. We bought our tickets and hurried across the cloister, barely pausing.

Then we entered the Treasure. And there, in that room which she makes holy and mysterious, there she was, beyond the high arch, on her dais. There she was all alone, like a fragile child reaching out, entranced.

In that stilled moment, awed and torn with tenderness, the top gone from my head, I saw not only her, Sainte Foy, but shadowy figures around her. They were standing, tall and slightly bowed, dark presences without substance, like guardian angels, not clearly defined but there, even as the monks who watched over her through the ages, even as the Ancient of Days.

I could feel the stirrings of that long procession of human beings who had come here down through time to fall on their knees and pray for her help, again and again in their devotion renewing her life—this eternal girl-child, daughter becoming woman, who held within herself the promise of all that is good and beautiful and healing, and all that is bountiful.

For a long while I did not think that I could speak of this, not even to Jack. And even after I began to write this, my Book of Sainte Foy, I still thought for a time that what I had seen then was too sacred, too tremulously personal, to be written down and woven into the work. I did not then know from whom it came, my vision, entering my mind's heart in a wave of light, and engendering all that would grow from it—at first through reading, and then through our returns to Conques, and our long sojourns.

Now, crossing the cloister, I watch a breeze flowing upward through the leafy green woods of the gorge wall beyond the Ouche. The chestnuts are coming into bloom and soon the woods will be burgeoning with the pale yellow sprays of their lovely Roman-candle blossoms. A dog starts to bark down at the trout farm at the bottom of the gorge.

When I enter the Treasure, Père André in his white monk's robe is sitting in the chair in his tiny library, which adjoins the entrance. An ample, solid man of more than sixty years, gentle and balding, he has fallen asleep for a moment after lunch. I pray for his health as I pass, and for his long life. He has been very kind.

No one is in the room as I enter, no one save Sainte Foy, that is, and I walk directly up to the raised altarlike place beyond the high arch where she sits, holding out her delicate gold hands, which grasp tiny tube-vases for flowers, her arms outstretched from the elbow, shyly, as if to receive one, yet a trifle tentatively. One must come close, but one may come no closer than the invisible flowers.

Today one of the lights that illumines her has gone out, and she has never looked lovelier. Shadows become her—little virgin, very pure, who died for her faith when she was but twelve. So they sang of her in sacred canticles, for so she answered the Proconsul Dacien, though she knew that she would die for it: "My name," she said, "is Faith. And I am a Christian."

That was at Agen in the year 303 in the reign of the Emperor Diocletian, at the time of the last of the terrible persecutions—the Great Persecution it was called.

And she is here now, for her bones worked miracles. She was brought to Conques, to this remote abbey in the mountains of the Rouergue, from Agen on the Garonne, where the coastal plains begin more than one hundred miles to the west. She was brought here in about 866 by the monk Aronisde, called since that time the Pious Robber and Author of the Furtive Translation. It was her holy bones he stole, together with other remains—her belt, a small purse, a few amber beads, and bits of woven cloth, the precious tissues the Christians had used to wipe the blood from her skin when, in the night of her death, secretly, they took her body from the public square to a hidden place away from the city, high on the rock plateau called Pompejac.

"There they could not bury her body," they would sing in the "Song of Sainte Foy," written down in the Provençal (or the ancient Occitan, as they prefer to say now in this country) of the eleventh century. "They made a kind of nest for it like that which the ostrich makes in summer, and entombed her thus in the rocks. They wept, grieving with their tears so piously, watering the ground around her humble sepulcher. They had no means to honor her better. Sorrowful they were, and miserable, grieving. They were anguished, like fugitives, guarding her tomb by day and by night, afraid the evil would come again."

And she is here, the bones of her head within the heart of her statue . . . here, looking out of her smooth gold face with her slightly slanted obsidian eyes, looking out from across the centuries with an expression of majestic courage, with the expression of one whose mind is on eternity, while yet she hears the beating of our hearts.

Protected by glass on her dais, still somehow the energy of life flows into her through her raised and partly open hands, through her thumbs and forefingers and the tiny tube-vases, the unseen flowers, and outward toward whoever may come to her.

She is a touching figure, less than three feet in height; her head is large, her body small, thin. Not a likeness in any ordinary sense, her statue is, rather, symbolic. It is a shrine. And in some mystic way it suggests to the mind's eye more strongly than any imagined likeness could the presence of Sainte Foy herself as she was, with her young fresh skin and the radiance, the life, in her face, the light, and as she is: bone and spirit come to God.

She sits like a sacred child bravely bearing the rich and fragile finery made to adorn her, like a queen, sovereign yet delicate, tender and gentle, but with a wild, mysterious power. Bride of Christ, she holds the Mystery of the Word within her—*La Majesté de Sainte Foy, Maiestas Sanctae Fidis,* seated on her throne, bearing gold and precious stones, in carved intaglios and cameos, the splendor and magic of the ages, come to her from ancient times and places far off

to the East and the South, from Rome, from Egypt, from Greece
and the Holy Land, from Persia, Byzantium, the Spain of the
Moors, and from the griffin-guarded land of the Scythians, treasures of kings and the emperors of old, treasures brought home to
France by the Crusaders, treasures of the barbarian warriors, and
of the ancient Gallo-Romans, those poets and masters of eloquence, who once traveled the whole civilized world and returned
to their vast estates with their vineyards and their fine libraries,
which then, in the fifth and sixth centuries, were ravaged, burned,
taken over entirely by the invaders from the north, treasures plun-
dered, bought, traded, guarded in castles and holy places, bestowed, received, treasures carried off secretly by the fleeing
Gaulish refugees and handed down from generation to generation
from antiquity through the Dark Ages, until they came to rest on
her, brought to her by the pilgrims from far and near who came in
their need and with their fears to adore her in fervor and seek her
protection, for her healings and her blessings knew no bounds.

Sainte Foy, radiant saint! Still after centuries the bones of her
mind, the stuff of her soul breathes her life, her presence, into this,
her reliquary statue, which is the work of many hands over many
hundred years, all drawn to and inspired by this little holy martyr.

"*Génératrice* of art," Père André calls her. The exact date of the consecration of her statue is lost; the origin of its head is shrouded in
mystery, but the statue was present already in the year 940 when, it
is recorded in the abbey's cartulary, Étienne II, Abbot of Conques,
the son of Robert, Viscount of the Auvergne, having been elected
Bishop of Clermont-Ferrand, and soon to complete the cathedral
he was building there, prepared to effect the solemn translation of
her mortal remains from Conques to Clermont-Ferrand. But she
would not be moved. She was heavy as a mountain and as firmly im-
planted.

Three times they gathered in as many weeks, the monks of the
abbey, the bishops and notable lords of the Rouergue and all the Auvergne, three times they gathered, having fasted and cleansed
themselves of all sins and possible sinners, three times they gath-

ered before the altar of the Holy Savior, and though each time their prayers were more fervent, and the chanting of the litanies and the psalms was more heavenly and prolonged, still, when they attempted to remove her, neither her statue nor her holy casket could be budged, not even an inch. The bells of the church rang out and angels sang somewhere aloft as it was concluded by the learned churchmen that it was her wish to remain where she was at Conques and God's will that she do so.

The work on her statue—all wonderfully wrought and filigreed and inlaid with jewels and precious enamels—went on over seven hundred years. The latest scholarly investigation—that undertaken by Jean Taralon, Director General of the Bureau of Historic Monuments, at the time of her restoration in 1954—determined that the body of wood had received its first covering of gold before the ninth century was out. Her arms and hands and the tiny tube-vases were fashioned in the sixteenth century, replacing earlier arms and hands with bracelets. But the head is older. It is thought to date from the fourth century, the century of her martyrdom, and is made of gold repoussé laid over with gold leaf. Although the fashioning of the hair makes the work appear to be Byzantine, and the head is thought to have been originally that of a late Roman god-emperor, laurel-crowned, the face resembles the mask of a Celtic god or goddess; through this head originally not her own, through its dark enamel eyes, blue as midnight, her spirit emanates with its mysterious, radiant calm.

"*Génératrice* of art," Père André says again, as one who causes art to happen, to be generated, and he speaks of "her luminous life of prayer."

Somehow her genius breathed through the hands of that first worker who began to give her shape, so that as he formed her body from two pieces of the root of the yew tree, joining them at mid-thigh, working with his chisel, smoothing over with his rasp, hollowing out the cavity in her back to enclose the bones of her head, he caught the very presence of her spirit. Though he was not skilled at carving statues, but rather (it is thought) had worked his lifelong making wooden shoes and other useful objects, still, by the very accidents of his innocence, and with his innate awe and love, he captured

her very breath and her particular power; and when the god-head
he'd held and measured was fitted over the wooden neck he'd shaped
and smoothed for it, her head, which centuries later critics would
note was too large for her body, was tilted in such a way (thought also
to be awkward) that it would convey the sense of her listening, with
Christ encompassed in her rapt mind, the skull of which, bound with
strips of silver, and wrapped in imperial purple silk brocade in Byzantium, was ritually enclosed within her statue.

By the presence of her relic, then, was she mystically there to
imbue the antique head of her statue with her own grace and
trancelike power, which could be, was, and even now sometimes is
thaumaturgic.

"*Génératrice*," pronounces Père André. She was here as magnet,
here as source. To her came the crown of Charles the Child to become the crown of her martyrdom, and the golden doves of the
Abbot of Beaulieu to adorn her throne. To her came the builders,
the sculptors, the poets. To her came the goldsmiths who worked
through the years embroidering her golden gown and outlining her
full falling sleeves, her collar, her hem, with pearls of gold, and setting the whole with gemstones of every color until, encrusted, she
shone with a light like that of the heavenly Jerusalem—with emeralds, marvelously luminous; with rubies and garnets which, the ancients believed, shone with their own light; with sapphires, pearls,
topazes, opals, and hyacinths blue as the heavens; with jade and
Byzantine bloodstones, with beryl green as sea foam; with jasper of
magical properties, and nicolo; with carnelians, and amethysts, ribboned agates, and cloisonné; with onyx and sardonyx, which, with
its three colors, red, white, and black, signified, according to the
eleventh-century poet Marbodus, those who carried in their minds
the memory of Christ's passion. To her came crystals clear as water,
and crystal balls like those found with the grave goods of Childeric,
the last of the pagan Merovingian kings, who died in 482. To her
came one who thought to set the aquamarine in the shape of a tear
in the center of her forehead, amidst the gold-beaded net that binds
her hair—the tear she shed at the last moment, this young girl who
so loved life she went, fired in her love, insisting on the truth, into
her passion and eternity.

Brought before the proconsul Dacien at Agen on the sixth of October in the year 303, she said, "My name is Faith, and I am a Christian."

She said, "Since I was a little child and first learned of Him, I have loved the Lord Jesus Christ."

She said, "I have served Him in every way as best I could."

And Dacien—for the girl they had led to stand trial before him was so young, of noble blood, and the most perfect beauty, luminous as a white flower and radiant with roses in her cheeks—Dacien said, "Your mother and father await you now in the house of your birth. Think of the grief you would cause them. You, their beloved daughter, their firstborn."

"It is Him my soul loveth," she said. "His name is Adonai."

("Fides, your earthly time passed as swiftly as that of a flower that lives but a day," opens a canticle of old, sung by the Christians in her great church.)

"Come, come, my child," said Dacien, "sacrifice to Diana as your parents would have you do."

"I pray you, Lord, help now as you promised," she said softly, and with her three fingers she made the sign of the cross.

"No," she said in a voice of great strength. "No, I will not."

Then Dacien spoke seductively. Quietly, almost whispering, he said, "Ere long your parents will prepare for you the wedding gown and ointments. The bridegroom will await you, and in the nuptial chamber the lamps will burn for you. The perfume of love will be there, the branches of hawthorn, and love you will breathe as your bridegroom embraces you. The beloved task of bearing children will be yours, and you will be blessed."

And Fides, her voice clear and natural, replied, "I want to take pleasure in my Lord, it is with Him I want to laugh and be gay, it is Him I would take as bridegroom, whether it pleases you or not; for

to me He is fair, to me He is altogether lovely. I will not lie: If I cannot have Him, there is nothing that will heal me."*

"Come now, my child," said Dacien. "You speak so charmingly. I
have no wish to torture a girl as tender as you. Come sacrifice to
the goddess, sacrifice to Diana. You need only reach out your fingers and touch a grain of the salt and the incense placed on the altar
there before you. Do that. Just that. And I shall release you."

A hush fell over the mob. Fides did not move her hand.

"Thus would the State have it!" said Dacien.

Holding her young head high there amid the symbols of power,
Fides spoke to the tribunal, and not only Dacien but the whole immense crowd assembled in the square at Agen that day heard her.
"Your gods and goddesses are but demons," she said. "They are evil
spirits. As their statues are the work of men's hands, they are the
product of men's imaginings. Neither are your emperors gods:
Diocletian as Jupiter and Maximian, his Hercules, are only men,
and corrupt men at that. As are you, cruel Lord Dacien.

"There is but one God—He who came down from heaven for us
and made himself man very gifted, who healed the sick and the lep-
rous and gave us baptism in water, He who suffered and died for us
on the cross, and rose again from the dead, destroying dark hell,
and went unto the Father.

"No, I will not sacrifice to Diana, nor will I touch your incense."

And as the torture was prepared, and again later, walking toward
the block, her head held high—the exquisite skin—she spoke as
she would in her Song, saying, "It is Him I would take as bridegroom . . . for to me He is fair, to me He is altogether lovely."

>Sainte Foy, virgin and martyr, pray for us.
>Sainte Foy, beloved of God, pray for us.

* So have her words, recalling the imagery of the "Song of Songs," come down to us in
the "Song of Sainte Foy." It was understood in the Middle Ages by the Doctors of the
Church that as in the "Song of Songs" the perfume of the bridegroom lured and excited
the bride's attendants, so the perfume of the martyrs, of flowers such as Sainte Foy,
lured humankind toward the love of God, and that miracles, together with the presence
of holy relics with their power, made certain statues, places, temples, however pagan in
their origins, sacred, for miracles proved beyond the shadow of a doubt that God held
them in His favor and worked His wonders through them.

Prayers whispered across the ages. Prayers whispered in their time in a thousand chapels dedicated to Sainte Foy across the face of Europe and along the great pilgrim route to Saint Jacques de Compostelle. Prayers chanted in Latin and sung as hymns, prayers shouted, cried out, sobbed forth in the language of the people here, in the langue d'oc, prayers borne here silently by those who came with their precious stones to pin them, as it were, like flowers, with their burning hopes, onto her golden gown.

So Bernard, the scholar-churchman of Angers, found her when he arrived not long after the turn of the millennium (when many men had thought the world would end), and indeed, when he first saw his Sancta Fides gleaming in her candlelit sanctuary, he was quite shocked.

He had come south from Angers by way of Poitiers, Limoges, Tulle, and Aurillac; the journey had taken weeks, and the last part, up into the mountains of the Auvergne, was the most arduous. Three days after he and his companion left Aurillac, having crossed the River Lot, still to this day called, farther upstream, by its ancient Celtic name, Olt, they entered the Rouergue, the ancient country of the Ruthenians, and arrived toward evening at the abbey of Conques, where they were led to the place reserved for the relics of Sainte Foy.

"There," Bernard wrote in his *Liber Miraculorum Sanctae Fidis,* written between 1013 and 1028, "in a space too confined a multitude of people was pressed together, all kneeling on the ground in front of her statue, addressing their supplications to it.

"The crowd was so thick," he said, "I was unable to fall on my knees. I had to remain standing to address my prayer to her." And this he did very carefully, making it clear in the words of his prayer that it was to Sainte Foy herself and not to her statue that he addressed his prayer: "O Sancta Fides, thou whose relic is enclosed in this statue, help me on the Day of Judgment" *(Sancta Fides, cujus pars corporis in presenti simulachro requiescit, sucurre michi in die judicii).*

Then he turned to his companion, the *ecolâtre* Bernier, and gave him a significant look, saying privately so he could not be overheard, "Venus! Diana! A pagan idol!"

And afterward, he reported in his *Liber Miraculorum Sanctae Fidis,* he regretted this exceedingly. He said that his first impressions had been insensitive, that his understanding had not been entirely clear. "This statue is not a worldly idol," he wrote. "It is not an object of worship in itself, it is not an oracle one consults or an idol for sacrifice. It is, rather, a pious memorial in front of which the faithful heart implores the saint with the greatest fervor. Even more it is a shrine which encloses the entire head of the holy martyr—it is only that the goldsmith has simply given this shrine a human form. Furthermore, God Himself intervenes to justify the worship given this statue, by working numerous and shining miracles for those who kneel down to invoke the martyr. Not only that, He punishes, sometimes in the most terrible ways, those who attempt to do her harm, or even those who neglect to render her honor when they find themselves in front of her."

Yet it was no accident that the goldsmiths had given Sainte Foy's head-reliquary a human form, and in the thirteenth chapter of the first *Book of the Miracles of Sainte Foy,* Bernard explains that "in all the country of the Auvergne, the Rouergue, and the country of Toulouse, as well as in other neighboring countries, it is, after an ancient custom, the practice that each church has had a statue made of its patron saint in gold or silver or some other metal, according to its resources, and there the people have enclosed with honor the head of their saint or some other part of their saint's body. This statue has become, to all appearances, the object of their worship.

"I do not wish to injure anyone's feelings, but such a rite," he says, "is considered by some learned men to be the remains of worship rendered of old to the images of the gods, or rather, I should say, demons. I also thought this way, though I regret it now. In fact, I was at first incensed at the sight of such worship—of a multitude of men and women provided with reason praying with abandoned fervor to an idol—without words, without sense. I thought it absolutely opposed to Christian law.

"When my companion and I first arrived in this country and went to venerate the relics of Saint Géraud at Aurillac in the abbey church that bears his name, we saw on the altar a statue of this saint resplendent with gold and the most precious stones. His face was so fashioned as to make him appear to be alive, and his eyes seemed to fix themselves on whosoever was before him praying. The people even pretended to discern in the *éclat* of his regard whether or not their prayers would be answered.

"I couldn't keep from smiling. (I confess my error.) I turned to my companion, Bernier, and said in Latin so that I could not be overhead, 'What do you say, brother, about this idol? Jupiter or Mars—would they have found this statue unworthy of them?'

"Bernier, who shared my feelings on the subject of this statue, began praising its traits with lavish irony. Not without reason. Since in the universal church worship is due to the supreme and sovereign God alone, it is the custom to fashion such statues only of our Lord on the cross so that His image may excite our pity for His Passion. To bring the saints to the memory and to the eyes of men, one must be content with veridical writing from the book or with painting that reproduces the saint's image on walls covered with colors. To make such statues of the saints—we would not know how to tolerate it except for the fact that in the countries where this is done, the custom is of such antiquity and is so deeply embedded in the souls of the simple people that it is irreformable.

"Had my companion and I been overheard casting aspersions at the statue of Saint Géraud, we would have been fallen upon by the people, stoned, and driven from town. We would have been considered criminals."

Bernard, in coming up into these mountains of the Auvergne and Rouergue, into the lands of the ancient Celtic peoples, had come upon a custom the origin of which was older than Rome, older than Christ, for whom the saints had given their lives. For to the relics of their deeply Christian saints these people brought their age-old beliefs in the magic power of the human head preserved, and in a vivid afterlife. As formerly they had taken their gold and silver as votive offerings to sink down into the sacred lakes and sources, so now they brought them to their saints, who lived on in their head-reliquary statues, which resembled the masks and images of their ancient gods and goddesses; and the religious fervor in the blood of these people was touched by the hand of God and transformed into Christian awe: Miracles occurred.

Here, then, to this wild gorge, to this place named Conques by

Louis the Pious, to this green chasm where the ancient sacred source the Plô with its healing waters gushed forth before the abbey church doors, they came to the shrine of Sainte Foy, and the blind could see again, the deaf could hear, the paralyzed could walk once more, the crooked stood straight, and those covered with sores were smooth and sweet of skin again as they had been in the spring of their youth. Dead babies in the arms of their weeping fathers and mothers woke and lived to play their childhoods through.

For in this apple-scented abbey, with its bees on the hillside making their honey, with its terraced gardens of herbs and roses, its fruit trees and vegetables and grains, and its vines with their grapes ripening in clusters, its many springs all flowing pure, and the rushing waters of the Ouche filling the valley with soothing sound; here in this abbey founded and endowed in the year 801 by Louis the Pious, then King of Aquitaine, together with the holy hermit Dadon, who dwelled here in penance; here in this place with its hundreds of monks—goldsmiths and ironworkers and artisans and builders and workers of every sort, as well as contemplatives, scholars, poets, and scribes, all devoting themselves to God following the rule of Saint Benedict; here, as in other places too in these ages when the shrines of the interceding saints were like portals into the halls of the supernatural, angels sang and church bells rang out and the Holy Ghost was everywhere present, for this was where Sainte Foy was, enshrined in majesty in her statue; and had not Jesus said, "He that believeth on me, the works that I do he shall do also, and greater than these shall he do, for I go unto the Father."

"Her statue is of antique confection [*ab antiquo fabricata*]," Bernard wrote, "yet it would be considered the most ordinary of jewels were it not for the fact that since the amazing miracle [about 982] performed in favor of Guibert, called the Illuminé [the restoration of his sight], riches have come to the monastery, poor until then, in such quantities that not only has her statue itself been entirely re-covered with gold and her gown ornamented with great art to its very borders with myriads of precious stones elegantly set, but her head is crowned with a rich diadem of gold starred with jewels; golden bracelets decorate her golden arms; and her throne, which is surmounted by two golden doves, fairly disappears beneath plaques of gold and the glimmer of the gemstones set thereon. Furthermore the many glories of the Treasure that surrounds her have been fashioned, and, too, the great altar of the Holy Savior, nearly six yards in length, has been covered with gold. . . . Although at the church of Saint Martin in Tours there are two altars as large as this, the gold here has been worked with an art so exquisite it would be impossible to find another so beautiful—except on the summits of heaven.

"Not a ring or a fibula is left in the province," he adds, "so thorough has been our saint in her quest for gold and gemstones."

Now, another millennium almost gone by, I stand before her in this museum, where she looks out toward the shadowy walls on which hang the tapestries that tell the story of her passion, and between them in lighted cases the Treasure is displayed.

A foreigner in her country, I come awkwardly, an anachronism, I suppose, and yet she came to light my life, to lead me into regions heretofore unknown to me, and I could not for the world give her up.

She came as a gift. Although since the time of my confirmation in a white dress at the age of thirteen in the Episcopal Church, I had loved and revered the language of the Nicene Creed—"God of God, Light of Light, Very God of Very God"—and although I almost swooned over the mystery of Holy Communion and its accompanying language spoken by the tall bishop of Southern Ohio and over phrases like "Therefore with Angels and Archangels, and with all the company of heaven, we laud and magnify thy glorious Name; evermore praising thee, and saying HOLY, HOLY, HOLY, Lord God of Hosts, Heaven and earth are full of Thy glory . . . ," and although I had repeated how many times in my life, "I believe in the Holy Ghost: The holy Catholic Church; the Communion of Saints . . . ," I did not understand the meaning of "the Communion of Saints," and it seemed that almost nothing in my prior religious life, which had remained, I think, peripheral, or in the content of my education had prepared me for this work, this devotion. For in some way without my knowing or preparing, I had been coming toward her my life long, and all that she would bring with her.

"At first I didn't see what it was that so excited you," Jack said. "I thought Conques was a sad place. I remember looking out of our hotel window in the evening after dinner and seeing our waiter come out into the empty street and walk off toward wherever he stayed and thinking what a bleak place this was. Sad."

And at that very moment I had probably been lying on our bed and reading in a stilled and blessed state, finding out what I could from the books we had picked up in the abbey bookstore. Reading French was still for me like trying to make things out through a thick mist, but with the help of my old college *Petite Larousse Illustrée* and battered Funk and Wagnalls French-English/English-French dictionary, I found that there were stories that sprang from Sainte Foy and were spun around her like the gold filigree, the beading and the gemstones around her crown, her collar, the borders of her sleeves, and the hem of her dalmatic robe, like the Gothic cincture round her waist, the shrine, through the glass quatre-foil cross of which we see, surrounded by the winged symbols of the Four Evangelists, the cloth that enwraps the bones of her soul.

I came to see how she lighted these stories with the breath of her life even as she gave her life with her death to Christ, and I was filled with the vision of a book of Sainte Foy.

Albi, with its fortress cathedral, I understood from the first, was about power, while Conques and Sainte Foy were about survival.

This insight had for me a kind of shining urgency, but I was working on another book, and more than a year would pass before I really began my studies for Sainte Foy.

For the time being those April days—we had come to stay for one night but we ended up staying three—I was on a holiday journey with Jack, and we fell into a happy rhythm of going in the morning to see Sainte Foy and the Treasure, then walking through the cloister and around the back of the perfect Romanesque church, delighting in the forms of the seven radiating chapels of its *chevet* (apse), and walking on round past the stark, cold northern wall of the church to reach the western entrance, where we gazed up at the great Last Judgment of the early twelfth century.

We entered the portals beneath it into the cool stone depths of
Sainte Foy de Conques. In the nave we stood rapt, going then
slowly forward, moved by the heavy musical grace of the rounded
arches rising up and up and over, in tiers, the eloquent intervals of
the columns repeating, varying, the pale yellow stone illumined
here and there by soft slants of sunlight, the light permeating the
air and the forms of the church with a stone grayness that sheltered and lifted our heads, our hearts, toward the high barrel
vaulting, and brought a holy comfort to the soul.

At noon we took a lunch basket, Jack and I, and walked up
through meadows high above Conques, breathing in the April sunlight, the songs of birds, the sounds of running waters. I gathered
flowers to press in my notebook, and we picnicked on a rock in the
heather high up, looking down on Conques, built into the steep
mountainside—compact and old and mysterious, the stone of its
roofs like dragonfly wings, and the yellow stone church of Sainte
Foy rising up in its somber majesty above everything.

Later in the afternoon we would return to the hotel for a bath
and a nap and then for tea and to read in the Hôtel Sainte Foy,
which I loved because it had a hushed charm, as if it were a dedicated place, like a library.

Before six I always went down again to the Treasure to see Sainte
Foy and stood before her awed, a lump in my throat. In that first
rushing descent into the grayness of the Treasure, in my first moment of seeing her, through the violent tenderness she tore from
me, and the ecstasy that transported me—it was like aesthetic ecstasy but it was other—I saw, I think I saw, both her statue and
somehow, by her statue, through the walls of what we ordinarily
call reality, her body, her face, all light, and the angels who stood by
her, the angels guardian presences, Sainte Foy form and light, not
with individual features but living, feminine, light which was mysteriously flesh and at the same time its clothing, the fair life-
dwelling, her body and soul, her self, standing as I saw her in the
place her majesty occupied, standing both there beyond and here,
at the brink of life and death, at the pitch of rapturous dedication,
to the Truth, to Christ, to Life Everlasting, standing here (bathed in
the light of vision), as I would later learn she had stood in the hour
of her trial and passion, alone in the square at Agen.

At Agen, amid the symbols of power, she had said to the proconsul Dacien that it was Christ her soul loved, it was Him she would
take as bridegroom, whether Dacien liked it or not.

As the lictors took hold of her and tore the clothes from her
back, the mob cried, "Sacrifice! Sacrifice to Diana!"

"As befits your age and sex," said Dacien loudly over the mob.

The lictors held her girl body naked before the people and beat
it so the sounds of their rods were like frenzied drums.

"The blood that streams from my body now is writing in praise
of Him, the very scarlet of the blood that is drawn speaks the holy
name," cried Faith so all could hear; and Dacien, hearing, felt a
shiver of dread run down his spine, for those same words had been
cried at Merida the previous January by another child martyr, the
girl Eulalie. Tears were running down the face of Fides.

"All right, I give you one last chance, my little lady!" Dacien
shouted.

Young virgin, girl of twelve, for your courage and your faith, for
your love of the Lord Jesus Christ, you were tied to the brass bed
(called the grill), and the coals were lighted in the braziers beneath
you, and you suffered the torture without a sound. So God came to
you. A dove in a cloud flew down and covered your nakedness with
a cloth, whiter than snow and brighter than sunlight, and the dove
made the cloud to rain so it put out the fires in the braziers beneath
you, and the dove held above your head a golden crown that glowed
with jewels.

There were some in the crowd who cried out in pity for your
suffering, and seeing your shining face, they began to believe.
"What evil has she done?" they cried. "What evil?" they cried, as the
executioners took hold of you once more.

And when the sword flashed in the October sunlight and your
head fell, they cried out your name, "Faith! Faith! Radiant girl!"
Falling on their knees, they spoke the name of Jesus. "Adonai," they
said. "Lord have mercy on us." And they died with you, bludgeoned
by the mob.

Golden spark, little saint, come down through time; like a star in
infinity, you shine in eternity. Carried at first in the minds, in the

hearts, of the Christians who survived the killings in Agen that day and came secretly by night to wipe the blood from your skin with their precious tissues and take your body to the hidden place high on the rock plateau called Pompejac.

There, in time, from your grave came a fragrance like the scent of roses, and moving away the stones, they found your body, perfect in flesh without any blemish, the color returned like blood to your face, and around your neck where it was cut through, a line of vermilion like a line of paint. So they would sing long after in your *canczon, chanson*. "They [the Roman governors, the cruel pagan mob] sent Him flowers such as these, whose colors are fair in Heaven," they sang. "Sweet and fragrant are their odors, and whoever breathes them, takes Him in love, and in His body grows in strength."

> *Cist l'en trameiron aitals flors*
> *Q'en Cel es bella lur colors;*
> *Dolcz e suaus es lor olors,*
> *E qi la sent, pren l'en amors*
> *E en sun corps creiss l'en vigor.*

Golden spark, little saint, elevated by Saint Dulcidius when a hundred years had passed, moved to the church he had built for you outside the city walls, guarded and loved then at Agen four hundred years and more, until in the years of the Norman destruction, in 866, the monk Aronisde took you from your marble tomb and brought you here; blessed by more miracles, guarded then at Conques safe in the wild mountains of the Rouergue, embodied in this your reliquary statue sometime before the year 900 to become Sainte Foy in Majesty, wearing a crown like that revealed to Saint Caprais when he watched your passion from a hiding place high on the rock called Pompejac; guarded forever after, in the centuries of your glory, in the centuries of decline when the Black Prince pillaged Languedoc and the English came up the river Lot and took Quercy and held even Rodez for seven years (1360–1367) and the monks fled with you to the Château of Lunel, and later, for more than three hundred years you lay, buried in the stones of the church as the religious wars raged on and subsided, and the plague in 1628

killed nearly all who dwelled in this town, you lay in darkness,
waiting.

Golden spark, little saint, come down through time, you who
through the ages stayed steadfast and survived, you who with your
girlish gaiety and your fierce protectiveness stood for healing, for
justice, and for the bringing forth of new life, hear my prayers, O
my saint. Hear us now as the hour of the second millennium draws
near and the continuance of life on earth lies in the balance, threat-
ened, help us, intercede with all the saints, with God Himself, that
men may hear and the eyes of power be opened while yet there is
time.

Like Saint Paulinus, who went to the shrine of Saint Felix of Nola
"To guard his altar through the silent night, / And sweep his floor
and keep his door by day; / And watch his candles burn," and who
wrote year after year for his saint's feast day (January 14) an ode—
"Spring wakes the birds' voices but for me / My saint's day is my
spring," making for his saint a small contribution to literature, so
would I with you, Sainte Foy.

Père André comes into the room with a small group of tourists to show them the glories of the Treasure. His large wan face is kindly and tired. The Germans took him prisoner in the war and broke his health.

He told us that on the first day we came here. He was talking to us in English (which he never did again); he was talking very painfully and insistently with an accent so bizarre I could barely, and then only with the greatest effort, make out some of what he was saying. (It was a lesson to me in how my French must have sounded when I got intense and tried to really say something.)

Père André said, "Martin Luther should have been a great saint of the Catholic Church. Reform was needed. . . . When the Church is rich and does nothing for the poverty of the people . . . and in that time it still exacted tithes from the poor and sold spiritual indulgences to the rich . . ."

This was part of a complicated idea, but I had not been able to follow him. There we stood, Père André, Jack, and I, in that April hour of 1975 that stands at the very beginning of everything that has happened since in my mind, in my heart and soul; there we stood, we three, tilting in the shadows amid the holy concentration that hung in the air of Sainte Foy's presence as hushed as the tapestries on the wall, while all about were ranged the gleaming gold surfaces, the glowing gemstones, the polished crystals, the mysterious forms of the other reliquaries—the *A*-shaped reliquary called the *A* of Charlemagne, the silver arm called the Arm of Saint George, the lantern of Saint Vincent, the object called the Reliquary of Pepin II, and two others built as if they were houses with steep, many-sided roofs, the crosses, the chalices, the portable altars, the little trunk that holds the bones of Sainte Foy's body, and the silver reliquary of the Blessed Virgin Mary, crowned and seated on her throne, holding on her knees the Christ child-man, who, smiling in all confidence, raises His hand in blessing.

I stood—my mind immense with ecstasy, my throat constricted
with awe and tenderness—straining to listen to Père André, who
seems, as he is in my memory of that first day, to be totally unlike
the Père André I know now—except that the problem of the
Church and the poverty of the people still preoccupies him.

"Hannah!" Père André says when he sees me. He sounds the ini-
tial *H* in a special learned way. At first when he began to know me
better he called me Madame Hannah, but now he says Hannah,
often repeating the *H* and saying my name over—"*H* . . . annah,"
and Jack, whom everyone else in Conques calls Jacques or Monsieur Jacques, he calls John-Jack, carefully repeating his two names
in English and beaming with pleasure at Jack's presence (rarer here
than mine). "Monsieur Rousseau," he says ever since Jack jokingly
linked Père André's John-Jack to Jean-Jacques Rousseau, surprising
Père André, who did not think an American would know the name,
not to mention the work, of Rousseau. "Monsieur Rousseau," Père
André says, his hands crossed over his comfortable stomach, looking up at Jack and laughing in low ripples. Not knowing Henri
Rousseau, Le Douanier, who is in his art revered kin to Jack, Père
André does not know the extra pleasure his little joke brings us.

When he is happy there is no one with such largesse as Père
André. Everything about him seems to be large—his heart, his nature, his ample white monk's robe, his face, as noted, with its large,
rounded jaw and big cheekbones, his high wide forehead with deep
creases, his blue eyes behind his thick-lensed glasses, his voice,
above all his voice, which is as warm as he is, and rich and deep.
When he lifts it in song to chant the mass, his voice seems to come
from God.

He has a perfect musical ear, and I have seen him—on the famous (to us) day when we went with him to Rodez to visit the
Musée Fenaille, though he was hurrying us through, afraid of returning late to Conques—I saw him stop, bend over an illuminated
manuscript, an antiphonary of the late fourteenth century, and
slowly begin to sing the written notes. Raising his hands as the
priest does at certain points in the mass, he sang, going on so his
wonderful voice filled the old dark-beamed room and touched the
sweet face of the Virgin of the Annunciation in the next room and
the stilled, tranced grief of the Virgin of the Pietà, and drifted out

into the lovely glass-covered court and down in praise of the Christ in marble relief from the altar of Deusdedit, fashioned for the cathedral about the year 1000; his voice reached even, I liked to imagine, the whiskered-faced menhir (standing stone), which comes from St. Sernin on the Rance and stands now in the Musée Fenaille on the ground floor off the court, with several other graven menhirs, all cut from the *rougier,* the reddish sandstone of the Camares in the southwest of the Rouergue, the modern Department of Aveyron.

We were alone in the museum, which had closed for the season, with Monsieur Balsan, the curator, Conservateur des Antiquités de l'Aveyron. Scholar, archaeologist, and speleologist, Monsieur Balsan was dressed in white shorts and high white socks, a white shirt and jacket and safari hat. All set, he looked, on a sunny November day in Rodez, set for a summer dig in the Levant, a small, wiry, witty man of over seventy, kidding Père André about Sainte Foy. He declared it was Sainte Foy that Père André had in the mysterious suitcase he'd brought in from Conques with him, to carry whatever it was he was picking up in Rodez for himself, Père Gilles, and Frère Isidore.

Showing us his Celtic goddesses from the period of La Tène, one of them unearthed when they were building the hospital in Rodez, and the other from near the Trou de Bozouls on the Dourdou, Monsieur Balsan bragged that *his* goddesses were a thousand years older, at least, than Sainte Foy, whom Père André had concealed there in his suitcase. Monsieur Balsan tapped the suitcase. It was not hollow. Père André smiled. Taking us around behind his favorite goddess, Monsieur Balsan said, "Note the lovely spirals of her coiffure—characteristic of Celtic art of the period of La Tène." (The same spirals, I see, reappear in another form on the gown of Sainte Foy.) "Note her ears," said Monsieur Balsan.

Sitting there carved in stone, breathing from a distant age, she is the ancestress of our virgin, who in essential ways resembles her (as she does the other goddess, too). The eyes of this goddess, Monsieur Balsan's favorite, appear to be closed, and her mouth is open as if, in her heavy dignity, she were speaking in sleep. She holds a sceptre.

Another time when I asked him, Père André sang for me the Gregorian chant in the *Collectaire* of the fourteenth century, open under glass in the Treasure. When I thanked him, telling him what a grand voice he had, he replied simply, "I know it well for it was given to me by God—*par le bon Dieu*. By my parents, too, of course."

"Père André has a *diction extraordinaire,*" says Jean Sègalat, Conques's artist—"the true Rouergat artist," Jack says with passion in his voice. Sègalat says: "He has a marvelous vocabulary. He speaks French with perfection. He has no accent. When he recites the early mass it is clear, it is beautiful. I asked him one day where he came from. I could not figure it out. From Anjou, perhaps, I thought, or the Touraine. But he is from the Auvergne, from a village near Chaise-Dieu, between Chaise-Dieu and Le Puy. I complimented him on how beautifully he speaks. He said, 'Oh, no, no, don't compliment *me*. It is a gift—*C'est un don.*' When Père André was at the Abbey of St. Michel de Frigolet, it was he who was chosen to sing the Passion during Easter week because of the beauty of his voice."

"Faith is a great tree, an oak tree rooted deep in the heart of France," the poet and philosopher Charles Péguy writes, and Père André is of that tree with its rough old bark. He is of the people, of the French people, or, rather, of the Auvergnat French people—"nurtured on the milk of the patois," he says of himself in what he is writing about the "Song of Sainte Foy," challenging accepted translations of certain lines. The "Canczoun de Sancta Fé," he says it should be spelled and pronounced. "I know the patois not by learning, but from within," he says. "It is my mother tongue. And I know a number of its dialects as well—from Clermont to Nice and from the Savoy to Toulouse and beyond." ("*La langue romane,*" Père André calls it in what he is writing, rather than the "langue d'oc" or, as I've observed, the now fashionable "Occitan" or the traditional "Provençal."

"Oh, perhaps I exaggerate there," he said, when I questioned him, "but you see I spoke only the patois, I spoke no French, until the age of six, when I first went to school. So for me French is a learned language and the patois my mother tongue, and because it is the patois of the Auvergne, I know most, no, not all, but most of the words of the patois of all Languedoc and of the Rouergue, and even of Périgord. Not all the words, mind you; sometimes I hear a word I have never heard before. But I can understand all these dialects. And then when I was at the Abbey of St. Michel de Frigolet in Provence—you know where it is, between Avignon and Tarascon—there I learned the Provençal. There are many dialects, too, in Provence, but I think it would be safe to say that I could understand them all—oh, I might have to question to get the meaning of certain words."

The village he comes from in the region of Le Puy is called Bobosc. It is eighteen kilometers from Chaise-Dieu. "Yes, it is a very little village," he said. "There were nineteen *feux* or *foyers* at the time of the Revolution, nineteen 'hearths,' or 'households,' you would say in English." He says these *Hs* carefully, breathing out the "*heh*hearths," the "*heh*house*heh*holds." "And now there are only five *foyers.*

"My father was a farmer. He could not read. He could count, he was very intelligent, he could make calculations very quickly in his head, but he could not read. Or write, of course. Not until he was much older. He was in prison for four months and he learned to read in prison. It was in 1943 or 1944, and he learned to read then."

"In prison?" I asked. "Was it the Germans?"

"Oh, no, no, no. It was an *affaire.* He was in prison for four months and there was a trial, a court trial, and he was acquitted. It was an *affaire.* I am going to write something about it someday, about my village, too."

"And your mother," I asked him another day. "Could she read?"

"Oh, yes, my mother could read, and she could write very well. She kept all the accounts for my father. He would sell a calf at the fair and he would bring the money to her. She would enter it into her books. She could write very well." He began to show me a letter he has saved that she wrote him, years ago, before the war, in 1935, when he was already a young seminarian. "*Mon cher Abbé,*" she addressed him. "It is all personal things," Père André said. "She was worried because she had seen my room, she knew how cold it was.

She had sent an extra blanket, and some wool socks she had knitted." We came to the second page. *Her stomach is troubling her.*
Père André brought the letter back to his heart and holds it there.
"Her stomach troubled her for a long time, she had troubles always
with her stomach, and then she died. I think it was from the First
World War. I was born in 1914 just a few months after the war
began. I never saw my father until I was five. He was away all that
time, in the north, at the front. He didn't come back until 1919. I
remember he came into the house, he went to take a match from
the place where they were kept near the stove. He was going to
light his pipe. I ran up to my mother. 'Maman, Maman,' I cried, 'the
man has taken one of your matches!' The man," Père André said. "I
said, 'the man.' He was my father.

"He was my *father*," Père André repeated (and I, moved, was
struck, too, by what he took for granted—his child self's anxious
awareness of the preciousness of a single match).

"All that time he was gone in the war," he continued, "she had
so many cares. Food was scarce. And she was doing so much, just
to see that all of us were fed, that was her concern, and then she
wouldn't sit down. After we were fed then she would eat, she
would eat standing, eat potatoes with vinegar." He imitated how
she stood eating. "Chewing nervously—like a squirrel," Père André
said. "It was all that time, that hardship. I think it was the vinegar,
the vinegar, all that vinegar, it damaged her stomach, and she was
never really well after that. Her stomach always troubled her, and
then during the Second World War, during the time of my captiv-
ity, she died."

Another day, talking to the young Valerie Norlogue, who assists
in the mass and reads from the Old Testament, and comes often to
see Père André, he was asking her about the dance, the dance and
the fire on the eve of the fête of Saint John (June 24). "Oh, my
mother," he said, "when she was young, when she was your age, Valerie, how she loved to dance, to dance the *bourrée,* the dance of the
Auvergne. Oh, how she danced, she could make the walls shake.
When she was still young, your age, Valerie, still living with her
parents, she had to be home and in bed by nine o'clock. And on
nights when they were dancing the *bourrée* in her village, she would

get into bed, but she would hear the music, and her feet would begin to move under the covers, and she would be unable to bear it. She would get up, get dressed, and ooooop!" Père André made the motion of pushing up the window, opening the shutters. "Out she would go!

"Oh, my mother loved to dance. She could make the walls shake!"

We *feel* Père André's faith, Jack and I. It is as natural and everyday as daily bread. But often he has a hard time of it. It is cold in the Treasure for much of the year, cold and damp in the entrance where he must stand, sometimes for hours in the summer season, taking tickets. And the day of our trip to Rodez was a notable exception in Père André's life, for Père Gilles, who is the head, the abbot, of this tiny branch of their order—they are Norbertine fathers, Premonstratensians—grants him almost no respite from his task. Day in, day out, year in, year out, Père André is here from nine to twelve and two to six, the guardian of the Treasure.

And he suffers, this sociable man, in spite of his faith and his devotion to Sainte Foy, both from the constant confinement and the loneliness of his position and from its petty demands—the perpetual interruptions.

He is a thinker, a philosopher, a questioner, and though there is a heavy stubbornness about him, he can be quite nimble in his thinking, elegant and profound. He has ideas he wants to work out. There are things he has come to understand about Sainte Foy, things he wants to write down and to publish so that people who come here can understand.

He is meticulous. He worries at things. He goes through painful periods of depression. Distraction. Irritability. At these times he cannot write—not even a letter. His eyes give him trouble.

Then his peace returns. It is a wonderful thing to see him on the rare occasion when, released from his duty for a quarter of an hour, he rushes, bulky and joyous, his white robes blowing in the wind, down the middle of the main street of Conques to the post office to mail a letter or make a phone call.

"Priests, too, need time to pray," he said to me one day in a state of some distress.

"But no matter what I may go through from time to time," Père André said another day, "it is never like that." He meant the years he spent as prisoner in Germany.

In Conques, in this tiny town of less than two hundred year-round inhabitants, I have already found five men who were held prisoner by the Germans in the war, and another three who were taken to Germany after the Germans occupied Aveyron in 1942 for *travail obligatoire* as it was called. "There was no choice, no choice if you came of age during the years of the Occupation," said our friends Janine and Roger, who come down here each fall from Paris to spend a week or so of their vacation time in Rosalie's house. "Either it was the *travail obligatoire,* and you were, more than likely, taken into Germany, or you went underground into the Resistance. . . . Or the *melice*—collaborators," they added darkly, almost hissing.

"You freed us," says Monsieur Geneste—Monsieur Denis, we call him—who lives in the house just below us. "What? You have never been to the beach at St.-Malo? But you should go there! Every American should see that! Omaha Beach. It was a great feat! You should be proud. Without you I wonder if we would ever have been liberated.

"Five years I was there in Germany, a prisoner. Five years! And you Americans"—he touches Jack—"you freed us." He smiles. "I was worked on a farm like an ox." He hunches his shoulders as if he were an ox pulling a load. "There were high barbed-wire fences." He looks up to show how high. He has a handsome boyish old face, blond hair gone gray, and blue eyes. "The guards wore silver belt buckles that said '*Gott mit Uns.*' Ha. Ha. Ha." He laughs his sad laugh. He was a shepherd here when he was a boy. He points off across the gorge of the Ouche to the plateau above Montignac. "Up there," he says smiling joyously. "I went up there with my sheep. Then I went into the army. I was in the north. I was there to help in the evacuation at Dunkirk. I spent one night in England. One night in England and in the morning I was sent back to France. I tried to escape. I hid in barns all day, and by night I headed south. I was trying to get home to Conques. But the Germans caught me. One night in England and five years in Germany. An ox. A human ox. And that is the extent of my travels." He laughs his sad laugh again. "Oh, but I was lucky they didn't shoot me when they caught me. I think it was my blond hair that saved me. My fair skin. I looked like one of them. So they let me live. Five years they let me live—a prisoner, a human ox. And all I could think of was home. Home. Conques." Sometimes when he is a little drunk he tells us the German words he knows, because German is *his* foreign language. He tells us the German for "sun," or "moon" or "rain" or "my darling." "*Mein liebling,*" he says.

"There must have been thousands who were taken prisoner in the war the way you were," I said to Père André one day.

"Not *thousands,*" Père André said. "There were *millions.* There were three million. More in the beginning. There were nearly four million. They took the *whole* army, you know. Even those who were sick. We were prisoners of war. Many of us died there. We had universal conscription, you understand. We still do. Every young man must serve his eighteen months in the army. It is the same now. I was at Belfort in Alsace. It was June 1940, when the Germans invaded and we surrendered. We were told we were being sent home. We were marched onto the trains. It was night. There was music playing. Gay music as we marched onto the train." Père André hummed the tune that was playing in an ironic mocking voice. "We thought we were going home. Hah! In the morning we understood the train was going east. It kept going. It never stopped until we had crossed the mountains into the Sudetenland. We were held there as prisoners. We were worked in the coal mines. We were slave labor. But mind you, we were treated as prisoners of war according to the rules of the Geneva Convention. Our fate was not at all that of the others the Germans deported—the Jews and the members of the Resistance. As you must know. Before the end of the war some of us were sent home. I became so ill I was useless. They sent me home to die."

It was in the house of his parents in the little village of Bobosc in

the country near Le Puy that, as he slowly returned to life, Père
André made the decision. The war not yet over, he wrote to the
Abbey of St. Michel de Frigolet and asked permission to join the
order of Norbertine Fathers, the Premonstratensians, who, as it
turned out, had been since 1875 in charge of the parish of Conques
and the guardian of its Treasure.

It was only later, though, during the years of his studies for the
priesthood at Rodez, that Père André first came to know Conques
and Sainte Foy, who would become in time the center of his life, a
life devoted to God and to guarding her "whose message" he wrote
on Easter Monday, 1953, "is this luminous life of prayer which in-
tercedes strongly for the oppressed and is generative of true art, of
the *caring* of true art, and opens souls, inspiring them to surpass
themselves."

He meant not only the caring of the art of the Treasure, he meant
that of the achievement of the Romanesque basilica, with its elegant lines and its beautiful proportions, and he meant the fullness
of care in the art of the famous tympanum over the western doors
of the church.

Care-taker of this radiance, Père André signed himself in English in
the book (*Le Glossaire*) he gave me when I had finished after much
labor translating the description of the objects in the Treasure from
French into English for him. "Care-taker of this radiance," he pronounced it aloud very slowly. "Can you say that in English?"

"Oh, yes, that's very beautiful," I said in English, overcome, forgetting myself.

"Very beautiful," Père André said laughingly, imitating my English. He is extremely emotional and at times (as just then) he turns
bright red.

"He is blessed," Jack said. "He is blessed by his work. And he
blesses. He is her guardian. Think of that! *He* is *her* guardian."

"But still," Jack said another time. "Even though it is true that he
is blessed by his work, still, no wonder . . .

"It is cold in there in winter. It is cold in there for most of the
year. Cold. Dark. Damp . . ."

.   .   .

"It isn't fair. It isn't fair of Père Gilles," said Mademoiselle Fau. "He ought to give Père André an afternoon off once a week, just one afternoon even, so he could go out on errands or walk in the village and talk to the people, or just be out in the sunshine. And he should have a holiday, not a long one perhaps, but *something*. It isn't right that he has to be in there that way all the time. *All the time*. He is lonely. *Il s'ennui*." She moans "*Il s'ennui*" with heartfelt sympathy, the way people here do.

They don't use the noun *ennui*, or *s'ennuyer* as a reflexive verb, the way we do, as meaning bored or filled with the feeling of tedium. No. For them it is an active heart suffering "*peine très vive*," says my *Petite Larousse*. Sometimes it is a general condition, such as Père André's, in Mademoiselle Fau's view; sometimes it is a longing like homesickness for companionship or freedom; sometimes it is a need for a particular loved person, a love-longing that has become a pain so terrible it is a torment.

My yellow Larousse French grammar says that in the seventeenth century *ennui* was used to mean great sorrow caused, for example, by mourning; but that the writer who uses *ennui* in this sense today is committing an *archaïsme*. Yet this is the way the people here talk, and it is only one example of an older French that survives here along with the ancient langue d'oc.

I noticed this use of *ennui* for the first time one day when Madame Benoit was dressed for a trip. She had on a pretty straw hat, a special dress with a jacket for traveling that I had never seen, and a little valise. She got into Madame Fabre's gray *deux-chevaux*, which was parked in the garage at the back of our house. Madame Fabre was driving Madame Benoit to the train station at St. Christophe. She was going to visit her sister-in-law. She didn't want to leave Conques, she didn't want to go, not one bit, but, explained Madame Fabre, Madame Benoit's sister-in-law wasn't well enough to travel, and "*Elle a ennui de Madame Benoit*." She has *ennui* for want of Madame Benoit. What can Madame Benoit do? Of course she must go. She would be back in five days. "*Au revoir*."

"I am not afraid," said Madame Benoit. "The Virgin Mary will protect us." Off went the little car. Up the drive and out of sight past the Tour Garrigue, as Mademoiselle Fau calls this tower from

the old rampart wall, still standing solid and thick and ancient, with
wonderful pink flowering weeds growing out at angles to its
stones. Down and around and through the Arch of Vinzelles went
the car; down through the Place du Château, where we could see
them bumping over the cobblestones, past Rosalie's kitchen garden. Rosalie waved. Everyone waved. Madame Benoit waved.
"What else can she do?" everyone said. "Her *belle-soeur* has *ennui* for
her. Of course she must go. *Au revoir!*"

When fall came and little Lucie's young parents, who had turned
eighteen and were going to marry, took Lucie off to live with them
in Paris, Dany Geneste could not bear the pain of the separation
from her granddaughter. When Dany and I saw each other up by the
boules court, Dany grasped my arm and said in her anguish, "*J'ai
ennui de Lucie, j'ai ennui de Lucie.*" She was almost wailing. "It is I who
cared for her since she was first born, since she was . . . ," and she
raised her hands to show me how tiny the newborn child Lucie had
been—Lucie, whom she had nurtured and cared for and loved with
her whole heart from that moment on, gone now, just like that, off
to live in Paris with her parents for good, or so it seemed in those
pained weeks. "Lucie is *mignonne,*" darling, said Rosalie, as if that
explained everything.

"*Il s'ennui,*" said Mademoiselle Fau, drawing out in sympathetic
anguish her *ennuuuui,* sitting there at her desk in the back of her
shop, surrounded by lovely painted faience—egg cups, pitchers,
vases, plates, and some perfect tiny things she has made herself and
painted and glazed and fired, dishes painted with flowers, a cross, a
statuette of Sainte Foy with her grill and her martyr's palm in
painted faience, blue and white, and one of Saint Jacques with his
pilgrim staff, his scrip, a scallop shell upon his hat—things she has
made at Rodez, where she lives in the winter, this beautiful dignified woman of seventy-two who will sit here through the summer
and until just after the festival day of Sainte Foy in October, sit here
among these things she will sell and *give* to friends and to the children who dash in to visit her in the midst of their furious play. Also
there are photographs, postcards, enameled-copper jewelry made
by the artisans of the region, and several impressive stacks of
books, including the book about Conques by her nephew, Jean-

Claude Fau, Conques's distinguished art historian, who like Jack is almost fifty now. She'll sit at the huge desk in her tiny shop, which is the former *cave* of her little medieval house. This house and the others on the Place de l'Église to which it is joined make a kind of quarter-moon across from the western face of the *basilique*.

———————— ⬤ ————————

"Au Tympan de Conques," says the long, glazed brown pottery sign that stretches across the front of Mademoiselle Fau's shop over the door, for from here one can look directly across the Place and up to the tympanum over the western doors. "One of the four marvels of the world," says Rosalie, my friend, her face shining with delight.

And here it is, one of the four marvels of this world, a Last Judgment completed most probably between 1135 and 1150, and almost perfectly preserved. Even the colors still cling to the stone in places and grow luminous in that hour just after the sun has gone down—the blue on the robe of Christ the Judge in Heaven seated in His almond-shaped glory, His mandorla; the yellow on the wings of the angels above Him, come to sound their trumpets; the blue on the mantle of Mary, who stands near Him to the right at the head of the procession of the elect, her hands held together in prayer; the reddish-purple cast of hell, and its ochres; the blue on the robe of Sainte Foy, who, "in her corner of force," Père André says, is repre-

Tympanum above the western door of the Basilique of Conques

sented not in heaven, but *here, at Conques, here in her church,* fallen on her knees, praying for her people, praying for the souls of the dead, still, on the last day in time; and the hand of Jesus reaches out, down through the cloud waves of heaven, to touch, to almost touch, her head.

For the great Last Judgment of Conques is not a vision of the all-consuming apocalypse such as we see at Moissac and at Beaulieu and elsewhere. It is not a vision of eternity, with Christ the Judge appearing in His glory, old like God the Father, crowned like an ancient king, seated on His throne in majesty, and surrounded by angels and the four Beasts of the Book of Revelation—the angel (Matthew), the lion (Mark), the ox (Luke), and the eagle (John); it does not have the swirling music of the tympanum at Moissac. It has, rather, something quiet and vast and peaceful and burgeoning as a wheat field on a summer day, brilliant as the sun shining down, and yet turbulent, in part, as the life of the creatures invisible within the myriad green stems; it has music, but not the music of eternity as does the Moissac tympanum; it has rather the music of the earth and heaven, and that of hell: and as one must listen to music in time, as one would listen to poetry or to a story, so must one look at the tympanum of Conques in time, with time. It is not set in eternity but rather, like a novel or a chanson de geste, it is set in time, with eternity shining through.

One can absorb the beauty of the tympanum at Moissac in a long regard, for it is a vision of eternity, it is happening forever and all at once. As a work of art, it is sublime: one could gaze on it again and again and dwell on its details and on the yearning of the beautiful beasts and never cease to feel the terrible rapture of this vision, described by Saint John in the Book of Revelation.

In order to absorb the whole vision, the rapturous form of the tympanum of Conques, on the other hand, one must both look on the face of Christ and on His body come in glory, and also regard the whole arc part by part, scene by scene, back and forth, until it is all absorbed, even as one might listen to and watch the miming of the alternating laisses of the "Song of Roland," or the "Song of Sainte Foy," and need to hear the whole to know it.

The core of the vision of our tympanum and its structure comes

from the mouth of the Lord, from words He spoke in the Gospel of
Saint Matthew in Chapters 24 and 25. It shows us what-is-to-be
breaking into what-is; the blessed and the damned appear to the
right and to the left of Christ, and below Him, inspired as they
most surely are by the breath of heaven, yet nevertheless, down-to-
earth—Conques-en-Rouergue earth—people in their particular-
ity, carved by a sculptor whose genius lay beyond skill in his
marvelous ability to see and to render human nature exactly and in
all its variousness, with its highest capacities and with its weak-
nesses and its wickednesses, and to portray in stone at once the
full-bodied and the sublime. The face of Mary, the faces of the angels, once you have seen them, make you gasp.

This work proceeds, then, from Scripture, and from the iconography it dictates.

For as the lightning cometh out of the east, and shineth even
unto the west; so shall also the coming of the Son of man be.
(Matthew 24:27)

Immediately after the tribulation of those days shall the sun be
darkened, and the moon shall not give her light, and the stars
shall fall from heaven, and the powers of the heaven shall be
shaken:

And then shall appear the sign of the Son of man in heaven:
and then shall all the tribes of the earth mourn, and they shall see
the Son of man coming in the clouds of heaven with power and
great glory.

And he shall send his angels with a great sound of a trumpet,
and they shall gather together his elect from the four winds,
from one end of heaven to the other. (Matthew 24:29–31)

When the Son of man shall come in his glory, and all the holy
angels within him, then shall he sit upon the throne of his glory:

And before him shall be gathered all nations: and he shall separate them one from another, as a shepherd divideth his sheep
from the goats:

And he shall set the sheep on his right hand, but the goats on
the left.

Then shall the King say unto them on his right hand, Come, ye
blessed of my Father, inherit the kingdom prepared for you from
the foundation of the world. (Matthew 25:31–34)

Then shall he say also unto them on the left hand, Depart from me, ye cursed, into everlasting fire, prepared for the devil and his angels. (Matthew 25:41)

But as Jesus was made incarnate and stood in history speaking of what lay beyond time, though nigh, so is what we see in the tympanum time-based, earth-based, at the hour the vast lightning of eternity breaks through with the coming of the Son of Man.

Sainte Foy is at Conques, in her church, with the manacles of prisoners freed through her intercession with the Lord hanging above her; Sainte Foy is still here, praying for her people, praying with all her might. And the hand of Christ reaches down through the cloud waves of heaven.

Near her in another scene is a closed sarcophagus, and then in a strip like a film clip an angel comes to lift its lid, and we see its occupant rise up with the lid, then higher and higher; while on the scales in the lower center of the tympanum beneath the feet of the risen Christ a poor terrified soul is being weighed; and though the devil has his finger out trying to tip the scales in his own favor, the small crosses on the scales on Saint Michael's side seem to be winning the soul for heaven.

It is a vision at the rim of time, which implies thus possibility. And it portrays individual people and brings them to life as it stresses the humanity of Christ and of His crucifixion, showing "the Son of Man coming in the clouds of heaven with power and great glory," come as Judge and yet bareheaded, at the age He was when He hung on the cross, which, heavy and solid, appearing in the sky as His sign, rises behind Him, held by two angels, who bear, too, the instruments of His passion, the nail and the lance, while the sun and the moon are there as they were, conjoined, in the hour of His death, and darkened as they would be at the hour of His coming.

This vision, held together structurally by the cross and by Christ in His mandorla and His large, strong hands, the right hand raised, the left hand lowered, is at once whole and composed of scenes— from the angels on high sent with a great sound of trumpets to gather His elect from the four winds, to the scenes below on either side of Christ, those to His left in hell, and those to His right in heaven or at its doors, with eternity shining through not only in the person of Christ but also in the faces of those elect who are coming forward to know eternal bliss, and in the faces of those who, already gathered into the bosom of Abraham, dwell beneath the arches of the Heavenly Jerusalem; for, taking place on Doomsday when these things are coming to be, Christ the King on high surrounded by His angels has said to those on His right hand, "Come, ye blessed of my Father, inherit the kingdom prepared for you from the foundation of the world," and to those on His left hand, "Depart from me, ye cursed, into everlasting fire, prepared for the devil and his angels." These words from the Gospel of Saint Matthew are borne forth by two angels, who hold them in abbreviated form on two banderoles at the top to the right and to the left of His almond-shaped glory; to the right the angel's banderole reads I PATRIS MEI FIDELES, and to the left the angel's banderole says HVC DISCEDITE A ME REPROBATI; while below on either side of the mandorla two angels hold huge candles to light the darkness so that we may read and see, for Christ has said that in those days "the sun shall be darkened, and the moon shall not give her light, and the stars shall fall from heaven, and the powers of the heavens shall be shaken."

Lines of perfect leonine verse, written no doubt by a poet-monk of Conques, are inscribed in Latin on the stone ribs that form the roofs and divisions of heaven and hell and delineate what is depicted in the balanced alternating sculptured scenes moving from the right to the left and back again, and divide and arrange the entire composition, which is both narrative in its structure and a timeless vision at once universal, eternal, radiant, and personal, individual, specific to Conques and its people, its history, its legends, its saints and its miracles; showing in its portrayals of everlasting time in Hades a good deal of wild verve and humor as well as, in one place, the real horror of war, contrasting with the bliss of peace that graces those who go to Christ on the other side.

With all this I only begin to describe this most marvelous work in its majesty, the sweet and terrible beauty of the whole, with aspects as manifold as the personages it contains, all worthy of a long gaze, and of thought, each individually, and in their groups, and in those that relate to them and those that contrast.

It contains, if I have counted them correctly, 126 personages, if you count as personages the angels and archangels, and the blackened busts of the sun and the moon personified, and if you count all the demons and the monsters crowded into the chaos of the red, purple, and ochre inferno; if you count for example that rabbit who, with tall ears and long front legs like arms, holds, with the aid of a demon at the other end, a spit to which is tied a wicked hunter who had poached on the abbey grounds and robbed the monks of their wild game, and now is being turned and roasted over flames by one of his rabbit victims; and if you count, finally, that poor damned soul who has disappeared, all but his feet and ankles, into the jaws of the great Leviathan. And if you count the Leviathan himself, of course, and the tiny terrified soul on the scales, undergoing psychostasy.

"Look!" says Margot, as I have come to call Mademoiselle Fau. We are poring over photographs of the tympanum, which she has just received from a friend. She speaks with awe and reverence, showing me a photograph that has revealed for her and for me the tear on Mary's cheek, the tear that time has given her, it seems. Then "Look!" I say, for it seems, though her other eye is in shadow, it seems a tear has just come out of that eye. "Ah, her face!" says Margot. The face of Mary is solid yet shining, a country face with the fine clear features of this region, lit by the glow of heaven within her—the wide high forehead, the straight long nose, the curved lips, the cleft chin, the direct, clear gaze. (And the tear, the two tears, that have come with time.) Charlou, Rosalie's husband, could be descended from her, I think, for his face is her face.

"Oh, and look at Sainte Foy's face," I say, moved. We are bending over the photograph of Sainte Foy on her knees, praying for her people—her face no longer the hieratic face of her statue, nor that of the young lady of rarest loveliness, barely nubile, who appeared in visions around the year 1000; her face has become like that of a young mother, care-worn, tired, loving, like that of a nun, worked to the bone in loving service and prayer, tired, yet going on, intensely spiritual and very strong. It is her strength, her humble power, her endurance that we see here in her face, in her large strong hands, and the soft, small female body beneath her nun's robes, as she prays open-eyed; and the hand of God reaches down through the cloud waves of heaven so the orb of the halo around His hand overlaps the orb of the halo around her head.

I sit in the chair Margot keeps beside her at the desk for whoever may come in to visit—her sister-in-law, Madame Fau; her nephew Jean-Claude and his wife and their children, her great-nieces and great-nephews; and her old friends who come to Conques, come long distances sometimes, to see her. She has many friends, this beloved and revered woman. They come and sit a while with her for the privilege and the pleasure of spending time with her and to help her endure the hours she must spend in her shop, here in the back at her desk, where, no matter how hot and sunny it may be out on the parvis before the church, it is always cool, and in cold or rainy weather miserable. Often I come upon her shivering at her desk, and her bony hands when we greet are icy cold. She suffers a great deal from the cold and the damp in here. I feel there are sorrows heavy in her heart. I hear them in her voice, see them in her beautiful eyes. Her eyes are a greenish gray, old with soul. "I see my face when I go to Brittany," she says. "I see it everywhere." It is a long, oval face with high rounded cheeks and a long, hawklike nose, a firm cleft chin; like all the Faus, she is somewhat dark of skin.

Her family comes from the plateau, from the village of Campuac up there, and their name, Fau, is an old langue d'oc word (*fagus* in Latin, *fauen* in Breton), the word in the patois for beech tree—*hêtre* in French. "On Sunday afternoons or summer evenings on special holidays when my father was a boy in Campuac," she says, "my grandparents used to walk up to the hilltop there, where they could see, far off to the south, the cathedral at Rodez. That was what they did for pleasure then. That was the grand event!" Her father became a doctor in Rodez, and she, like her mother before her, was sent to a convent school. In her generation, to her regret now, they no longer spoke the patois.

Margot Fau went off as a young woman to Toulouse to the university, to the École des Beaux-Arts, to study to be a painter, and after that to Paris, where she was still working as an artist when, as

SAINT

45

the Germans approached in June 1940, she fled with two friends who had just married that day, leaving everything, all her work, behind with friends; she went with the thousands who left Paris that June in terror of the Nazi occupation, along roads that were being bombed sporadically. She escaped from Paris, only to be in Rodez with her mother (for her father had died) when the Germans came to occupy the town in 1942. "It was frightful!" she says, still trembling with outrage at what the Germans did. "Oh, it was frightful. The war broke all our lives."

But then, changing the subject, she says, "Père André is a more cultivated man than Père Gilles. He used to teach my nephew Latin when the abbey had its school up there." She waves her arm toward the hill beyond the basilica.

"I am glad," she says, "I am glad that you go so often to see him. It is not easy. No, Père Gilles is not very nice with him."

It occurs to me that Père André is the only man in all of Conques who clearly is not his own boss. Even Le Fraysou, as people call him, making the diminutive of his last name, Fraysse (meaning ash tree), even Le Fraysou, the garbageman, who also digs the graves and rings the bells for the marriages, the baptisms, and the deaths (is, that is to say, the sexton of the church) and sings, too, in the choir in his hauntingly beautiful tenor voice—*is* the choir, on certain occasions—and cuts down brush with his scythe, working by the hour, and rebuilds the walls that hold and terrace the earth when they begin to give way, Fraysou, who does all the work that no one else will do, seems somehow to be rather like the captain of his own enterprise, as he mounts the *côte* singing on his tractor, pulling the garbage of Conques behind him up to the plateau to the dump. And Frère Isidore, who, like Père André, owes obedience to Père Gilles and, tiny, old, and hunchbacked, sits in his white robe guarding the church door, seems, in fact, to be there sometimes and not others. Often I find Frère Isidore, dressed in trousers and a sweater, having a coffee in Rosalie's kitchen, where all the world comes for joy. And Monsieur Charlou, after he's told one of his favorite jokes about the monk and the bull, claims that he has also told this joke to Frère Isidore. He told it to him down in the abbey garden, where he goes to draw the honey out of the abbey's hives for Frère Isidore each September.

And Père Gilles, while he handles with skill his most delicate position and is most certainly, as Père André has said firmly several
times, a good priest, seems, nevertheless, somehow to live the life
of Riley, comparatively speaking. "He is a good priest," Père André
says, repeating, as if to settle the pricks of resentment he must feel
at certain times. Actually, he is encouraging me to put aside my shy-
ness and go and talk to Père Gilles, who knows, Père André says,
more than himself about Conques's history, and has, too, certain
books I want to borrow that Père André does not on his own have
the right to lend me.

"But Père André makes me think of Gimon," I say to Mademoiselle Fau.

She looks puzzled.

"Gimon," I say again. I think I am not pronouncing his name correctly. "Gimon, the warrior monk, who was Sainte Foy's guardian
in the days before Guibert the Illuminé. Gimon. He is in the *Book of
Miracles.* Gimon the old warrior-monk. Père André stands like that
in the long tradition of her guardians."

"Ahh." She smiles. "Gimon. Yes." She seems to like that.

Everyone who reads the *Book of Miracles* becomes fond of Gimon,
and so, it appears, was Sainte Foy herself.

"Père André is ardent like Gimon and somehow *rough* the way he
was, and like him *devoted,* somehow innocently and naturally, ut-
terly *devoted* to Sainte Foy." I say that to Mademoiselle Fau, or
rather, that is what I try to say in my still-halting French.

"The marvelous and amazing things I am going to tell you about the
monk Gimon, prior of the monastery, have been related to me by a
multitude of persons, still living, who knew him," writes Bernard
of Angers, in the twenty-seventh chapter of the first *Book of the Miracles of Sainte Foy,* compiled from the stories he gathered (and au-
thenticated) on the first of his three pilgrimages here to her shrine.

> This Gimon, in donning his religious habit, did not leave be-
> hind the ardent warrior's temperament that he had possessed in
> the world. He kept it to turn against evildoers. In the dormitory
> he hung at the head of his bed, alongside his religious vestments,
> his cuirass, his shield, his helmet, his lance, his sword, and all his

arms and armor. And in the stable he kept his courser of combat, all equipped and, like him, ever ready to go forth to stop an attack against the monastery or an attempt to pillage its lands.

Sometimes the valiant Gimon rode out alone to carry out this duty. And many a time he warded off an attack thus with a few words shouted fiercely from atop his prancing horse. At other times, when there were a great number of men on the rampage, he would lead a whole troop of monks to the defense, riding out ahead of them, enflaming them with courage, bolstering the fainthearted, shouting of the glory that would come to those who bravely fought to defend the territory of the holy martyr Fides. The effect of all this was such that as the warlike band of monks approached, the malefactors would quite often take flight, and combat was not necessary. Sometimes, however, emboldened if they were numerous, the miscreants would decide to fight; and then Gimon would yell out prayers to Sainte Foy to grant victory to himself and his band of monks and chase off the pillagers. These prayers cried forth in the pitch of battle had such an effect that often a small troop of monks with Gimon could beat off a large number of aggressors.

Sometimes, although it was rare, the multitude of marauding horsemen was so immense that there was no hope of winning. Then Gimon, seeing the situation, turned round with his men and retreated to the safety of the walls of Conques. Leaving his men to man the ramparts, Gimon, still armed, rushed into the sanctuary to the foot of the tomb of the martyr and began addressing his prayers to Sainte Foy in the most fiery and familiar fashion. He'd tell her *she had to help, she had to help right away!* He didn't lower his voice, he shouted. He even went so far as to threaten to strike her statue if she didn't help, or he'd say to Sainte Foy that if she didn't punish these criminal aggressors upon her territory, he would throw her statue in the river or down a well.

These pious outbursts of passion did not keep him from addressing the most humble and urgent prayers to the saint. I deem that God Himself inspired this naïve form of prayer. At any rate, if it sounded strange and menacing, it came from a heart so pure and so right that God nearly always granted his prayers, rude as they were in their expression, for they came from one who was irreproachable in his works and his deeds. And these impas-

sioned supplications so frequently tore out of heaven the divine
assistance that when Gimon and his brothers were too weak to
defeat great numbers by the force of arms, it happened (often)
that these brigands would perish miserably—some hurling
themselves over the cliffs, others choking when they ate; still
others were seized with a crazy fury and turned their daggers on
themselves and died. Thus did the hour of punishment come to
them with death presenting itself in a variety of hideous ways.

Gimon, as prior of the monastery, was charged not only with
watching over the monks, that they observe the Rule of Saint
Benedict carefully in all its aspects, but also he was the guardian
of the sanctuary.

In Gimon's day the church was not yet enriched as it has been
in our time by the affluence of the thousands of pilgrims who
have come here since the healing of Guibert, called the Illuminé.
The church was not then lit with the magnificence with which it
is lighted in our day. There was at that time but one lamp burning in the sanctuary and watching through the night on the holy
altar.

As it often went out, the guardian monk, according to custom, got up and relighted it. And when Gimon, overwhelmed
with weariness from work or drowsy from his prolonged
orisons, was conquered by sleep, he would feel a hand lightly
touch his cheek, and he would hear a sweet voice telling him he
must relight the lamp. Wakened by this, he would get up quickly
and, seeing the lamp was extinguished, go to it immediately; but
just as he reached out with his hand to take hold of the lamp, he
would see it being relighted by a heavenly hand. Sometimes it
was completely extinguished, and it could not be relit of itself.
Then he would carry it to the live coals to light it there, and on
the way the lamp would miraculously light up in his hand.

He would go back to his couch, but hardly had he tasted a moment's repose when the same apparition returned. As if she were
playing, Sainte Foy would touch his cheek again and call to him
in her sweet voice, three or four times she would wake him up
and force him to get up in spite of his groanings and his protests.
She would make him think he *had* to get up and light the lamp
that burned on the holy altar near her statue. And again, as he
would approach, the lamp would flare up on its own. Finally the
old man, boiling with impatience, burst out with the most lively

recriminations against Sainte Foy; he would tell her that she simply must stop tormenting him when there was no reason. He
gave vent to these outbursts of anger in the idiom of the country
of his birth. Having thus, finally, put a stop to the little miracles,
he would go back to his couch. Or, by then thoroughly awake, he
would spend the rest of the night singing psalms or chanting
prayers, and so would he watch through what remained of the
night.

For the rest, he practiced meditation with so much constancy
that he often employed it all day and all night. Often he was
heard murmuring some prayer without cease. Sometimes during the night, when he was exercising his functions of guardian
in the church, he heard the metal of the golden statue of Sainte
Foy resound, and then, obedient to this warning, he would hurry
to relight the lamp in the way I have already described. It was for
him a habitual favor, and more frequent than for any other, to
enjoy in diverse manners these conversations and divine signs or
notifications. One is not astonished to find him worthy of these
sweetnesses, for nothing impure could find access either to his
body or to his soul. Always ready to do works for the good of his
brothers, he could be surpassed by no one in the virtue of obedience. As for the vivacity and the ardor of his temperament, he
conformed to the precept "Let your indignation burst out, but
guard you from sinning." The eminence of his virtue was such
that he exercised an ascendancy not only on the other brothers
but on the abbot himself. He ranged all under the yoke of a perfect discipline, not by the effect of his learning or his discourse,
but by the force of his example.

So Sainte Foy played, touching her beloved old guardian Gimon
fondly on the cheek (as later she would touch her blinded jongleur,
Guibert), announcing through the small miracles with which she
teased the rough old warrior that if the light was taken away, she
could bring it back. "She favored Gimon as no other with these
sweetnesses," says Bernard, and so, it seems to me, she favors Père
André. Tested and tormented as he often is, for his life of service to
her is a very hard one, yet—as in another age the lady from time to
time favored the troubadour who was ready to die in service to her

whom he loved, to her he celebrated in verse—Sainte Foy, shining in her golden aura, touches her old, prickly, kind Père André with a thousand graces, lighting up his life of bondage. Pledged to obedience, following the rule of the Order of Saint Norbert, he grabbed up my hands warmly one day when I walked in and said, excited, "Oh, Sainte Foy is good! Sainte Foy is good! She still works miracles!" Just then a group arrived, and they had to have their tickets taken. When I returned to talk to Père André, I asked him what he had meant. "Oh, it is not something I can talk about," he said. "You understand that. There are things that are too personal. One cannot talk about them. You understand that, Hannah. I know that."

"Yes," I replied. "Yes, I know."

After the early mass, when the women of Conques linger in the chapel of the Virgin Mary in the north transept to recite their rosaries in unison, I have seen Père André go and fall on his knees in the south transept in the chapel before the altar of Sainte Foy and remain there a long time, rapt in prayer, a lone figure in white in the shadows of the church with its thick, tall stone columns, its arches high above.

"The Church frowns on that," Père André replied benignly when I inquired about the women reciting their rosaries aloud.

But the instructions to do this came from the Virgin Mary herself. Madame Benoit told me about it. "There is too much evil in the world now, too much caring for material things, too much sin. The Very Blessed Virgin Mary, Mother of God, urges us to pray, to pray, to receive the Eucharist daily if possible, and to recite our rosaries. We must recite our rosaries when we are alone, and we should recite them aloud together when we can—in groups, in families." Madame Benoit told me this urgently in a low voice so as not to be overheard. "The world will not end, but a great change is coming," she said.

All this came to her from Mama Rosa Quattrini at San Damiano in northern Italy, where every Friday between 1964 and 1970 the Virgin Mary appeared. "She appeared to Mama Rosa about noon in her garden. There is a pear tree there and a plum tree," Madame Benoit said. "When she appeared to Mama Rosa the first time it was as if she came in a cloud of gold and silver surrounded by stars and roses of every color. She said that her Son could no longer carry His cross, and that we must pray, we must pray, we must recite our rosaries, that she came as the Mother of Love, as the mother of us all, the good and the bad, and that because she loves us and because she loves her Son she urges us to pray. She ordered Mama Rosa to announce to the world what she said. Mama Rosa said no one

would believe her, an ignorant peasant woman. The Virgin Mary,
Mother of God, said she would leave her a sign: The pear tree
would bloom. It was a gloomy and rainy October, but the pear tree
flowered there in the garden of her little farm, and part of the plum
tree, too, that part which was touched by the Very Holy Virgin.

"Oh, and they gathered a great *corbeille* of pears that Christmas
and some plums as well," said Madame Benoit.

"The Virgin Mary appeared to Mama Rosa after 1970 also, right
up until the hour of her death in 1974. Every Friday at noon she appeared, and on all the special fête days of the Very Holy Virgin, but
in 1970 Mama Rosa's bishop ordered her to stop transmitting the
messages. Mama Rosa was obedient," Madame Benoit said.

Madame Benoit took hold of my arm. In her low voice, almost
whispering, she said, "Every day between noon and twelve forty-
five is the hour of the Virgin. Pray to her then. Ask for her protection. The birds fly around for her then." Madame Benoit waved her
short arms around like the swallows flying around the church for
the Virgin Mary.

"Or pray to Sainte Foy. She will protect you. It is the same thing
really. The same thing." She smiled. She shrugged. She was happy.

"I like you very much," she said.

I feel the light of the lovely intelligence of her blue eyes, and the
perfect comfortable harmony of her being, both soft and strong.
Henry Adams was carried away by his perception of the *energy* cre-
ated by the Virgin Mary, the energy that built the cathedral at
Chartres in the twelfth century. Here at Conques in this century
the Virgin Mary fills a very old woman to whom she has appeared
in vision with the sweetest of graces. Madame Benoit's white face
glows with the purity of her smile.

"France is consecrated to the Virgin," Madame Benoit proudly
declared. "May is her month."

She belongs to an organization called Les Esclaves de Marie, the
Slaves of Mary, and she can be almost pugnacious in defense of the
Virgin. The men of Conques tap their heads when she gets going.

"*Toc, toc,*" says Rosalie, but in truth Rosalie is as susceptible to all
this as I am, and she wears the medal of the Madonna of the Roses
that Madame Benoit brought back to her from San Damiano, where

she goes every fall with Madame Fallière before the fête day of
Sainte Foy. They go together in an enormous bus with all the other
pilgrims from this region, and they sing, they sing, they sing, all the
way to San Damiano, Madame Benoit says. And when she gets back,
joyous and renewed and full of energy, she sings us the songs they
sang on the way, and she gets more and more excited telling us this
and that. There is something about water, about a well Mama Rosa
had had drilled, something about Father Pio, and something about
an enormous church that had been built, but they were not allowed
to go in. I do not understand everything she says when she gets
going too fast.

"They always see something," says Madame Fau—Babet—her
eyes alight with pleasure. "If not the Virgin herself, a chalice, perhaps, or a monstrance."

Out in her kitchen garden, Rosalie gives Madame Benoit a bouquet of dahlias. "They are not for me. They are for the Virgin Mary,"
Madame Benoit says. Rosalie pretends not to hear that. Madame
Benoit goes off proudly with the flowers to take them up the winding stairs to her apartment.

She puts them in a vase on the desk, where she keeps the little
white statue of the Virgin of San Damiano, the Madonna of the
Roses—below the picture of the face of Jesus as it appeared on the
veil of Saint Veronica (meaning "true image") and a photograph of
the pope.

"Now he is somebody!" she said to me approvingly as she looked
at the face of Jean-Paul II.

Nearby on her desk was the handsome old-fashioned face of her
husband with his smooth brow, his large dark eyes, his dark hair and
mustache. He died of tuberculosis nearly sixty years ago. On the
wall opposite, in the corner, there was a tiny faded photograph of a
young girl standing in her First Communion dress, Madame
Benoit's beloved firstborn, her daughter, Germaine Fides, who
died of the same illness the year after her father.

"I named her Germaine Fides rather than Foy," she said another
time, "because Fides is more beautiful."

"*Une brave dame!*" Père André says of Madame Benoit. He is very
fond of her. She loves to discuss theology and Church matters with

him. "He has faith, he is pure," she says of Père André. She does not think the same of Père Gilles on either count.

And when the women of Conques begin in the first light of morning, "Ave Maria, full of Grace . . . ," Père André falls down to pray before the altar of Sainte Foy. He told me that at nine o'clock, just before he turns on the lights and opens the iron gate to the Treasure each morning, he always prays to Sainte Foy there in the dark. He prays that it will be a good day. And he prays for everyone who may come into the Treasure that day.

"Hannah!" Père André says now when he sees me. "I didn't see you come in." We shake hands.

His handshake is, like his intellect, firm and extraordinarily powerful.

"I was very quiet," I tell him.

"*Coquine!*" (hussy), he says, smiling broadly.

Père André goes to one of the lighted cases so he can press the button to make first the *A* of Charlemagne and then the reliquary of Pepin II turn round for the tourists. Like the reliquary of Pepin II, which was given originally to Conques by Pepin II, king of Aquitaine, the *A* of Charlemagne was considerably refashioned at Conques in an atelier of goldsmiths, that flourished here for several centuries. Some of the work on this *A* dates from about three hundred years after Charlemagne, Protector of Holy Places, gave to Conques the *A* of his kingdom, for its abbey school was first in the realm.

"The emperor together with the empire shall go to school," Charlemagne declared.

He conceived the thought, as I imagine, that Conques should have this *A* on one of the sleepless nights when, as Einhard tells us, he used to practice his letters on the slate he kept beneath his pillow. When he came here in the last years of his life, carrying on his person, as was his wont, a relic of the true cross, Charlemagne brought two precious relics he had got from his uncle Carloman at Monte Cassino: a piece of the foreskin of the circumcised Christ, and a piece of His umbilical cord; and arriving here, Charlemagne fell down on his knees at the Porte du Barry and crawled on his knees up the hill from there to the door of the basilica of the Holy Savior.

On the tympanum above the western doors to the church we see the crowned Charlemagne in the procession of the elect, being led forward by the hand by a bishop-abbot toward Christ the Judge in heaven. On the face of the aged king there is an expression of gentle but resigned uncertainty; his shoulders are a bit stooped, his step not sure; he seems to have been wakened from a dream, the dream of his long-ago life, which he wears like a mantle, to find himself dazed and slightly sad in this amazing light among so many strangers being led toward the Lord; while the face of the young bishop-abbot who leads him is filled with the intense and joyous calm of bliss. He knows. In 1165, not long after the tympanum was completed, Charlemagne, the most human of kings, beloved hero, glorified in poetry and exalted in iconography, was canonized. It is as if symbolically, in humbly presenting the most holy relics and honoring this abbey by his imperial presence, Charlemagne, sometime between 801 and 814, prepared the way so that more than half a century later Sainte Foy would be brought here to fill the hillside with her roses.

"What have you there?" her father said, catching her, finally, stealing bread from his kitchen to take to a hungry family in the city.

"Flowers, father," she replied.

"*Flowers*," he said, scoffing. "Let me see your *flowers*."

And she pulled from the folds of her dress a bouquet of roses red as the dawn and alight with drops of morning dew.

Her father turned purple in rage. He knew then that she was Christian. But not that roses were the symbol of celestial bliss, nor that they would fill the hillside gardens and climb the walls of the houses of the little town that, off to the east and up in the mountains, would grow up around the bones of his daughter in another culture and another time.

.   .   .

It is the only miracle of her short lifetime before the Acts of her Martyrdom that has come down to us in legend. And so she brought them here, her roses, her miracles, to "her country of election," Père André says, "where she never ceased to work miracles of every sort.

"She worked them for the sake of justice; she worked them out of pity for those wronged or oppressed or afflicted. And then she worked them, it seemed, to amuse herself, as if she were playing. She was famous for her *joca,* the people called them."

"*Joca,*" Bernard of Angers wrote, was what the people of this country, "in their rustic language," called the playful, teasing miracles she worked by the hundreds with such facility, and the funny things she made happen sometimes in the midst of her grander operations.

"You know the story of the bon mot of the countess Bertha, I suppose," says Père André.

"Yes!" I say proudly.

I like it especially because, serious as he is in his purpose, even ponderous, at times, in his painstaking efforts to prove himself no liar, Bernard cannot help but be infected by a certain glee, so charming and triumphant is his subject. And it is in this spirit of gleeful braggadocio that (sounding at moments not altogether unlike a modern-day society reporter) he describes the occasion of the statement of the venerable countess Bertha. It was, according to Bernard's editor and translator, the abbé Bouillet, sometime between 1004 and 1012 that the very reverend bishop Arnaldus of Rodez convoked for his diocesians the synod described by Bernard in the twenty-eighth chapter of the first *Book of the Miracles of Sainte Foy.* "All the golden majesties of this country were brought by their diverse congregations of monks and canons to the prairie of St. Felix about a mile to the north of the hill on which the city of Rodez is built, and there," reports Bernard, "these shrines were ranged in the tents and pavilions which had been set up for them. The golden majesty of Saint Marius, confessor and pontiff, was there, and that of Saint Amans, also confessor and pontiff, as well as the *châsse* [reliquary] of Saint Saturnin, martyr, and the golden statue of Saint Mary, Mother of God, to whom the cathedral at

Rodez is dedicated, and finally, the golden majesty of Sainte Foy. There were other shrines present too numerous for me to name on this occasion when the goodness of the All Powerful deigned to glorify His servant by a signal miracle.

"A young boy child afflicted since his birth by four infirmities—he was deaf and dumb and blind and lame—was brought by his parents to the foot of the dais on which the majesty of Sainte Foy had been placed with honor. The child lay there for about an hour. His mother and father and all about were praying for him when the divine intervention was manifested. The little boy stood up and looked around. He could see. He could hear. He began to walk and he walked perfectly. Then he began to talk. At this the amazement of the crowd burst out into what seemed to the bishops, sitting on an elevated platform at a little distance, to be a most terrific uproar.

" 'What on earth can be the cause of this popular clamor?' the venerable bishops were asking each other.

" 'What,' replied the countess Bertha, 'could it be other than one of the typical little *joca* of our Sainte Foy.'

"As word of the miracle spread," writes Bernard, "the whole great assembly, filled with astonishment and elation, began unanimously to celebrate the divine praises. And all, drunk with joy, were pleased to repeat, one to the next, the comment of the venerable countess on the subject of the little *joca,* the playful *jogs menuz* of Sainte Foy."

"Oh, how greatly favored this country / To which God had brought so powerful a saint. / She made for them great miracles, / and very pretty things [*plaiz molt gentz*] and little jokes [*jogs menuz*]," they sang in her song.

Sainte Foy could be quite fierce, and her fury could be final; she could be a warrior when she had to be, but for the most part she took on the character of a charming child, affectionate and loving and lovely, young lady, girl of almost thirteen, full of gaiety and humor, going after, for instance, the jewels of special beauty that she wanted, as if it were to satisfy her feminine vanity. So she lived out in her miracles in the people's minds the rest of the young years she had denied herself.

"*Joca Sanctae Fidis,*" Père André says in Latin. "*Joculatrix. Joglaresse*

the troubadours called her when they sang her glories, when they
sang, for instance, the story of how she obtained the golden sleeves
of Arsinde, the wife of Guillaume Taillefer, Count of Toulouse.

"And she was a *coquine!*" Père André says. "The way she teased
and played with her old guardian Gimon, for example. You know
that story?"

"Yes," I say, smiling happily and wondering if maybe Gimon
hadn't looked a bit like Père André. Certainly he would have had
hands of extraordinary power, like Père André's.

"They say it was Sainte Foy's own father who turned her in,"
Madame Benoit said in a low voice as if she were telling me a confidence about a neighbor.

"Her mother was Sophie. Her little sister was Alberte," she continued. "Her mother sympathized but did not have the courage to
be Christian. It was Sainte Foy's nurse who taught her the Christian
religion and took her secretly, when she was still very young, to
Saint Caprais, the Bishop of Agen, to be baptized. And Saint Caprais
instructed her then. As a pupil she was extraordinary. *Extraordinaire,*" Madame Benoit repeated, throwing her head back and smiling with pride. "Sainte Foy was very intelligent, you know.
Precocious, you might say—the first in her school in the arts of
rhetoric and grammar, ahead of all the boys, and these gifts she used
when she went with the bread or flour from her father's kitchen
stores to give to the poor in the city, to tell them, too, the things
that Jesus said, and the things He did, and how He was God, and
how He honored them. She was very learned, and she was radiant
when she spoke of Christ. And she was gay! She was warm! She
laughed and joked, and she played with the children and the babies,
and she comforted tired mothers, and she talked seriously with the
girls of her own age. She took them presents, too—toys and little
jewels and warm clothing, everything of worldly value that she had
outgrown. Certainly she was not hated. At least no one would have
thought so. *Au contraire:* She was beloved! So when the news came
that the proconsul Dacien was on his way to Agen, Saint Caprais
fled the city, taking with him all the Christians, to protect them

until the danger was over, but he left Sainte Foy there in the care of her family because she was still so young. She was only twelve, you know. He had no reason to think she wouldn't be safe. They were a family of noble blood. A proud Nitobridgian family of ancient Celtic stock. Her father had a position of importance in the provincial government. Certainly he could have protected her. Probably he just thought he would teach her a lesson. He didn't know. No, he didn't know what strength she had, his Faith."

In her parents' house as the proconsul Dacien approached the city, everyone slept, even the servants, but the young Faith lay wakeful in the silken sheets of her bed. She could hear the rumble of the mob without. The hot light from their torches seemed to throb through her room, lighting the wooden cross that hung there. There was no one to talk to. Her nurse, her beloved Martha, had gone.

"The bishop, the young Caprais, he is taking us up there," Martha had said, waving her arm toward the wild white rocky mountain and plateau beyond the Garonne. "There is a cave up there where he will hide us. Until the danger is passed, my little lamb," Martha said, embracing her fondly and stroking her hair. "They say this is the most terrible of all the persecutions until now. The emperors aim to annihilate us—each and every Christian. But we shall be victorious in the name of Jesus Christ our Lord." And she made the sign of the cross on the forehead of her Faith. Martha was gone.

Faith got up and dressed and lighted the lamps in her room and went to walk by the marble pool in the atrium. A beam of moonlight shone on her fragrant hair. A yellow leaf floated in from somewhere out there above the turbulence in the night. She gave a gasp of delight and leaned down to pick it up and gaze at it—the leaf so lovely, the delicate perfection of its lines, pale gold in the moonlight. It seemed to have come from heaven to comfort her, and she smoothed it against her cheek and kissed it, even as she saw the trembling surface of the pool, and the faint red shaking there, reflecting the fires carried by the running mob.

Passing through the columns of the peristyle, she returned to her

room. On scrolls of papyrus from Egypt she had carefully copied,
under the tutoring eye of Bishop Caprais, secretly, after school,
passages from the Gospels, and these she drew out from the
drawer, where she kept them hidden. From Saint Mark she read the
words that Jesus spoke on the Mount of Olives against the temple
as the time of His death drew nigh.

> . . . and ye shall be brought before rulers and kings for my
> sake, for a testimony against them.
> And the gospel must first be published among all nations.
> But when they shall lead you, and deliver you up, take no
> thought beforehand what ye shall speak, neither do ye premedi-
> tate: but whatsoever shall be given you in that hour, that speak
> ye: for it is not ye that speak, but the Holy Ghost.
> Now the brother shall betray the brother to death, and the fa-
> ther the son . . . (13:9–12)

"And the father the daughter," Faith heard herself saying, and she
turned to Saint John, reading through her tears, things that Jesus
said to his disciples when His hour was come and Judas had gone
from the room to betray Him. He said, and she read, speaking,
hearing:

> And I will pray the Father, and he shall give you another Com-
> forter, that he may abide with you forever;
> Even the Spirit of the truth; whom the world cannot receive,
> because it seeth him not, neither knoweth him: but ye know
> him; for he dwelleth with you, and shall be in you.
> I will not leave you comfortless: I will come to you.
> Yet a little while, and the world seeth me no more; but ye see
> me: because I live, ye shall live also. (14:16–19)
> These things I have spoken unto you, that my joy might re-
> main in you, and that your joy might be full. (15:11)

Now Faith knelt down before the cross. She prayed. While the
roar of the mob raged on through the night of the city, and the proconsul Dacien slept, guarded by soldiers, Faith prayed to Jesus for
strength in the day ahead. She prayed that the words that came to
her lips, like those that came to Esther of old, would be words that
pleased Him.

She called up the image of Him in her mind, of Christ the Son of God, of Christ the Lord, of Christ the teacher, Wisdom, the Word made flesh; she thought of His body on the cross, of His agony, His death. She thought of His resurrection to go unto the Father, leaving His word: "And this is life eternal, that they might know Thee the only true God, and Jesus Christ, whom Thou hast sent" (John 17:3). She gazed up at the cross through her tears, dwelling first on the idea of Him as Truth, and then on His suffering, and on the mystery of His triumph.

She closed her eyes again to pray. She prayed. She prayed until, at last, like Thecla, in her heart she sang, I keep myself untouched for you, tending my gleaming lamps. Bridegroom, I come to you!

And when, as the sun rose, the soldiers came for her, she was ready.

"Let them take her," said her father. "It is the only way for her to learn responsibility."

She could hear her mother weeping in her room beyond the atrium. "Tell my mother not to grieve. I go in joy," she said. "This will be my wedding gown, Father." Weakened a moment by her father's power, she laughed a nervous laugh. Her lovely hands brushed the cloth that covered her small body. She had chosen her most beautiful dress, a rose-pink brocade with white. "Tell nurse Martha I went in joy, will you, Father, when she comes back?"

The soldiers took her roughly.

"Wait!" her father called.

> Lo corps es belz, e pauce l'estaz
> Lo sen es gencer, ge dinz jaz.
> Los oilz a gentz, e blanca faz;
> El senz des cor es mais prezaz.
> Antz qe doz anz agges passaz,
> Tal obra fez qe Deu molt plaz:
> Martiri pres, e fort assaz,
> Tal con ligez e con cantaz.
> O Deus! tant n'es est monz honraz!

Lovely her body and small in size;
Fairer still the sense within her.

White her face and pretty her eyes;
The sense of her heart is yet more prized.
Before she passed twelve years of age,
Such works she did that God was pleased:
Martyr she was, and very awesome,
Such as you read it and as you sing it.
Oh God! How the world is honored in her!

"Sweeter and more fragrant than honeycomb" is this song which sprang from her young martyr-death (love-death) and was written down in the language of the people, to be sung and danced to. For this song, composed of 593 octosyllabic lines arranged in monorhymed strophes—*laisses*—of varying length, "is a song made for dancing," the jongleur sang (or clerk or monk). The people listened and, slowly, gravely, began to dance in the presence of her statue on the eve of the vigil of her passion, after the liturgical office and the reading of the *Passio* here in the church built for her relics, for her body entombed behind the altar of the Holy Savior, and for her—spirit-bone, encased in wood, covered with gold, studded with gemstones, shining forth from her dark heart chamber.

When Père André is happy there is a joyous lilt to his voice, and it is a pleasant thing to hear him speak, as he does now, shining his flashlight into the solar center, the hemisphere of polished rock crystal at the summit of the *A* of Charlemagne.

"The *A* of Charlemagne is famous," he says to the tourist group. "Here at Conques it is as celebrated as Charlemagne is in the world at large."

As he tells them the story from the *Liber Mirabilis,* the early chronicle of Conques, of how Charlemagne gave the *A* to Conques because its abbey school was first in the realm, he continues to let his flashlight shine into the hemisphere, which suggests the sun, held in place as it is by three slender bands of gold (gilded copper) that meet in a radiating starlike center.*

Père André begins to move his flashlight to illumine the gemstones and the lovely filigree work that surround the solar crystal. He speaks of the exquisite workmanship, the rare elegance of design, and he shows how as the filigree descends the legs of the *A,* the gemstones are arranged in an alternating pattern, two small, which are hemispheres, one large, which is ovoid, from the summit to the base.

"There are amethysts, garnets, agates, emeralds, and carnelians," he says. The stones glow with their various colors as he moves his light across them. "It is a scroll pattern such as one finds in illuminated manuscripts of all epochs from the ninth through the thirteenth centuries," he says. "The *A* is made of gold and gilded silver covering a base of oak wood," he says. "Its total height is 42.5 cen-

* As Christ is identified by the Alpha and the Omega, symbol of eternity, from the Book of Revelation—"I am Alpha and Omega, the beginning and the ending, saith the Lord, which is and which was, and which is to come, the Almighty" (Rev. 1:8); "I am Alpha and Omega, the beginning and the end" (Rev. 21:6); "I am Alpha and Omega, the beginning and the end, the first and the last" (Rev. 22:13)—so is He identified also with the sun.

timeters, and it is 40 centimeters wide at the base" (16.7 inches by
15.7 inches).

There is no need for Père André to describe what one feels if one
is here: that these reliquaries are not cold, as precious stones and
metal might suggest, nor do they give off a feeling of riches in the
cold material sense. Rather, they are warm. They suggest the richness of the earth, its lights, its colors, the immense variety of treasure, of things that can be found in the earth and its rocks, and at
the edges of its seas. And, further, looking at these objects closely,
one feels the warmth that comes from the caring that has gone into
them through the centuries, the caring of the hands that touched
them in reverence, and of the hands that worked with amazing skill
to make them beautiful, changing them as skills were developed, as
more riches were acquired, and as ideas of the beautiful were trans-
figured, then patching, preserving, for there were those other
meaty hands that came with knives to cut away gemstones and
pieces of goldwork in greed. Here and there gemstones are missing, and there is a certain tattered quality that makes the oldest of
these reliquaries moving. Further still there is the warmth, the life,
the gentleness, that comes from the fact that each was made to contain, to honor, to elevate to a shining beauty that could transport
one, some tiny fragment of human matter long preserved, or of
wood that was said to be the wood of the True Cross soaked with
the blood of Christ, or of wood that had touched this sacred wood
and had thus acquired its healing oil and its power. And these tiny
crosses and bits of bone and hair and cloth still remain, some visible and some hidden, identified in writing on pieces of parchment,
within the reliquaries made for them. Some of the writing is in
Merovingian script, some Carolingian, and so on, up through the
ages.

"We cannot be certain that Charlemagne brought the precious
relics of our Savior here in this *A*," Père André says, "but we do
know, at any rate, that the work on this side of the *A*—not the base,
which was added much later—but the work on this side of the *A*
belongs almost certainly to the Carolingian period. And the form
of the *A* before the base was added resembles that of certain capital
*A*s found in Carolingian manuscripts.

"Bernard of Angers tells us in his *Liber Miraculorum Sanctae Fidis,*
written between 1013 and 1028, and considered, by the way, by
many scholars to be one of the pearls of the literature of the Middle Ages"—Père André waves his white-sleeved arm grandly to
point out Conques's copy (a fragment) from the eleventh century,
lying open across the room in the case with the trunk that holds the
bones of Sainte Foy's body—"Bernard tells us that when the statue
of Sainte Foy was taken in procession to another place it was 'always
accompanied by the reliquary brought here, they say, by Charlemagne.'

"So even then, a little after the year one thousand," Père André
says, smiling, "even then the tradition of Charlemagne coming here
existed, and even then there was some doubt.

"The coming of Charlemagne to Conques had long since taken
on the aura of legend. The *A* of Charlemagne seems to have been
borne here, as it were, on the wings of the 'Song of Roland'; yet
there is no reason to suppose on this account that Charlemagne did
not come here. He was the most human of kings. 'And when
Charles died,' wrote Einhard, 'the world lost its father.' He traveled
widely. He was crowned emperor at Rome in the year 800. He visited his uncle Carloman at Monte Cassino in the south of Italy. It
would have been most natural that as emperor he come to visit
Aquitaine, the kingdom of his son Louis the Pious, and that while
here he visit at least one among 'the twenty-six fair abbeys of
Aquitaine' that Louis the Pious founded or endowed and then took
under his protection. Of these 'twenty-six fair abbeys' Conques is
mentioned especially by Louis's biographer, the anonymous Limousine astronomer called Astronome; and alone among the fair
abbeys of Aquitaine, Conques is described in detail by Ermoldus
Nigellus, Ermold Le Noir, in his 'Poem in Praise of Louis the
Pious,' written down about 826. It would seem that very early
Conques held a special place in the imagination of the people, possibly because of the legend that had grown up around Dadon, our
holy hermit. Datus he was called in Latin from Deodatus—given to
God.

"Ermold tells us that Louis the King himself gave Conques its
name and that he had the route of access cut through the moun-

tains, a considerable achievement in itself, and therefore, I ask myself, why would the great and fatherly holy Charles not have come
here to this monastery, still young and poor, newly submitted to the
rule of Saint Benedict, and already boasting numbers of monks and
a very fine abbey school. Both Ermold's account and an early charter set the date of the founding, or rather we should say the *re*-
founding, of Conques as 801—the year, that is, when it would have
been refounded under Louis's protection and dedicated to the rule
of Saint Benedict. Surely Charles, in the years between then and his
death in 814, could have come in all reverence, bearing the precious relics of our Savior to this abbey dedicated at that time to
Him, the Holy Savior.

"I say refounding, by the way, because although the earliest written document is the charter of 801, both tradition and archaeological evidence would set the existence of Conques much further
back. Tradition has it that there were hermit monks here as early as
the late fourth century. One of our ancient writers described Conques as having been in those early days 'a veritable Thébaïde' of hermit monks, all inspired by the example of Saint Anthony of Egypt,"
Père André adds. "And beneath the stones of the church they
found, toward the end of the last century, a circular foundation
which may have been a Druidic temple. As is the case with many
holy places, Conques was holy, no doubt, before the time of Christ.

"Now although I am almost certain that Charlemagne did, as our
chronicle, the *Liber Mirabilis,* states, bring the precious relics here in
this *A,* it could be, as Alfred Darcel, our great authority on the Treasure, suggests, that this *A* was originally made to hang from the
right arm of a crucifix such as that you see in Toulouse at Saint
Sernin, and that it is what remains of two enormous images of
Christ on the cross in silver, ornamented with gold and precious
stones, which were given to Conques and to the Nouvelle-Conques
at Figeac by Abbot Aigmarus, who governed Conques and its dependent abbey for thirty-two years beginning in 816."

Through the years Père André has developed certain strong (even
headstrong) ideas of his own on certain questions in Conques's his-

tory (he told me he has prayed to Sainte Foy for guidance in these matters), but all that he has just said about Conques's history is precisely what I have gleaned from my reading; and in describing the Treasure, apart from his own expression of feeling, which is very tender and aesthetically open, he follows for the most part the study made by Alfred Darcel, whom he has just mentioned.

Alfred Darcel, Attaché à la Direction Générale des Musées Imperiaux, having been, he wrote, led here "as if by chance" in 1860 to find (like Prosper Mérimée before him) such riches as he never suspected, returned to this valley—"still," he wrote, "the *vallis lapidosa* of the chronicles"—and walked the twenty kilometers in from the train station at Marcillac, carrying his archaeological sack on his back, and a book in his hand to read when he tired "of the wild grandeur of the scenery." He stayed to make a thorough study of the Treasure and of the antique intaglios on the statue of Sainte Foy and the other reliquaries.

This he did with the help of the curé, Monsieur l'Abbé Turq-Calsade, taking the objects from the big armoire behind the high master altar in the church, where they had been kept, he said, since the loyal inhabitants of Conques, who risked their lives to save them during the Revolution, had brought them back once the danger was over and the church reopened for worship. Both the reliquaries and the relics they contained were exposed to the veneration of the faithful on the grand feast days of the year, Alfred Darcel said, and in the meantime he took them, one by one, to the *presbytère,* where he made detailed drawings of every object to scale, and took wax molds of each intaglio and every cameo. He also, clearly, read all the relevant documents in Latin, and possessed a broad knowledge in the field, as well as a fine romantic, intuitive temperament, and his study remains one of the most detailed and authoritative to date, together with the study of the statue of Sainte Foy made by Jean Taralon at the time of its restoration in 1954, which used photography and advanced techniques for dating and, incidentally, proved Darcel correct in his estimation that the statue dates from the ninth century.

.   .   .

"The Alpha and the Omega," Père André tells the tourists, "traditionally appear as signs in early medieval art on either side of the crucified Christ, as they do in Toulouse at Saint Sernin, or of the Christ in Glory, as they do, for example, in the lovely eleventh-century marble relief from the antependium of the altar of Deusdedit, now conserved in the Musée Fenaille in Rodez.

"There you see the Alpha and the Omega, once filled with a luminous substance, on either side of the beautiful Christ in Glory, seated in heaven, holding the Book of Life in his left hand, and displaying the host, also once filled with a luminous substance, in his right hand."*

"Or as they do here." Père André points and then crosses the room to show them the Alpha and Omega on either side of the minute portrait of Christ in the portable altar in alabaster and gold and enamel cloisonné from the eleventh century. It is called the Altar of Sainte Foy.

"Now!" Père André presses his hands together as if in prayer and holding them out before him he walks rapidly back across the room, his white robe flowing, and the tourists trailing after him. "Now!" he says again, turning toward them and beaming. He presses the button, and the *A* of Charlemagne swings slowly around to reveal its reverse face. "Look at this stone," he says, shining his flashlight into the center of a large orangish intaglio in the center of the circular summit. "It is a carnelian," he says. "And on it is engraved a Winged Victory. One of her feet is raised and resting on a shield. She holds the other shield on her knee and she appears to be writing on it. Nearby is a tree on which hangs a trophy. It is of the Greek epoch. It is 11 millimeters (0.43 inches) in width. Think of that. Eleven millimeters in width, and all that is carved on it, very beautifully carved on it. One wonders how it could be done. The details are exquisite. No wonder such stones were so highly prized in the Middle Ages. How awed they must have been by the work-

* So this figure, then, as the Alpha and Omega, stands for Christ who is Eternity, which is beyond time, outside it, yet in time, in the procession of the hours, the days, the years, in the person, the physical body of the historical Christ, who was and is and ever will be, by the ritual of transubstantiation, miraculously present in the consecrated host.

manship! The art of such carving had been lost. The iconography of antiquity, too, was lost, and the men who set this stone may have thought the figure was an angel. Saint Michael perhaps. Sometimes in the Middle Ages antique cameos and intaglios such as this came to possess magic and incantatory powers.

"Here below on this leg of the *A* we see a figure of Achilles engraved on nicolo." He points with his flashlight to a small bluish-gray stone with a lone figure carved on it. "Perhaps they thought it was one of the apostles," he says. "Or Lazarus risen from the dead."

Père André moves the beam of his flashlight to illumine the ravishing goldwork—tiny pearls of gold, like minute rosebuds, which surround in two circles the Winged Victory, and the third larger circle of crosses and flower patterns in enamels cloisonné—"all the work of the goldsmiths in the atelier of *orfèvrerie* that flourished here at Conques in the eleventh, twelfth, and thirteenth centuries," he tells me again, "as is the lovely filigree work that descends the legs of the *A* on this side."

"Now for the base!" Père André turns to beam at the tourists. He presses the button to return the *A* to its original position. He shines his flashlight to illuminate the inscription along the interior of the *A*. It says, "The abbot Begon had this object fashioned and placed herein the holy relics."

"Pay no attention to that," Père André says.

"This inscription seems to have been added posteriorly to the *A* itself and perhaps even to the base . . .

"You will see Abbot Begon's charming funerary plaque above his *enfeu* (wall-niche tomb) on the south side of the abbey church. It shows Christ in Glory with two angels and Sainte Foy with the abbot Begon raised into heaven. The inscription there in Latin verse reads:

> HIC EST ABBAS SITUS
> DIVINA LEGE PERITUS
> VIR DOMINO GRATUS
> DE NOMINE BEGO VOCATUS
> HOC PERAGENS CLAUSTRUM
> QUOD VERSUS TENDIT AD AUSTRUM

GESSIT ET ALTERA PLURA

SOLLERTI CURA BONA

HIC EST LAUDANDUS

PER SECULA VIR VENERANDUS

   VIVAT IN ETERNUM

REGEM LAUDANDO SUPERNUM

Here lies an abbot
Versed in the divine law;
A man agreeable to the Lord,
He was named Begon.
He built this cloister
Which extends to the south.
He performed his cares with diligence,
And accomplished several other works as well.
A venerable man, worthy of praise
Across the centuries,
Let him live in eternity
Praising the supreme King.

"Prosper Mérimée," he says, "who came here in 1836 for the Bureau of Historic Monuments and, 'astounded to find such a treasure as Conques in such a desert,' managed by his report and his action in our behalf to save the church from destruction and what remained of the cloister—three sides had by then already been taken down, destroyed forever—Prosper Mérimée was the first in our time to note how fond of poetry the monks of Conques had been. Eight hundred years before him, Bernard of Angers had made the same observation.

"Now, the abbot Begon, to whom we owe so much at Conques and here in the Treasure, governed the abbey from 1087 to 1107, and we do indeed attribute to him—to his abbacy—these angels on the base of the *A,* as well as several other reliquaries.

"Look at these angels. Look at them!" Père André smiles with pleasure as he stands back and shines his light. "Observe the modeling. How supple it is. How graceful. They are barefoot and they are swinging censers. See the expression on their faces. They are standing in the niches dear to the Romanesque sculptors' hearts, and they resemble not only certain large figures of the time, sculpted in stone, but such figures standing in illuminated manuscripts of the Romanesque period. There is no doubt that these angels were fashioned under Begon III.

"I want you to come with me a moment to examine the reliquary that we call the Reliquary of Pascal II because it was built for a piece of the True Cross that Pope Pascal II sent to Abbot Begon III as the century turned in the year 1100."

Père André moves forward to the next case and directs his light on a wooden cross revealed by the opening in the beaten silver on the undulating, slightly slanted jeweled rooftop.

"This reliquary has been so considerably refashioned that it is difficult to tell what remains from the original," he says. His flashlight illumines the figures of Christ on the cross, of the Virgin Mary and Saint John standing below it, and the two figures in the disks of the sun and the moon above. "These figures seem to date from a later period. [Jean-Claude Fau thinks they date from the fifteenth century, but almost certainly they replaced an earlier crucifixion scene.] Now! Look at this!"

Père André lights a tiny fragment, a face, shown on a velvet stand. The face has a ravishing beauty and is almost exactly the same as the face of one of the angels on the A.

"It is by the same hand," Père André says quietly, "the hand that made the angels on the base of the A, and we think it is a fragment of the original crucifixion scene on this reliquary.

"And now, come look at these portrait busts in relief on this reliquary, called the Lantern of Saint Vincent or the Lantern of Begon. These saints were fashioned, too, almost certainly, by the same artist who fashioned the angels on the A."

He moves back and presses a button so the Lantern of Saint Vincent begins to turn. A tall circular reliquary, square at the bottom and hexagonal where its windows are, with a roof in silver and gilded silver, its tiles all defined, it is like a tiny architectural model of one of those little towers called Lanterns of the Dead that used to burn in cemeteries through the night, and it resembles in style the small Byzantine towers on the domed cathedral of Saint Front at Périgueux or the domed abbey church at Souillac, both influenced, it is believed, by the style brought back to Aquitaine from Byzantium by the First Crusaders.

There is a jeweled ring around the lantern's top (turning, turning), and inside its windows lie three small bundles of relics enwrapped in red silk and identified in writing in a fine hand on a piece of parchment.

I cannot make out the writing, but I see it is signed by Père Marie-Bernard, who was the curé when Madame Benoit was a child. Her beloved Père Marie-Bernard. I have heard his name on her lips many times. It was he who wrote the Passion play that all of Conques acted in when she was a child. "Oh, it was famous!" she said. "People came from as far away as Toulouse to see it! We used the whole church, Heaven was up in the tribune. I was eleven the last year of the play at the fin de siècle. I was an angel," she said. "I came down on a pulley from the tribune, bringing a chalice to Jesus. Jesus was in the garden of agony and an angel appeared carrying a chalice and singing to him." In her high reedy old voice, still lovely, she sang the words she had sung as a child of eleven, bringing the chalice to Jesus. "Thou must drink it, drink it all down to the dregs, the chalice of sorrow and pain," she sang, "the chalice of death *affreux* . . . [dreadful].

"And when Jesus died and rose again from the dead, He ascended up to heaven in the tribune on a pulley," she said. "Oh, it was beautiful. It was a pageant! It was very beautiful." And then quietly: "It was that experience that made me become something more than a simple peasant woman. It gave me a certain culture. It was the beginning for me."

But talking of the Passion play, Monsieur Charlou, who was not born until 1921 but knows about it from his father, says, "We were oppressed, oppressed. We had to work very hard. We had to make our own costumes. The whole village took part. The Passion play was famous. People came from as far away as Toulouse to see it. But we weren't paid anything for all that work. The abbey took all the money."

Memories are long in Conques. Walking slowly up and down the Rue Charlemagne four times a day with his cane, his marvelously large red face aglow, his white hair and full white mustachios neatly

clipped, the shirt that covers his huge rounded belly stained with
red wine, comes Monsieur Rémy Montourcy, a living remnant of
the Passion play. He is called the Devil by the people of Conques.
Not because *he* played the Devil, but because his *father,* year after
year before the turn of the century, took the Devil's part in the
play. Monsieur Rémy has the erect carriage and the gruff correct
address of an old army colonel. Jean Sègalat says he calls him Monsieur *de* Montourcy because of his courtly manners and the elegance of his diction when occasion demands it. "*Bonjour,* Madame!"
Monsieur Rémy barks out, bowing slightly when he sees me. "*Bonjour,* Monsieur Rémy," I reply. (To most people here he is simply
Rémy or Le Diable.) For years he worked as a cowherd up in
Aubrac, staying up there in the mountain pastures all through the
summer. "He was a great horseman," Jean Sègalat said. "A true cav-
alier. They say he came into Conques on his horse, and when he left
he went so fast his horse's shoes made flames on the pavement."

Now in his old age, having never married, Monsieur Rémy
slowly climbs the Rue Charlemagne each day for his morning
drinks at Francis's *auberge-café.* You can see from the slight bow in
his short plump legs that he is a man who spent many years in the
saddle. And he brags that when he was in the army he was in charge
of seventy-five horses. Shortly before noon, he goes to Madame La
Combe's *boucherie-alimentation* for the meat for his lunch and a bottle of wine. He then descends down to his little ramshackle house
on the Rue Charlemagne, and there he cooks his lunch and dines,
listening to the radio. Then he naps amid his famous (in Conques)
filth and clutter; and toward three he ascends again to Francis's and
sits much of the afternoon in fine weather on the stone wall across
the street, as if to watch the passing parade. From there, if he
wished, he could turn his head and just see into the Place de
l'Église, and across it, to observe the kingship of his, or rather of his
father's, counterpart over the reddish goings-on in the hell of the
great tympanum. "The poor Devil," I heard someone say. "He for-
gets." He smells very strongly of urine much of the time, and Francis has to insist he sit out there on the wall when there are tourists.
It is a position that, at any rate, seems to be reserved for him. When
winter comes he suffers from rheumatism and pain in his legs, and

*M. Rémy
("Le Diable")
descending the
rue Charlemagne,
Conques*

he often goes then to the hospital. But he always returns in the
spring. "Clean," people say. "With the swallows," he says. And Jean
Sègalat told us he replies when he is told he should stop drinking:
"I shall not cease to drink."

If someone addresses him directly as the Devil or refers to him as the Devil in his hearing, he draws himself up and says in the most gruff and definite of tones, "It is not I who played the Devil: It was my father." Once, giddy, coming out of Francis's, showing off to a visiting friend, having just told this story about Monsieur Rémy, I approached him at his seat on the wall in order to get him to say in his theatrical fashion: *"Ce n'était moi qui était le diable: C'était mon père."* "Is it true, Monsieur Rémy, that you are the Devil?" I asked him. He replied rather gently, "Yes, but don't be afraid. I won't take you." And then after a pause, in mock-plaintive melancholy tones he said, "I can't anymore."

Shortly after the last Passion play, when Madame Benoit was eleven, there came the separation of church and state, and the monks of Conques had to go into exile, as did all the monks of France. "Père Marie-Bernard remained, though, because he was the curé," Père André said. "He was the curé until his death in 1912."

"We took our library with us when we left," Père André told me, "and we took our clock. You can see the empty circle where it was at the top of the old abbey building which we built, or rather re-built, when we first came here in 1875. The things we took with us then are still there in England," he said.

There is bitterness in certain quarters of Conques going back to this time. There were things that Père Marie-Bernard promised to the people of Conques (I have not quite got it straight), and some of these things are still locked up inside the old abbey building.

Père André, who has no say in these matters, is philosophical about it all. "We took *our* clock," he told me, "and so the town got its *own* clock. You know it—in that little tower above the public treasury" (where taxes are paid, and so forth). "Now *they* keep temporal time," Père André said, "and *we* the celestial. *They* ring the hours of the day and the night and *we* ring the hours of the angelus three times a day, and the hours of the mass."

Now in the chapel of the Treasure, Père André is drawing the tourists' attention to the portrait busts of saints that circle the Lantern of Saint Vincent just under the windows. Their beauty, both sensual and spiritual, is so sublime that if one stops to look closely, they take one's breath away. The modeling makes the metal seem to glow like the most exquisite skin; their expression is one of bliss, yet misty and vague, so they seem to be saints and angels appearing in vision blurred by light.

Though they are different, their faces bear a strong resemblance, one to the other; their eyes and their eyebrows and their hair all are gold, as are their stamped and wafered halos and the strip of wafered background. This gold lends the tint to the silvery skin of their faces. Their right hands are raised with the sign of the Word, and in their left hands they hold scrolls.

"Look at the supple modeling! Look at the smoothness, the delicacy. How beautiful they are!" Père André says.

"There is more to say about this lantern," Père André goes on. "We will be coming back to it even as we look at the reliquary of Pepin II, but first I want you to return to the *A* of Charlemagne.

"By the by," he says, "this is not the reliquary of Saint Vincent of Saragossa but of another Saint Vincent, a deacon of Agen, who was thought to have been martyred at the time that Sainte Foy and Saint Caprais were martyred, in October 303.

"And thereby hangs a tale," he says, for he is in fine fettle today. He does not intend to tell the tale, but I am astonished that he even refers to it, for one thing Père André is absolutely adamant about is that the bones of Sainte Foy were not stolen. "They could not have been stolen," he insists. "They were transferred here at the time of danger from the Norman invasions, just as the bones of Saint Philibert were taken by the monks at Noirmoutier in order to protect them from the Northmen. The monks of Noirmoutier took the bones of Saint Philibert and they kept watch over them, and during the next thirty years, between 836 and 875, Saint Philibert's body lay in five different places before at last he came to rest at Tournus. Those were terrible times in France," Père André says, "in all those places within easy reach of the sea."

Père André is sure that Sainte Foy's presence here at Conques came about similarly, in a perfectly orderly fashion, that she was transferred here for her protection. "After the siege of Toulouse in 862 the whole valley of the Garonne was vulnerable," he says. He becomes very excited and wants to have nothing to do with the story of the monk who returned to Conques from Spain with a wild tale about the bones of Saint Vincent of Saragossa, only to be cast out by his brethren at Conques as unreliable—to their regret. For the bones of which he spoke were afterward obtained and welcomed with joy by the Abbey of Castres, south of Albi. They began to work miracles and brought fame and wealth to Castres, while Conques, still poor, way off up in the mountains, and not knowing what to do to better conditions here, went off in search of another Saint Vincent, a deacon of Agen they had heard tell of, whose bones were in the place called Pompejac. The bones of Saint Vincent of Agen, which they brought here without any real trouble, didn't work: There were no miracles. They did nothing, those bones. But it was while the monks of Conques were at Agen obtaining the bones of this Saint Vincent that they first heard of the holy virgin martyr Fides. They heard her praises and they heard of the miracles that were occurring around her tomb. And thus the plot was hatched.

"The whole story was invented by the troubadours," Père André claims recklessly.

Now he shines his light again on the Abbot Begon's angels standing on the base of the *A* of Charlemagne, swinging their censers "as if," writes Jean-Claude Fau, "to forever perfume the relics contained therein." For dramatic effect Père André directs his flashlight then directly into the solar crystal at the summit of the *A*. "The relic is behind the crystal," he concludes mysteriously, and he moves on to focus on the Reliquary of Pepin II, which is, as a work of art, the most sublime in the Treasure.

A little child, who is with her mother, walks away alone from the cluster of tourists and up the three steps into the round-vaulted chapel-like space of the golden statue, where I am standing.

"*Pas beau,*" she says loudly, pointing up at Sainte Foy. "*Pas beau,*" she repeats, full of the devil, and pleased with herself. "Shh," her mother says, running up to her. She takes hold of her hand to lead her back to the group.

"The regard, fixed and somber, of this statue of gold, combined with the rigidity and the symmetry of the principal lines, give an aspect most strange, something of the mystery and solemnity of certain Egyptian figures," Alfred Darcel wrote.

"I find her *hideous*," says an Englishwoman who has just come in with a companion. "Simply *hideous*."

"Barbarous," is a word that well-dressed Frenchmen often use when they come to regard her.

Before leaving Sainte Foy, I always go around behind her statue, for there on the back of her throne, behind her neck, in the misty depth of an ovoid crystal, polished and engraved in the time of Charlemagne (when the glyptic art was being revived), Jesus hangs on the cross in the hour of His death, the sun and the moon above Him, the Virgin and Saint John below, while at the foot of the cross a large serpent writhes. The figures are white and appear in relief, as if they had body, so that looking in, you feel you are seeing the crucifixion through a glass at a great distance in the strange light of that hour when the moon, nearly two thousand years ago, passed between Jerusalem and the sun.

> *Black darkness covered*   *with clouds God's body*
> *That radiant splendour*   *Shadow went forth.*

As I start to go out Père André interrupts his lecture for a moment. He tells me he has something for me—some pages he has written about Sainte Foy, he says as we walk toward the table at the entrance to the Treasure where he takes the tickets. Something he has written, and also something written by one of his pupils when he was teaching up there—he motions toward the hill. And then too, he says, as he gives me the typed pages, he has a little booklet of the Canticles of Sainte Foy. You must please bring them back, he tells me. They are his only copies. I take them, shaking his hand. He wishes me *bon courage* for my work. I leave sublimely happy.

Outside in the sunlit cloister I take off my sweater. It is hot, this June. In the afternoon Jack and I will ride our bikes up to the high green plateau and then through fields of hay and grain—rye, barley, wheat, oats—past the dark fir wood where we once heard a thrush singing at midday as if it were twilight. We'll go nineteen kilometers—as far as Lunel, on the plateau of Lunel, from whence they brought the tawny yellow limestone to build the basilica.

I look up at the giant stones absorbing the summer sunlight into their age-old might and order, and I think of the massive size and grace of this Romanesque church—the *stones,* the *stones,* the skill that went into cutting these stones exactly to measure, each one, according to the master architect's plan, the work, the labor of transporting them such a distance across difficult terrain, the skill of the masons, both laymen and monks, who built with these stones, fitting them precisely, the strength required, the patience. The silence and peace now where once for more than seventy-five years, beginning in the time of Abbot Oldoric (1031–1065), were all the noises of building and all the sounds of the lives that went into it, and the deaths; the breath of faith, of hard work, of *art,* for this church was built with a wondrous perfection by those who were filled with the holy vision of the church of her for whom they built and who inspired their work, their art, their *joy*—little virgin, very pure, who in her majesty of gold sat within the older Carolingian church guarded by tall iron grillwork. ("This grillwork, forged entirely from the irons of the prisoners freed by her intercession and brought here ex-voto in such numbers that they were threatening to overwhelm the very monastery," wrote Bernard of Angers, "forms to my mind, apart from the glories of the Treasure itself, the most admirable decoration of the church.") They built for her, holy martyr who died for Christ, little saint who stayed earth-close so that she might play and joke and protect and heal and free those oppressed who prayed for her help. They built for her whose wonders shone with the light of heaven, as now, high up on a ledge, the top of a buttress, near the roof of her church, a poplar tree blows in the wind, and its silver leaves ripple like water in a stream running through the sky.

The town bell rings once for the half hour. It is twelve-thirty.

I enter by the door of the south transept into the cool shadowy depths of her church, where the Romanesque reaches toward its full height and the concept of the wall gives way to that of columns and arches and arcades rising in tiers to the barrel vaults that are so favorable to Gregorian chant. I pause to light a candle at the altar of Sainte Foy. Tonight when the church is closed we will peer through a crack in the doors to see this candle, perhaps, along with others, still burning in prayer in the dark church.

Back up at our house I see that Jack has finished repairing the tire. Our bikes are at the ready, leaning side by side against the stone wall near the fountain. In my shadowy workroom (I have partially closed the shutters so the flies will fly out into the sunlight), I set the typed pages and the booklet Père André has given me down on the table next to my typewriter. Through the cracks in the shutters I can see the cross that stands in the heather high up at the top centermost point of the Ouche river gorge—tall and thin and gray against the blue sky.

"*La croix!*" said Rosalie lovingly the other day, leaning way out of the window in her parlor and pointing up. Her view! From here— my view!—I can see straight down into Rosalie's kitchen garden with its roses and dahlias, its parsley and chives and tarragon and chervil, its flourishing rosemary bush, its vervain, and chamomile, its vines of grapes and its walnut trees. Lines stretch across it and sheets and pillowcases white as snow are hanging out to dry in the sunlight, along with one of Rosalie's flower-print dresses and a pretty nightgown and a pair of Monsieur Charlou's blue cotton-canvas work pants and jacket, and several shirts. They are the only family in Conques who still make their living entirely from farming. Monsieur Charlou states this fact with pride; and also the fact that all the products of their farm are "*biologique*"—grown without pesticides or chemical fertilizers. "*Tout naturel!*" Rosalie always says.

At the back of the garden, up against the hillside wall, hidden from my view, is a long two-story row of rabbit hutches. "Mi mi mi mi mi mi," Rosalie singsongs to them when she comes to feed them in the evening. I hear the squeak of the iron gate from my workroom, and then I hear Rosalie talking to her rabbits. "Mi mi mi mi mi mi." And they hop about in their grasses, their tall ears up, their mouths and noses quivering with nibbly movements.

Across the Place du Château from Rosalie's garden, rising up with its bleak and stolid tower, stands the fifteenth-century Château d'Humières, all pinkish like the rest of Conques. "A noble lived there once," Madame Benoit said. "I remember him."

"My château is down there," she added proudly, waving her hand in the direction of the church and the cemetery beyond.

Then Jack and I are off to Lunel, pushing our bikes slowly in the sun up the steep hill past the *boules* court to the *rocade,* and away.

II

Afternoon: Ascent to the Dolmen of Lunel

We are flying down the *rocade,* as the Conquois call this road built around Conques for trucks, and so that cars and tourist buses can reach the Parking without going through the narrow main street; we are going to Lunel on our *vélos* (the people here say *vélos;* they seldom say *bicyclettes*). And where the *rocade* rejoins the old road below the Gendarmerie just beyond the sign which means You are now leaving Conques, we begin our climb eastward up through the gorges following the way that leads to Sénergues, Espeyrac, and finally Entraygues (there is no direct road to Lunel from this side of the Ouche), up by way of *les côtes,* the slopes, to the plateau, through steep vineyards, the road bordered by apple and walnut trees, past the gray stone farm called Jordy, where Flora, the old sheepdog, always basks in the sun while her family inside the house down the hill are dining. When Flora sees us, she stands up, and we stop to talk to her. She becomes bashful. She lowers her head and she comes up to us, but shyly, not quite all the way, to let herself be patted.

"She smiles," I say. I can't get over it.

"She smiles," says Jack. He bends down over his bike to stroke her as best he can while she shyly demurs, her head down, her red mouth curling up, her pearly teeth all bright. Embarrassed, because she thinks she should be barking, she wags her shaggy tail. We are crazy about this delicate dog who smiles!

We always stop to make a fuss over Flora, and usually she is our first stop, because most of the time we set off earlier and picnic on our rock high up in the heather beyond Guillebastre; and the Conquois who walk out this way in the afternoon are still in their houses finishing their lunches. Usually, before we reach Jordy, two long bends in the road and several vineyards and some wild land before we get there, when we pass through the garden land of Monsieur Denis and Dany Geneste, who live just below us in Conques, they have not yet come out to their garden.

But today Monsieur Denis is standing there, his back to us, just beyond the old stone sheep barn, now his garage, which borders the road. Probably he has come out to get his car and they are going into town, to St. Cyprien or to Marcillac this afternoon, or up to the plateau to visit Dany's mother at Longueviale or Denis's cousin near Lunel.

Monsieur Denis appears to be gazing off down the grassy path, wide enough for a tractor, that descends gradually below the vineyards, down toward the river. Below him on the sunny south-facing slope is their vegetable garden, and above the road on the left among the trees they keep their chickens. Beyond the chickens' yard and house is a shady grassy knoll where often in the late afternoons before supper they sit in chairs, chattering with whoever may come by to visit, while little Lucie, their granddaughter, plays at their feet.

"*Bonjour,* Monsieur Denis," we call out as we approach, and he turns. "Oh," he says, squinting to see us. "Oh," he says again, moving toward us, holding out his hand for us to shake, and swaying a bit as if he were passing with difficulty through curtains of time, "I was standing here dreaming of my youth." He laughs at himself. "I used to gallop down this path with my sheep. Off I would go in the morning with my sheep, still a boy, off I would go galloping, and I would sing. Everyone could hear me back in Conques." He speaks with a slightly hoarse melodious voice, and he laughs the laugh of one who with every breath, it seems, is aware of the ironies of existence, of the tricks that time plays on us, of the sad jokes of fate.

"I would take my sheep down to the Ouche, and then up, up"—he motions with his hands—"up through the woods to the pastures above Montignac."

Looking across the thickly wooded mountain wall beyond the Ouche, I cannot imagine how he could have gone up it with his sheep. "Was there a path then through the woods?" I ask him.

"Oh, the woods were clear in those days," he says, "they were clean. Everything was used. Every bough that dropped. Every twig. Every bit of dead wood. Everything. The sheep could graze in the woods. You could spot a mushroom, a *cèpe,* at ten meters. And we gathered all the chestnuts, all of them. There were seven *séchoirs* [drying sheds] along through the woods on high, and another four lower down."

"We would gather all the chestnuts and dry them and feed them to the pigs and eat them ourselves. You know them, the dried chestnuts. They are golden. They are delicious. At Christmastime we would stuff a turkey with them.

"Ahh," he says. "Sometimes I wonder what the old people of my day would say if they came back now and saw what has become of our woods.

"You are going to St. Marcel?" he asks, because usually we take only a short bike ride of an hour and a half or so, stopping for our picnic and going on then up to the plateau to the Croix de Loubatières or perhaps as far as the Croix d'Aussets, beyond the fir wood, and then we return to work by way of St. Marcel.

"We are going to Lunel," we say.

"To Lunel!" He smiles, he tilts back his head. "You will gaze on Mont Kaymard. It is the highest peak in the region. Seven hundred and seventy meters, I believe."

After the war, he tells us, after the years of his imprisonment in Germany, he worked up there for the fluorspar mine behind Mont Kaymard. "I drove the truck down to the train station at St. Christophe. I'd make several trips a day. Back and forth. Back and forth." He moves his head back and forth, back and forth, laughing as he speaks. "From St. Christophe the fluorspar was shipped north, to Paris and beyond—to the steel mills in the north of France, to Belgium, to Switzerland." He looks up at the sky with his pale, dreamy blue eyes. He makes a sweeping motion with his arms to encompass the geography of Europe from the old fluorspar mine behind Mont Kaymard to the railroad line at St. Christophe and on to Decazeville, Figeac, Brive, then north to Paris and those faraway steel towns. "Then the fluorspar mine was closed down. Dany and I were married by then. Our eldest son was already born and Claudine was on the way. I went up to Paris to find work. I drove a truck there for the S.N.C.F. [*Syndicate National Chemin de Fer*—the French railroad]. For twenty-seven years I drove a truck. I delivered packages. For twenty-seven years! I delivered packages all over Paris. I know every elevator in Paris."

We part from him saying, "*À ce soir,*" and ride on, moved by him and marveling over him. There is no one quite like him. He is unique, and yet he speaks for every man. Perhaps because of his long and painful years of separation from his beloved homeland, during the five years of his imprisonment in Germany and then the twenty-seven years of delivering packages in Paris, he seems more than anyone else to be filled with nostalgic love for Conques, for this valley, this place, and to be at the same time partly removed, observing, observing even himself, like a bemused philosopher: He is distanced from the petty day-to-day struggles of the village, from the pricks of class differences, from old family feuds, and at the same time now in his retirement, his *troisième age* (third age), as the French say (not without thinking it is a hilarious expression), back in the country of his boyhood, he is continually aware of the inexorable circle of life, of man's fused relation to the earth, of the inescapable onrush toward age even as the earth turns and the sun and the moon rise and set. He seems to be filled with the wonder of nature, and to see this valley, this *conque* and the plateau as far as the eye can see, all bathed in the paradise light of his boyhood. He thinks how here in this place where he grew up he is now, year by year, growing older, recalling every inch of the land he gamboled over as a boy, as he moves toward the point where, walking slower and more stiffly, following the others, he will go to join those who came before him down in the cemetery below the church.

All this he accepts with a shrug of his shoulders, and that sad laugh, even as he breathes. What he bewails is the loss, the loss of the culture, the knowledge of his ancestors, along with their language.

In July a year ago, when beautiful Dany, brown-eyed, olive-skinned, dark-haired Dany, came down from the meadows above Conques with a huge bouquet of *marjolaine* (marjoram), she told us she would dry it and use it to flavor her sauces, her salads, her *pot-au-feu,* her *farçou.* She said she would make infusions with the dried flowers in winter to calm the stomach, to comfort the liver, to heal bronchitis or a cold.

And Monsieur Denis spoke, bemoaning: "After us, who will know these things? They will go to the *pharmacie* to buy these herbs. They won't know them even to pick them in the green meadows. Our language is dying, and with us all this old knowledge, the things our grandmothers knew, it will all die with us. No one cares anymore.

"When we were growing up, in our house—in all our houses here at Conques—as a matter of course, we always made the sign of the cross over the loaf of bread with the knife before we cut into it. We never would have done it otherwise. We were poor. Making the sign of the cross that way was a kind of silent thanks to the good Lord for the blessing of the bread. It goes way back. If I do it, my grandfather before me did it, and his grandfather before him . . .

"But my sons grew up in Paris. Theirs is another life completely."

We move slowly, pumping. The way is steep. It is five kilometers from Conques to the farm called Fonromieu at the top and it takes us half an hour or more to get there.

At Conques the elevation is about a thousand feet above sea level, depending on where you are: At the abbey, according to Abbé Bouillet, the elevation is 330 meters (1,082 feet) above sea level; but the village is steep in every direction and each of its hundred or so houses and buildings is higher or lower than the one next to it or across the way; and as for the houses themselves, they say in Conques that you enter a house by the attic and leave by the *cave*. "No wonder," we joke, when we walk back up the Rue Charlemagne from the Dourdou (elevation 260 meters), "no wonder Charlemagne fell down on his knees when he reached the Porte du Barry and crawled the rest of the way up to the doors of the church."

By the time we reach Fonromieu on the plateau we will have climbed almost a thousand feet and a bit more than that when we reach Lunel (700 meters; 2,296 feet, as Jack calculates it), and will stand on the plain of the dolmen gazing up, as Monsieur Denis suggested, at Mont Kaymard.

Beyond Jordy we go around a heathery rock outcropping, above a deep chestnut grove, where far below us the sunlight shines in lovely grasses and in the sliver of a stream rushing down to join the Ouche. We cross the stream, and the road switches back higher above the chestnut grove, following the mountain.

"*Les rochers!*" said Madame Benoit when we drove her once with us this way, her voice evoking all the wild mysterious beauty of these craggy rocks and wooded gorges, all the years that she had loved them, singing, as she then began to sing, "*À Sainte Foy la Grande, amour! Amour et fête!*"

> *Que la montagne aride au rocher la repète*
> *Que le rocher jette au vallon*
> *Ce cri d'amour des fils de l'Aveyron:*
> *À Sainte Foy la Grande, amour! Amour et fête!*

> May the arid mountain repeat to the rocks
> May the rocks cast into the valley
> The cries of love from the sons of Aveyron:
> To the great Sainte Foy, love! Love and rejoicing!

At the ridge, where the stone village of Guillebastre stands deserted and crumbling slowly back into rock, a rabbit, startled, runs out of a barn whose door has long since disintegrated. The rabbit hops, zigzags, and turns, running down the hill into the *séchoir*—another of the stone drying sheds with chimneys that were built here and there throughout the chestnut woods and at every farm village to dry the chestnuts and preserve them, for this abundant and nourishing nut was the staple food of the people here through centuries of their poverty.

"They say the Aveyronese are like the *bogue* of the chestnut," Père André said to me one day.

"The *bogue* of the chestnut?" I asked.

"That is to say, they say that the Aveyronese have a character that seems to be as prickly and rough as the outer burry shell, the *bogue* of the chestnut.

"But then," Père André went on, "you have watched the chestnuts; you have seen, have you not, the *bogue* in autumn, how it changes color, gradually, from green to yellow to almost brown, and then slowly it begins to open." Père André cupped his hands to show the two parts of the prickly *bogue* slowly beginning to open. "And inside," he said, "inside—gold!" He looked into his hands with wonder and pleasure as if he had just conjured up a perfect cluster of glossy brown chestnuts, which then—beautiful chestnuts, chestnuts joined with dozens of others—could be quickly cut up just so and tossed in the water and boiled up for supper.

"But you know the chestnut?" he said. "You have eaten it, haven't you?"

"Oh, yes," I said, smiling. I was quite incapable of replying with the world of things he makes me want to say.

"One could say the same thing of all the mountain people," he said. (Himself as well, I think.) "And of the Bretons, too," he said. "The word *bogue* comes from the Breton; it is, that is to say, an old Celtic word."

The *bogue* of the chestnut! Père André filled me with a need to express what was impossible for me to say in French and is difficult even in English. He made me want to express the overwhelming tenderness we feel, Jack and I, alike and together, for all these things—and it is more than tenderness, it is wonder and delight and admiration. It comes over us when a person we had not known before opens up to us, or when we come to know something more of someone we had known already, so that our life here is a continual adventure of discovery in which tenderness and delight are constantly at play and the strong emotion of love infuses the whole. I can only think it is Sainte Foy who has brought so many wonderful people together all in one place and has endowed the people, the children and the young girls especially, Jack says, with such beauty; and then that it is Sainte Foy who has blessed us in that we are taken in, it seems, by the whole population. Taken in generously. "But you are real Conquois," they say to us now, again and again. And it is true that all this has come to us slowly, as revelation, as the outer burry shell of the chestnut, the *bogue,* has opened; for when we first came here, coming as we did from Provence, the people struck us as dour, as pale and silent—they did not seem to have the rosy-faced buoyancy, the exuberance of personality we felt in the people around where we lived along the Route du Destet in the Alpilles; they did not automatically wave and greet us, strangers, foreigners, passing by. We felt the hardship of their life, the poverty, the pain that comes from generations of eking a living with enormous difficulty and hard work out of the mountain soil.

"Everyone knows you," says Monsieur Charlou. "Everyone. Between here and Senergues, and in St. Cyprien and as far as Marcillac. Everyone! 'The Americans,' they say, 'ah, yes! *Les grands Americains*—the tall Americans! The tall man and the woman with the'—he makes a wild wiggly gesture with both his hands around his head—'the woman with the curly hair.' " He laughs.

"Hannah and *le grand* Jack are Americans, but they are Conquois, they are perfectly integrated," says Monsieur LaPeyre, a Parisian, a retired government official—he was in the Ministry of Transportation and now he travels all over, free of charge, according to Rosalie, and he is president of Les Droits des Piètons de France (The Rights of the Walkers of France).

He bought his house after the war and built it up from a ruin, and formerly he and Madame LaPeyre, who died before we began coming here, came to spend the summers with her daughter and her daughter's family, but now his *belle-fille* uses the house through the summer and he comes for a week or two before and after the summer season; he comes, it seems, to regale us all, the ones he has chosen to admire, with his hospitality, and to make pronouncements as he observes the Conques scene. "Hannah is a *copaine* of Rosalie!" her buddy, he says, as if this were my final coup, the finishing touch, the real thing that has turned us, Americans, into perfectly integrated Conquois.

In the mornings, at a table strewn with papers, Monsieur LePeyre works on the Rights of the Walkers of France in the light of his balcony doors, and frequently then he drives off for lunch, perhaps even up into Lozère or beyond the Lot into Cantal to the Auberge Fleurie at Montsalvy, with Charlou's older brother Louisou at the wheel—his friend, the most intellectual of the three brothers Garrigue, he tells us. Louisou was until his retirement a *petit fonctionnaire,* he says, working for the Département of Aveyron, while Monsieur LePeyre, one gathers, was higher, in Paris, what the French call an *haut fonctionnaire.*

And in the evenings Monsieur LePeyre, this enormous presence,
this large—one might even say fat—but graceful, smooth-faced,
white-haired man of seventy-some years, this eater and drinker,
with his generous inventive sense of hospitality, of bringing people
together, invites us to come to dine—perhaps on one of Rosalie's
rabbits, stewing in a pot in his smoky fireplace while we drink fine
wines and not-so-fine wines (one cold autumn evening we had a
wine soup of red wine and bread, which Rosalie found detestable),
and he, with all his worldly wit and intelligence and always an
obligatory joke about *le dollar,* goes hither and thither between the
fireplace and the stove and the sink in the far corner and his long
table supported by a tree trunk, offering us bits of *saussiçon* to eat
while we wait for everything to reach perfection. At last, supper
served, he lolls back like an opera singer at his long table and beams
with satisfaction down the length of it. I imagine he will lift his
right arm and burst forth into an aria. Instead, as he has instructed
us, we all lift our glasses and sing the toasting song of the printers
union in Paris, which he has taught us: "*À la . . . À la . . . À la . . . À
la santé du confrère, qui nous regale aujourd'hui.*" (To the health of our
colleague, whom we toast today.)

He has told us that the printers sing this song on the occasion of
every wedding or birth or baptism among them, the bottle being
brought by the groom or the father of the child, and that in Paris,
when there are many mistakes in the newspaper one day, the people say, "Ah, they must have had an '*À la*' last night."

"Oh, but Anna," said Jean Sègalat, when I tried to express to him
our wonder at how kind and generous everyone is to us here, how
they fill us with joy, how it seems a kind of miracle to us the way
they have taken us in and made us a part of their village. "Everyone
here likes you and Jack. Everyone! 'Ah, Anna et Jacques,' they say.
You have understood how to respect the rules of each household.
With the Aveyronese if you take a wrong step, if you wrong them
some way—Out! Ooop! You're finished!" He makes the motion of
pushing, of shutting a door, of slitting his throat with a knife.

He, too, is an Aveyronese (the Sègala is the region, formerly very
poor, where nothing could be grown but the *seigle*—rye), but he is

an artist, an intellectual, an observer, removed from the people by two generations, and he comes here in the summers from the coal-mining and industrial town of Decazeville eighteen kilometers from here, where his father was a prosperous wine merchant and grocer; he comes from years of study as a young painter at the École des Beaux-Arts in Paris, and an early rigorous religious education at Sainte Marie de Rodez, where he was sent as a boarding student: and he is, he says, a stranger in Conques, a foreigner, almost as much as we, he says. He is a real artist, "the true Rouergat artist," Jack says often with strong emotion and feeling. "And he is proud to be a bourgeois," Jack says. "That's so exotic."

Sègalat is divorced and since the death of his friend—*mon amie,* he says, speaking of his life-love, Emanuelle (for whom his gallery is named)—he lives alone, and during the winters lives and works in his old family apartments above the store, closed since his father's time. He told us that a friend of his remarked that his house at Decazeville is ideally situated: close to and equidistant from the two *grandes départs* (the two great departures)—the station where one boards the train for Paris, and the church.

He is a *personage,* well known and well respected in Conques, and throughout Aveyron. "Monsieur Sègalat has gone to Montarnal to dine with the Préfet" (the equivalent of the governor of Aveyron), Rosalie says. He rents the attic room at the top of Rosalie's wonderful old house for the summer months, and she is proud to have him there. Not because she looks up to him—she doesn't—but because he's a feather in her cap.

"This house is old," Rosalie said of her house, her pride, when I came upon her one rainy day down on her knees, waxing the stairs. She rubbed a piece of worn purple sweater vigorously across the dark wood of the steps, making them shine. Later she gave me a piece of the sweater so I could wax my stairs. Her stairs are wide and a little crooked, tilted from age; the banister is charmingly carved; the stairs, like the rooms, are spacious, for this house was built in 1836 and was part of the convent. "This house is old," Rosalie said, "but it was here before us, and it will be here when we are gone." She stood up then. "Oh, my leg, my leg!" she cried out. A wave of pain passed over her face. And in the next moment she was smiling again, radiant, this marvelous woman who works all the time. "Come in! Come in! It is time for coffee," she said. We en- tered her kitchen. "It is the most beautiful kitchen in the world," I tell her often in the glow of pleasure when I come in. "*La plus belle cuisine du monde,*" she says laughing with delight at my hyperbole. But she believes it to be, at any rate, the most beautiful kitchen in Conques. It is her work, her art, her spirit, her caring, her energy, her joyous energy that make her kitchen what it is, and she fills it with the light of her face, her hair, her voice, her wonderful voice, and of the flowers from her garden she always has arranged just so in the tiny window over the sink.

Rosalie told me, whispering as if it were a secret recipe, that when she paints her kitchen she always adds just a touch of pink to the white paint, and it is for this reason, I see, that her walls have, quite literally, a rosy glow; and copper pans, too, glow on the walls; and her woodstove in summer is covered with red oilcloth, and a vase of lovely flowers stands on it; but in winter, when it (and it alone) warms the house—the kitchen, really—the last thing she does after she finishes washing the dishes is to vigorously rub the whole stainless steel top of the woodstove with a cloth until it, too, glows clean.

Père André made me think, too, of the time I went off with Ros- alie to gather chestnuts one autumn afternoon. We gathered them above Conques at the farm called Goubert (Rosalie had the per- mission of old Monsieur Goubert). There where the plateau slopes, gradually at first, toward the west, we moved along under the old chestnut trees, stooping over, picking up the fat and glossy chest- nuts, feeling their smooth surface, taking in their warm light—like firelight, somehow—one after another, one more wonderful than the next. "The light ones, the reddish ones are the best," said Ros- alie. We pressed our shoes on the prickly *bogue* to extract those clusters that hadn't yet fallen loose. We didn't talk much; we'd sep- arate and fill our baskets and then come back and empty them into big burlap bags, and all the while we were breathing in the lovely smell of the fall woods, we were sniffing the air on the mountain high up above the Dourdou.

Somewhere near, off in the birches above us, or rather in the chestnuts, the mushrooms were coming up. "The *cèpes,* perhaps," said Rosalie. "And the *trompettes*" (the *trompettes de la mort,* trumpets of death, black chanterelles, which come up beyond the ridge, farther down, on the north face). When Rosalie finds the *cèpes,* the most prized of all the mushrooms, she always cooks some of them fresh that very night, sautéed in olive oil with garlic and parsley. And the rest are sliced and dried in wooden boxes. "Two or three days in the sun on the roof, or if it rains, bring in the boxes to dry them on the woodstove," she says. The dried *cèpes* and the *trompettes* she uses through the winter to flavor the sauces of her roasts, her ducks, her chickens, and her rabbits. The dried *trompettes,* cut into tiny pieces, flavor her paté, too.

The mushrooms are a fever, a delirium that grips the whole population of Conques and fills them with joy as they go off to "*chercher les champignons,*" and grips Rosalie, too, who can sniff them out and spot them at a distance when I would see nothing but wet brown leaves. She guards the secret of where she finds the *cèpes.* She tells no one. But to me she has said that often there is a white mushroom, like a *girolle,* but not edible, and this white mushroom is scattered in the woods, here and there, like the path leading to the *cèpes.*

For now, though, we are concentrating on the chestnuts. The chestnuts are a necessity for Rosalie and she must have a huge quantity, too, to feed her rabbits through the long winter. The chestnuts come first. They must be gathered, dried out, and stored, enough to last a year.

"The chestnuts are a complete food," Rosalie said. "They have protein. They have minerals. They have vitamins. They have Vitamin B and Vitamin C.

"With all the unemployment," she said, "with all the unemployment and hunger, if only people would come to gather the chestnuts, there would be no unemployment, there would be no hunger."

By the end of the afternoon we had filled six bags, huge bags as high as Rosalie's waist, which must have weighed a hundred pounds apiece. "Fifty kilos, fifty kilos, at least," said Rosalie, lifting them

proudly. She was happy, she was peaceful. She loved being there on
the mountain where it was tranquil. Monsieur Charlou came for us
in his little *trois-chevaux* Citroën jeep just before dusk, and we
heaved the huge bags into the back and Rosalie climbed in and sat
on top of them, insisting that I ride in the front with Monsieur
Charlou. "Oh, it was tranquil," she said to him. "I was happy the
whole afternoon."

In her kitchen that night she would boil up a *poignée,* a fistful, for
supper and they would eat them—rich, warm, sweet, filling chestnuts. ("Gold!" says Père André.) "In the old days," says Rosalie,
"sometimes there was nothing to eat but chestnuts. The people of
Conques and the *pays* of Sénergues made their bread from a flour of
pounded chestnuts."

Rosalie makes a chestnut cake as delicious as anything I can think
of. "You cut the chestnuts like this." She shows me with her knife.
"So the shell will peel off after they are boiled. You take a demikilo
of them and boil them for half an hour in water with a little salt.
Then you take off both the shell and the outer skin, and you put
them all through the food mill. Afterwards you mix in 150 grams of
butter, and 150 grams of sugar. You mix 50 grams of cocoa and a
spoonful of milk together and then mix all the ingredients together.
You put it in a pan to set. Then you make a sugar glacé to color it
and give it a *bon aspect.* You put it in the *frigo* to keep until you are
ready to eat. And *bon appétit!*" Rosalie smiles, radiant.

She remembers the grilled chestnuts. "They must be fresh chestnuts when you grill them," she says. "The dried chestnuts are not
good for that." She loves to organize an evening party, a *grillade,* when
the chestnuts are fresh, and to grill them over an open fire. (In her
own house, the fireplace in her parlor has been closed over to keep
out the drafts, and the fireplace in the kitchen is given over to the
woodstove.) "The chestnuts are grilled until they turn black on the
outside," she says. "Then they are wrapped in a cloth to complete
the cooking and someone must sit on them a while to bring them to the
point of perfection." There are many little jokes on these occasions, I
have noticed, directed at the one who is sitting on hot chestnuts.

Rosalie and I are going to do a cookbook together. When I have
finished writing this book, we will do the cookbook. She'll tell me

the recipes, and I will write them down in English. She is excited about this, and she is in a hurry to get started. "Look! Look!" she said to me one day when I came in. She had her book of songs open, an old paperbound book with the words of songs in the patois and in French translations. She has covered it with flowered paper. The night before for hours she and Dany Geneste had been singing songs in the patois of their villages up on the plateau in the country of Sénergues. (Ten kilometers from here, but it is another country, another *pays.*) "Songs of *la vielle France,*" Jean Sègalat told me. "They were so beautiful I came down and sat on the stairs outside the kitchen to listen to them."

"Look, Ahnnah!" said Rosalie. "I found a song in my book! Look!" she said. "You could finish your book with this song." A lovely sad sweet song of farewell it was. She made me want to cry. "You can borrow this book," said Rosalie.

We stop at Guillebastre to drink from the water we carry and to look back for the last time, as it were, at Conques, which from here in the still golden light seems to be a mirage magically hanging in the lush wild green of the gorge, the white chapel of Saint Roch glowing off alone on its high rock perch, as if in the next moment the mirror would turn and Conques would be gone into the green. We listen, for it seems one could hear Conques from here, but its sounds, too, even the music of its bells, are washed away into dream by the rushing waters of the Ouche down below.

So it is as if we see this valley as it was when the first breaths were drawn. Here, deep and enfolding, the waters flowed, the source and the little streams, the Ouche and the Dourdou, filling the air with the sounds of falling waters rushing like the sounds of thousands of hands clapping, clapping as they would, in waves of applause down through ages, as the sun and the moon and the stars in their turn moved slowly across the sky; and there seemed to be in the rhythm of the seasons, in the growth, in the life, in the very green of the place through the long summer, some secret—as if (as is the case, I have come to think, in other holy places, too) something in the conformation of the earth has preserved since the earliest days the mysterious energy of God's presence somehow concentrated, so that in these places, as here, it, His presence or whatever it might be called, can be felt as spirit-energy in the mystery of the earth and in its beauty, but it is something more than beauty that dwells in these places.

When the Druids came to build their circular temple, this valley, this *conque* with its sources of pure water, may have already long been a place of pilgrimage. A road, following, as Roman roads did, older routes, came through here. Vestiges of it have been found coming across the plateau from Lunel at Reyronie, and then descending, passing under Le Puèch and coming out above Conques near the place called L'Estoulène.

The ancient name of the valley is gone, erased, washed away with the waters. Vallis Lapidosa it was called in Latin, according to the chronicles of the abbey, before it took the name that Louis the King gave it in the language of his people.

"There is a place, a much reputed center of devotion to which the Emperor himself gave the name of Conques [Concas]," wrote Ermold Le Noir in 826 in his "Poem in Praise of Louis the Pious." "Formerly this place, harsh and rugged as it was, harbored only the savage beasts and the birds, who filled the valley with their melodious songs. Now it counts a brilliant legion of monks, whose reputation fills the skies. The monastery was built at the expense of the king, who, having founded it, endowed it, and took it under his protection. It rises in a deep valley girdled by a pleasant river and stands in the midst of vineyards, of orchards, and abundance. It owes to the king as well its route of access, which was cut through the rock at the cost of the most laborious efforts.

I love this long green climb in the sun. I do it slowly, just at my pace. Jack passes me and eventually he is far up ahead. Coming down to Conques this way in their cars, friends from this country wave, or gaily honk their horns. Strangers from other Departments make a great fuss when they get to me. They take their hands off their wheels to turn them in bicycle-pumping motions, or they raise their fists in signs of Bravo! or they call out, *"Doucement! Doucement!"* *"C'est dur,"* says a walker. *"Ça monte,"* says another.

A hard climb? I feel myself dissolving into the golden air. I look at the heather, the ferns, the broom, at the chestnut trees coming into flower, at the locust-tree leaves and the lovely watery birches, at the grasses and flowers at the road's edge. I breathe in the fragrant wild mint and the *serpolet* (wild thyme). Gathered in the morning in June and July and dried in the shade, *serpolet,* an infusion of *serpolet,* is good for the circulation of blood, says Rosalie. A tisane of dried mint leaves, a tea, she says, makes you amorous.

I carry my notebook and pen in my tiny deerskin bag with its bursts of colored Indian beads, and I climb, pumping my bike, praying that if I don't try for it, a sentence will rise as perfectly formed as the beads in the gilded netting that binds the hair of Sainte Foy, that a detail will come, as delightful as the lantern earrings that hang from the golden lobes of her ears. I see wild strawberries here and there, and I smell them, ripe beneath their leaves along the roadside.

I look across and down into the deep wooded chasm where, in 1976, when we came back to Conques the first time, we saw a whole rainbow, not just the upper arc but the whole circle, the bow, with its colors, suspended in this gorge, where it was raining in a burst of late-afternoon sunlight; and in the part of the rainbow that spanned the sky the luminous rims of violet, indigo, blue, green, yellow, orange, red, were more sharply defined, while in the part below they were dimmer, half veiling the woods and the rocks and the heather beyond. It remained there suspended, the entire rainbow, a long time, and the raindrops were falling through it while we stood in its spell, not wanting to move. "It's a sign," Jack said then, long ago, it seems. "It's a sign," he said. "This is our place."

It was October 1976, a year and a half after our first visit here in April, and we had come back to France to winter again in our same house along the Route du Destet near Maussane-les-Alpilles. Early that summer I had finished turning a small part of my "College Days" into a publishable story and then, unable not to any longer, I had laid aside the manuscripts of my "College Days" and my "Dreams and Early Memories," and had begun my studies for Sainte Foy. I abandoned myself to the rapture of learning. I spent the summer in the library at New York University in a kind of illumined fever—reading, reading, going from book to book by way of its neighbors on the shelves, by way of footnotes and bibliographies. I was gathering knowledge (wonderful knowledge!), discovering things, finding books, thinking, making connections, coming to understand things I had never known before, and writing in the giant new notebook I had begun for my Book of Sainte Foy. I wrote down thoughts, feelings, phrases. I copied poems and passages of prose, made efforts at translations and set them down in a rush, partly in English and the rest left in French. I was listening to the voices of the ages, absorbing a spirit, a feeling, a whole realm of faith—its structures and symbols, its life. I was looking for everything that might relate either directly or indirectly to Sainte Foy and to Conques, its people, their language, its architecture, its art, its history. It was only the beginning—the summer of reading—of what would become almost a new life for me.

The first line of my notebook was, I see, looking back, "My head sets off in longing, ready for this pilgrimage." And below that, after a gap, "The sense of hundreds of years, thousands of pilgrims, footsteps and miles and miles of land, of mountains, of rivers crossed, all with an object—that golden statue, and in it the bones of that young girl who perished centuries before, who perished for her faith, for her pure courage."

And then here we stood, Jack and I, looking out at our rainbow; here we stood, having driven up from the silvery dry country of olives, deep into the green mountains of chestnuts, coming north this time by way of the Pont du Gard, and continuing north through the Cevennes to Florac, where we spent the night. The next day in wild curiosity we climbed the steep road up to the Causse Méjean (as high and barren and dry and mysterious as Nevada, it seemed); and then, after an hour or two, we plunged (these roads were scary) down into the golden-pink granite gorges of the Tarn, and up again we drove into wooded mountains where we saw our first purple cows (lavender-brown to be more exact), and the French parking their cars at every viewpoint to get out and gather chestnuts by the roadside. Down into the valley of the Lot we drove and up again and down and up, using our detailed Michelin maps, following the narrow roads, on one of which we now stood, having walked out from the Hôtel Sainte Foy before dinner.

It was a Sunday evening. We had come for five nights so that we might be here for Sainte Foy's fête day, October 6, which fell on a Wednesday that year. We didn't know until after we had been in Conques several days that the celebration of her fête fell, as it always did, on the first Sunday following the sixth. Sainte Foy would be carried forth from the Treasure and borne in procession into the church to the festival mass in her honor. We missed the procession that year, 1976, and the next year as well (for we were back in New York by then), but my heart was filled with the sun-full moon-full autumn silence of Conques. And Sainte Foy was there in her statue, just as she was when last I saw her gazing off into eternity, her little hands upraised.

On the day of her fête, in the morning, after I had visited her in the Treasure, I went—shyly, awkwardly, because I didn't know quite how to do this yet—to buy a candle and to light it and pray before the altar of Sainte Foy in her chapel. "As you follow the Lamb in heaven, light my way here below."

There was a soft light in the high lantern tower above the choir of the church (at the crossing of the transepts and the nave) and warmth in the yellowish stone of the tall columns, the arches, the tiers of arches. The whole church seemed to speak of some grave purpose lit by grace. And down in the chapel of Sainte Foy I put my hand on an ancient column that forms a part of the wall of her chapel, as if to take in some strength from the weight and the harmonious structure of the great stone *basilique*.

The gray schist stones of Conques, mixed here and there with blocks of the red sandstone of Combret, which form the walls of the chapel of Sainte Foy in the south transept as they do the chapel of the Blessed Virgin Mary in the north transept, date, it is thought, from the earliest campaign of construction of the present church (from about 1040) before the quarry of yellow limestone at Lunel was discovered, or at any rate before it was decided to put it to use at Conques; but Sainte Foy's chapel, with its ancient columns and the Celtic basket-weave crossings of the carvings of the capitals, feels so much older than the rest of the church that I do not laugh, as one American scholar told me she did, at Frère Isidore's notion that it belongs, in fact, to the earlier Carolingian church. "We think . . . ," Frère Isidore had said. If you spend much time in the church you begin to think as he does that Sainte Foy's chapel was part of the earlier Carolingian church (its proportions fitting perfectly as the south transept chapel of the much larger new church, where it was dedicated to Saint Peter), just as you think the columns devoted to Saint Michael, now mysteriously in the sacristy (one column and capital inside a cupboard of liturgical objects), were surely once part of the chapel of Saint Michael. This was mentioned in passing by Bernard of Angers, for Guibert the Illuminé ran up and through it when he was escaping, after he had, by miracle, gotten back his eyes, his sight (his delight!).

That morning of my first fête of Sainte Foy, I knew nothing of the waxen figure of Sainte Foy lying in *repos éternel* on her satin-fringed pillow behind the wooden panels below her altar (for she is revealed this way only on the vigil and through the Sunday of the celebration of her fête). I stood there in the somber light reading the inscriptions on the marble plaques given ex-voto and arranged on the walls on either side of Sainte Foy's altar. Then one by one I copied down those I could see into my notebook.

Reconnaissance	Gratitude
à Ste. Foy	to Sainte Foy
pour une heureuse	for a happy
maternité	childbirth
5 Fevre 1911	5 February 1911
Remerciements	Thanks
à Ste. Foy	to Sainte Foy
pour l'heureuse	for the happy
naissance de ma	birth of my
fille	daughter
Marie Thérèse	Marie Thérèse
1915	1915
Remerciements	Thanks
à Ste. Foy	to Sainte Foy
pour la naissance	for the birth
de Foy de Benoit	of Foy de Benoit
1919	1919
Reconnaissance	Gratitude
à Ste. Foy	to Sainte Foy
pour l'heureuse	for the happy
naissance	birth
de notre fille	of our daughter
Marie Thérèse Alauze	Marie Thérèse Alauze
Reconnaissance	Gratitude
à Ste. Foy	to Sainte Foy
Miracle dans un naufrage	for a miracle in a shipwreck
Prière pour trois voeux	Prayer for three vows

Reconnaissance	Gratitude
à Ste. Foy	to Sainte Foy
pour la guérison	for the healing
de ma fille	of my daughter
1936	1936

Merci	Thank you
Ste. Foy	Sainte Foy
pour grâces	for blessings
obtenues	received
1911	1911

J' ai prié Ste. Foy	I prayed to Sainte Foy
accablé de douleur	overwhelmed by sorrow
Elle a intercéde	She interceded
pour moi près du Sauveur	for me near the Savior
1913 C.D.	1913

Reconnaissance	Gratitude
à Ste. Foy	to Sainte Foy
C. P. Janvier 1930	C. P. January 1930

À Sainte Foy	To Sainte Foy
Reconnaissaner	Gratitude
pour ma guérison	for my healing
Lors de la consécration	at the time of the
de sa Basilique	consecration of the basilica
C. M. Bennett	C. M. Bennett
Supérieur du	Superior of
la Grande Séminaire	the Grande Seminary
Rodez, 1909	Rodez, 1909

I didn't know then about the Belt of Sainte Foy with its "mysterious power," but I sensed the power from the marble plaques that spoke of these daughters born early in our century safely, happily, thanks to Sainte Foy; I thought of how these expressions of gratitude represented other mothers, other daughters, of this century and centuries before, who gave thanks to her not with gold-lettered inscriptions but with prayers and a few *sous,* with whispered tales of miracles, and lifetimes of devotion to her who protected mother and daughter, to her who almost a thousand years earlier had, according to Bernard of Angers, inveigled the golden sleeves of bracelets out of Arsinde, Countess of Toulouse.*

I found the story of the golden sleeves as Bernard of Angers told it in the nineteenth chapter of the first *Book of the Miracles of Sainte Foy*.

> Now it happened in those days when Sainte Foy was occupied gathering gold and jewels and gemstones for the great altar of the Holy Savior, that Arsinde, the wife of Guillaume Taillefer, Count of Toulouse, and the daughter of Geoffroi Grisegonelle, Count of Anjou, was the possessor of two gold bracelets, or rather, I should say, sleeves, for they covered her arms from her wrists to her elbows, and were of a most marvelous workmanship, set with precious stones.
>
> One night when the lady Arsinde was alone in her noble chamber in the country of Toulouse, she saw as if in a dream a young virgin of the most shining beauty pass by close to her bed.
>
> The countess Arsinde was awed by the incomparable grace of this young lady, and she asked, breathlessly, "Tell me, my lady, who are you?"
>
> "I am Sainte Foy," replied the saint in a sweet voice. "Banish your doubts, noble lady: I am here, I am Sainte Foy."
>
> "O my holy lady," the countess Arsinde said in a suppliant tone, "why have you deigned to visit a sinner such as I?"
>
> "I have come here because I wish you to give me your golden sleeves," replied Sainte Foy. "I have come here to ask you to carry them to Conques, to the abbey church there, to take them yourself and deposit them as a votive offering at the altar of the Holy Savior."

*I did not obtain until later that year (from the library at Avignon, which ordered it from the library at the Sorbonne) a copy of the great Bouillet and Servières *Sainte Foy, Vierge et Martyre d'Agen* (Rodez, 1900), the chief source of everything on Conques written afterward, for, with the exception of the *Cartulaire*, already edited by Desjardins and published in 1878 by the École de Chartes, it contains every document of importance on Conques known at the time of its publication at Rodez in 1900, including a translation into French of Bernard's *Liber Miraculorum Sanctae Fidis* by the Abbé Bouillet, based on the manuscript of Sélestat, the most complete of the seven surviving manuscripts, which the abbé Bouillet had edited and published in its original Latin in 1897.

The lady Arsinde, prudent as she was, would not have parted with such a treasure without asking for some compensation.

"O my lady saint," she replied to Sainte Foy, "I shall carry out your orders with all my heart if you will consider obtaining for me, by the goodness of God, a son."

"The all-powerful Creator," replied the saint, "in consideration of his servant, will grant you this favor without any difficulty whatsoever, if you do not refuse my request."

The following morning the lady Arsinde went to some trouble to find out where, in what country, was this place named Conques with its monastery and its patron saint, Faith. At this time the clamor caused by the miracles of Sainte Foy had not yet resounded beyond the borders of the Rouergue as far as the country of Toulouse. When at last the countess had informed herself of the whereabouts of this Conques and inquired, too, about the best route to take to get there, she made the arrangements, and as soon as was possible, she set off on her holy pilgrimage. She carried to Conques herself, as Sainte Foy had requested, the golden sleeves; and when she arrived she offered them with great veneration to God and to His saint. And there at

The golden sleeves

Conques she remained several days in prayer, honoring by her
presence the solemnities of Easter.

Afterward when she returned to her country, she conceived
and brought forth into the world a man-child, and some time
later she had another son. The elder was named Raymond, the
younger Henry. And the golden sleeves, so beautifully worked,
were used as Sainte Foy had wished them to be in the confection
of the great master altar of the Holy Savior.

In the following century, in the time of Sainte Foy's great renown,
a song was composed in the langue d'oc that tells the story of this
same miracle, adding several charming details. It sings of the
sleeves of Arsinde, Countess of Toulouse, which now fall to the
ground, all worked with gold and studded with gemstones; and
when she sets off for Conques with them she is accompanied by a
most honorable company; and after she has laid her sleeves on the
altar of the Holy Savior, the countess of Toulouse is led before
Sainte Foy (Sancta Fé) and shown her in her majesty; and then the
countess tells how Sainte Foy appeared to her in vision and requested the gift of her sleeves; and she tells them, too, what she
asked for in return from the glorious Sainte Foy, *la gloriosa Sancta
Fé*. And so it was that soon after her return to Toulouse, the lady Arsinde conceived a child and without peril brought him into the
world—her son who was baptized Raymond. And not long after
that her second—Henry, he was called.

> *O Sainte Foy be praised*
> *O Sainte Foy be thanked*
> *O Sainte Foy be glorified*
> *And give us her love*
> *And that of God our Creator*
> *Amen*

Though I knew so little, still, on our first return, in October
1976, I felt all the long, homely mystery of love and of life, of body
and soul, held and sheltered there, beneath the roof and within the
stone walls of Sainte Foy de Conques, and I wrote in my notebook
in a rapture.

I wrote how that evening of her fête day toward six, as I was returning to the hotel from my visit to her in the Treasure, I saw that
the door to her chapel, which opens into her great church just off
the cloister, was still open, and I saw there were candles burning
before her altar in the nearly dark church, and I went in and stood
there and took in as much as I could by candlelight, wanting it to
stay in my mind—the candlelight flickering on the gold leaf of the
high rococo reredos of the seventeenth century with its gold-
winged pink-faced cherubims like children and its angels sur-
rounding the gold-gowned full-blooming Sainte Foy in the center,
and above her, Christ on the cross; and on the panels on either side
of her, leafed in gold, were scenes from the hour of her martry-
dom—her torture on the grill, the men with bellows fanning the
flames while above, the dove, Lord and Giver of Life, in a cloud
brings rain and a crown; and across from that scene, on the opposite panel, the executioner with his sword stands behind her as she
prays, and we see her soul as Saint Caprais saw it from the mouth of
the cave above Agen where he was hiding with the Christians, we
see her soul in the form of a dove being carried up to heaven by angels in a cloud of light. All this was lit by the candles in her chapel
and in the stone-arched church all else was still, save this chapel
with its candles and the last light of evening coming in the door.

After dinner Jack and I went back down to the cloister, and there
below was the valley of the Ouche in the full moonlight, remote
and wild in the far-off October stillness, with the waters rushing far
below. The yellow stone of the cloister was burnished by the moon,
and we got up close enough to examine the capital there that shows
the church builders rising above the tower they are building, holding their stone hammers and other tools, with a look of triumph on
their faces. One of them holds a horn up close to his mouth, so that
even then, in the moonlight more than nine hundred years later,
they looked as if they had posed this way for a portrait and would
soon begin to sing.

Jack and I decided the Hôtel Sainte Foy was our favorite hotel in
all the world. We loved the feel of the old stone *hostelerie,* which
was like a blessed refuge, with its thick walls and its generous
spaces; one felt a kind of stillness there the minute one entered

from the street. On the first floor up from the street, mornings were devoted to order, among the big sprays of flowers arranged in vases here and there, and to the pleasures of coffee, crusty bread, and butter and jam.

On that second visit, for our picnics at noontime, we went farther afield, following one of the walks described in a booklet called "Les Promenades de Conques," which Madame Cannes of the hotel had lent to us. (It was written and published, we learned later, by Monsieur LaPeyre and *Les Droits des Piètons de France.*) The directions were often hard for us to make out. The little arrow-signs had faded and often the paths were grown over, so that we'd return late in the afternoon hot and happy from our adventures, a bit sunburned and scratched from the brambles, and brushed with heather.

And then came the dinners, in the warm and spacious dining room with its panels of antique wallpaper and its ample solid tables covered with white tablecloths and set with hand-painted plates, large, heavy flatware, and vases of fresh flowers. We chose always from "*le menu*" and ordered, for instance, the *salade au Roquefort et noix* (walnuts) and the green *crêpes Auvergnats,* a favorite with Jack, made, I later learned, with the chopped green of the Swiss chard (the *côtes du blettes,* as they said at Conques, pronouncing both *côtes* and *blettes* with two syllables), the *pintadeau,* a bird, with wild mushrooms, the black-red wine of Cahors, the cheeses of the region—Roquefort, Cantal, Saint Nectaire, Bleu d'Auvergne, the *cabecous* of goat cheese. (The caves at Roquefort once belonged to the Abbey of Conques, and Charlemagne ordered wagonloads of the cheese drawn by mule from Roquefort to his palace at Aix-la-Chapelle.) The *poire Belle Hélène* was the best I ever tasted—the ripe pears of Conques! The warm bittersweet chocolate sauce!

The courses arrived in turn in the discreet and courteous atmosphere of the dining room, where all of us seemed to catch the whispered tones of the girlish Madame Cannes with her smooth skin, and her lavender-tinted glasses, greeting the guests individually and ushering them to their tables, moving about, long-legged, slender, soft, her wavy hair tossing, bending over to take, whispering, our orders, doing everything with perfection in her enchanting, graceful way. She was in her early forties then, about six or seven years younger than we. Only later did we come to understand that the charming sunbrowned Monsieur Cannes called Zée-Zée, with his sandy hair and his deep voice, the Monsieur Cannes we saw about the lobby and doing this and that, was not her husband but her brother-in-law, who had never married, and that her husband, Jeannot, whom we never saw until after we came to live in Conques, was the chef of the hotel.

The hotel had belonged to a great-uncle of the Cannes brothers, and then their father was the *patron* for many years. Madame Cannes had grown up in Rodez, the pampered darling daughter of the owner of a fine and fancy three-star hotel there; after we had come to know her well, she told us that her father was very displeased indeed when he learned that she was going to marry into the family of such an unimportant country village hotel, but that she had refused to change her mind. She had fallen in love with Jeannot, she claimed, because he was such a marvelous dancer. And that was that. But after they were married and she came to live in Conques, her father-in-law, old Monsieur Cannes, was very hard on her, Jean Sègalat told us. He tried to make her suffer. He made her wash the sheets in the icy waters of the village *lavoirs*. He made her do all the unpleasant chores. And she had been spoiled, Sègalat said, she had been given everything until then. But she was tough (*dur*). She endured. And after old Monsieur Cannes's death, she told Jeannot and Zée-Zée that she had a few ideas of what they could do to make over the hotel. They said, yes, wonderful, go ahead, we support you. So it was she, her genius, her taste, and the discipline, the talent, the hard work of all three of them that made the Hôtel Sainte Foy into the charming, elegant, and comfortable place it had become. (The Hôtel Sainte Foy had won two red houses and a red *R* in the *Guide Michelin*, meaning it was a very special though simple hotel with excellent meals at a low price.)

Dinner finished early. And the hotel was locked up by ten-thirty, or by eleven at the latest. Then in the quiet, as if in reaction to the decorum of the hotel and the holiness of Conques, there would come from one or another of the various chambers wild cries of sexual ecstasy or giggling hints of harder-to-figure-out goings-on.

We didn't think from the way Conques looked that there could possibly be any place to rent and stay, any more than we thought it would ever be possible for us to ride up these mountains on our bicycles. It wasn't until the following May, 1977, that we returned, coming by way of Notre Dame du Puy, following, more or less, the old pilgrim route, up and down and up and down, over the high mountains of the Massif Central, across the Margeride, covered with new-fallen snow that early May, to Aubrac and down to the valley of the Lot.

We returned determined to at least ask Madame Cannes. She welcomed us and called us *fidèle,* and led us, when we asked her, directly to Madame Fabre, who worked in the hotel and had a small house she wanted to rent for the month of June. It was already promised for the Pentecôte weekend at the end of May and for July and August. It was in this way, as we took up our life in Madame Fabre's house under the kind aegis of Madame Cannes, and later, when July came, spent two weeks in Rosalie's "Rooms for Rent," that we began to enter gradually into the life of the village, which has become by now our village, our life.

"I could deliver the mail," Jack says. "I know the names of all the dogs."

It was just here that we saw the rainbow three years ago, in October 1976, here where on the far side the plateau of Lunel juts forth like the prow of a ship as far as Calvignac (or Caubignac) and the Ouche forks, so we can see the humped wooded ridges of its gorge receding to the south and east toward its source on the plain near Lunel, and to the north and east toward its other lesser sources. Far below, down in the chasm, vast rocks rise like mountains partially covered with heather, the layered gray schist jutting forth at their tops like twisted, tortured towers.

"Oh, but there were castles down by the Ouche," says Madame Fau. "There were! There was a castle there on the rock where the little chapel of Saint Roch stands now. It tells about it in the *Book of Miracles.* There was a terrible lord, Raimond, he was called; he was wicked; he was planning to tear down the village of Conques, which had grown up around the abbey. Yes! He was planning to do that, and he began, although the people pleaded with him, he began, and so Sainte Foy . . . Sainte Foy who always protected the *good* people of her village, Sainte Foy destroyed the castle, she made it just crumble to the ground, and the cruel lord was killed and his sons were all struck down—I forget how—by some frightful disease, I think, and his daughters all ran off into another country with men of low estate. Monsieur Balsan is conducting some excavations there inside the chapel. He has found some Gallo-Roman artifacts.

"And there was another castle way down in the valley of the Ouche up toward Calvignac. It was a castle of the English. Or maybe the Moors. The people here called it Roqueprive. There is nothing left of it now but some stairs carved in the rock. But there is a story about it the people here loved to tell in the old days."

Madame Fau tells these stories excitedly, her blue eyes sparkling, she tells them talking fast, like a child, with gasps of glee. I think of her as being like a tiny benevolent dowager empress, living on in Conques, young in her age, innocent somehow in her charming enthusiasm, affectionate, making an adventure out of everything, walking everywhere, stopping to talk to everyone, trim and straight and nicely dressed, her hair a nice sandy blond, prettily waved. "*Ahh, bonjour, ma petite*," she says when she sees me, and she stands up on tiptoe, smiling, tilting her cheek for me to bend down to kiss her, first one cheek and then the other and then the first once more.

She comes from the south, from Béziers, and her father, Henry Parayre, who had been the head of the École des Beaux-Arts at Toulouse and was a fine lyric sculptor in the style of the turn of the century, retired to Conques and became in his retirement, for many years, Conques's mayor. After his death Madame Fau's husband, who was Conques's doctor, became Conques's mayor, and now Jean-Claude Fau, her eldest son, has become officially Conques's *conservateur*. He is a professor, teaching at the *lycée* in Montauban and is a noted art historian, specializing in the Romanesque in Conques.

"A 'dynasty!' " Madame Fau said when she commented on this.

"You see the young girl in the face of the old woman," Jack says of her. And another time he said, "Have you noticed how straight she stands and walks ever since that awful Blackou died?" (Blackou

was her beloved old muddy, matted, barking, black cocker spaniel.)
"Ever since that Blackou stopped dragging her around everywhere."
(Shortly before we first came here Docteur Fau and Madame Fau
together had been struck down by a car in a crosswalk in Toulouse,
and he had never really recovered from the accident; he was dead of
a heart attack in his office a year later; and she, stricken with grief,
was only slowly recovered—not helped, Jack insisted, by that
awful, demanding Blackou.)

"Jack is just the same age as Jean-Claude," Madame Fau says. "I
like you very much," she says. I love sitting in her living room, looking out over the valley, surrounded by her father's sculptures, several graceful Venus de Milo–like nudes, and some lovely paintings
of the Impressionist school, an old print or two of Conques (the
church before it was restored), and a kind of comfort that is rare in
Conques because her house has central heating. The mantelpiece,
the fireplace and the *boiserie* above and around it come from the
château at Pruines, beyond Lunel several miles to the south of
Mont Kaymard, on another upcropping of mountain.

She goes on to tell us the story of Roqueprive, talking fast, in little
bursts. "The people say the English, or maybe it was the Moors, they
say they captured a girl from the village and they took her up there to
their castle and they kept her there, a prisoner, a servant. But somehow or other she was able to communicate a signal, that when she
would hang a white cloth from the tower window, the men of Conques would know the English, or maybe the Moors, had feasted and
were sleeping; they knew it was a sign they could take the castle. And
they did. And they rescued her, the village girl. And then they set fire
to the castle and all the English, or maybe the Moors, were burned up
inside." Babet ends the story smiling, triumphant, like a child who has
managed to tell a whole story. She shrugs her shoulders in wonder—
it was all over so fast. "There is nothing left there now at Roqueprive
but some steps carved in the rock," she says. "We used to go there on
Sundays sometimes when the children were little. The path that leads
to it is all grown over now. Jean-Claude always took his trowel. He
was a historian, an archaeologist, right from the start. He always
wanted to dig for old artifacts, or dig for treasure."

. . .

High above Roqueprive, our road follows the mountain in long leisurely zigzags up through the woods and the heather, up through the vineyard and the high pasture land of the farm called La Combe du Notaire.

I can see the rims of certain fields on the far plateau—smooth as carpets laid down over the edge into the rough woods. And here I can look up through a meadow to see the sky through the legs of the cows on the ridge.

That is one way to describe this country as it is now, I once decided, a country where you can look up through a field, green as Ireland, and see the sky through cows' legs. Jack spoke one evening, in the midst of telling a story, of a cow looming up ahead of him. "Cows don't loom, Jack," said a friend who had come to visit. "What?" I said to our friend. "You have never been to Hong Kong?" Causing much laughter. (Kow Loon! Ha, ha.) But Jack is right. Cows can loom, and in this country frequently they do.

From behind comes the racket of a tractor wagon and above it a melodious tenor voice singing out over the valley. Then the toot of a horn. It is the Fraysou bringing the garbage of Conques up to the dump on the plateau. Presently he will pass me. He'll be up on his high seat with his hands off the steering wheel, he'll be flexing his muscles with his fists raised high, and he'll call out something unintelligible.

"I am a Gaul," he said to us one evening, standing by our table on the terrace at the Auberge du Pont Romain down on the Dourdou. "My family has lived in Conques for four hundred years." I wanted to ask him to sing a song in the patois, but Madame Odile of the Auberge wailed: "No, no, he must sing in French! If he sings in patois no one will understand." "I am a Gaul," said the Fraysou to us with the authority of Julius Caesar (though he knows he must accept Madame Odile's conditions for his singing), and he looks the Gaul with his ruddy weathered face, his short, comic strip–like muscular Hercules body with its short, bandy legs, and his bald head.

Rough and taut, he has an incongruously high voice—almost unintelligible at times, even to the French, when he speaks, yet singing out in church with haunting beauty the words of the mass, the Latin words, too, on Good Friday at the Stations of the Cross.

When, on the dark day of Christ's passion and death, the bells of the church are silenced, there is no Angelus, and the Fraysou leans out of the window of his house near the top easternmost part of the old village inside the Porte du Foumouze and blows his conch shell (his *conque*) to call the people to go to the church.

"It is a gift," he said touchingly when I told him how fine his voice was. "I had it always, even when I first started going to school."

"And your family has lived here in Conques for four hundred years," I said to him another time, wanting to go on with that conversation.

"Four hundred and fifty years," he said, raising his chin a little.

They were here then, either way, when the plague killed nearly everybody in all of Conques; they must have fled in terror up to the *séchoirs* in the woods with the few who eluded death. I do not say this. I wonder even if the year they came is not what he thinks, if they might not have come after the plague of 1628, come down to one of the houses left empty, to work, perhaps for the abbey, from some village higher up, long crumbled now back into rock along with the old ash tree from which it got its name. *Fraysse (frêne* in French), as noted, means ash tree in the patois.

"And before they came here, where did your family come from?" I asked.

He pointed with his chin. "From up there," he said, indicating the direction of Lunel to the east and a little south. "From a little village?" He nods yes.

"I am a Gaul." He said it again. It explains him, I think, to himself, explains the thing that sets him apart—his primitiveness, his specialness, his aloneness. He was here, one feels—his forebears were here, but he is like them somehow, a much earlier man—he was here millenniums ago, working, raising the immense stone of the dolmen at Lunel, here when the Celts came (between 600 and 200 B.C.), here to work building the Druids' temple by the sacred spring on the little plain at Conques, here when the Romans came to work building, or rebuilding, the road that came down from Lunel to Conques, here to pull stones, to lift, here a thousand years later at the quarry of Lunel, to pull, to lift the huge blocks of yellow limestone destined to be cornices and buttresses for the new

abbey church, to lift them onto the huge dray which the twenty-six
pairs of oxen described in the *Book of Miracles* would pull then from
the quarry above the source of the Ouche near Lunel, across the
plateau, and down the mountain into Conques.

I do not know why I think of the Fraysou, of his forebears, as working with stone down through the ages, not as skilled stonecutters but
as laborers used for their strength, but perhaps it is his physical
strength and the feeling I have that his skin is partly stone or rubbed
with stone; perhaps, too, there is something in the quality of his voice
which, filling the stone church with its haunting tenor beauty, seems
itself to be somehow cool, like stone, and to have within it some
tremulous granulated quality like the dust of stone, so that when his
voice, his gift from God, fills the air within the high stone arches, the
smooth Romanesque vaulting of this sacred shrine, singing in holy
adoration, "Hosanna! Hosanna!" it seems to be at one with the stones,
which stand so that the spirit of God may dwell within them.

Far ahead I hear his tractor horn toot again. He is greeting Jack.

The road enters a cool and sun-dappled shadowy oak woods; it is
climbing still, but soon I will emerge on the plateau, right by the
farm called Fonromieu, where Jack will be waiting.

He is standing, lithe and tall in his black jeans and his blue denim
shirt, beside his *vélo*. He is looking out with his binoculars across the
plateau to the north to the white church of Aubepeyre and the old
beech tree there beside it on the crest of the plateau beyond the deep
valley of the Lot—four or five miles away, perhaps, as the crow flies,
but it takes more than an hour to drive there from here. We greet, we
drink more water, we chatter, here by the farm called Fonromieu,
from Font Romieu, Pilgrim's Spring, for in this part of the country
since before the turn of the millennium the word for "pilgrim" has
been spelled variously, *romieu, roumiou,* and so forth. It was derived
from a kind of slang designating one going on a pilgrimage to Rome
and came to mean, by extension, all pilgrims. (In English we have
"roam," and though my *O.E.D.* says it comes from the Middle English
and that the origin is obscure, it is clear enough to me where it comes
from.)

I came across the word "*romeus*" in Bernard of Angers, who is fond of sprinkling his Latin prose with words peculiar to this country. At the very opening of the *Book of Miracles* we find it, for it is thus that the young Guibert is accosted, amicably, it seemed at first, by his terrible godfather, the priest named Gerald.

"Ahh, there you are, Guibert-Pilgrim," said this Gerald most affably. "I see you are making a pilgrimage." "*Je vois tu fais roumiou,*" writes the Abbé Bouillet in his translation of Bernard's Latin: "*Ecce, Guiberto, romeus, ut video effectus es.*" "Such," writes Bernard, "is the name given to pilgrims in this country."

"Yes, master," Guibert replied. (Guibert worked in the household of his godfather, whose business affairs he managed with diligence, writes Bernard.) "I am coming from the fête of Sainte Foy," said Guibert, innocent and unsuspecting. He had passed the vigil of her fête in the church at Conques, near her statue, and he wore still the sacred insignia of the pilgrim as he made his way home once more, on the day, even, of the fête, Bernard points out.

Gerald was on horseback but his men who accompanied him were, like Guibert, on foot, so it was easy enough for them, when Guibert's back was turned, to run as they were commanded and to fall on Guibert and bring him down.

I cannot pass Fonromieu without thinking that it was here where they would have encountered each other, stopping to drink from the source—Guibert having climbed up from Conques on his way home from the long vigil, from fasting, and Gerald and his servant men going down to Conques, to celebrate in feasting. Guibert was pinned to the ground, struggling to get free, and when he could not, he began pleading his innocence of he knew not what. "If not for my sake, then in the name of God and Sainte Foy, spare me, master," Guibert cried out.

"Neither God nor Sainte Foy nor your pilgrim's habit can protect you now," said the priest Gerald in his fury. "Thus did he blaspheme," writes Bernard, "possessed as he was by a secret jealousy he dared not let be known, for it had to do with a woman." He ordered his men to tear out Guibert's eyes. "Tear them out, tear them out," he said, foaming in his fury.

When they would not (yet they went on holding Guibert down),

Gerald got down from his horse and "with those very hands which had touched the sacred body of our Lord," writes Bernard, "the priest Gerald tore out the eyes of his godson and threw them with scorn to the earth."

At that, while the young Guibert lay there on the ground doubled up in his blood darkness, the servant men saw a dove white as snow appear out of nowhere and fly off with Guibert's eyes up and over the mountain in the direction of Conques. These men insisted afterward that it was a dove, but the priest Gerald maintained, and does, Bernard says, still, at the time he writes, claim it was a magpie that took the eyes of Guibert up and off over the mountain toward Conques. "But magpie or dove," says Bernard, as if chortling over the dispute, "it took up the eyes of Guibert in its beak and flew off toward Conques. All are agreed on that point."

"Perhaps," ponders Bernard, "the Divine Will would that the bird He sent be neither tout à fait dove nor tout à fait magpie, and the difference in what was seen could be laid to the fact that the servant men, being innocent, saw the dove, all white (appearing as the Holy Ghost appears), while the guilty priest, Gerald, already filled with remorse, saw the partial black of the magpie. And yet," continues Bernard in his pondering, "did not God send ravens to take nourishment to Elijah in the desert, and might He not as easily designate a magpie to save and guard over the precious eyes of Guibert."

"Magpies are known for picking up bright and glittering things," Jack says. "That's why they're known as thieves. They pick up bright and glittering things and put them in their nests. They've been known to steal jewels."

I hadn't known this and it delights me—another homey natural detail in this tale of miracle which is as human and down-to-earth as anything could be, both brutal and touching, though permeated with symbolism and metaphor, which in that age were not thought of as being simply literary devices; they were, rather, considered the real keys to reality, to the truth.

Bernard looks on the miracle of Guibert the Illuminé as the foundation of all the other miracles of Sainte Foy and he puts it therefore, first and foremost in his Liber Miraculorum Sanctae Fidis, not only because of its great fame, and because he heard the story from the mouth of Guibert himself as an old man whom he came to love, but also because of its symbolism; for more clearly, dramatically, and intimately than any other, Guibert's story showed symbolically how, through the intercession of Sainte Foy, God worked His wonders at Conques.

For eyes are like gemstones in that eyes, like gemstones, contain light and transmit light. And light is the Lord Jesus Christ who said, "I am the Light."

"The light of the body is the eyes: if therefore thine eye be single, thy whole body shall be full of light" (Matthew 6:22).

And Guibert's good and innocent body was, at the moment he was mutilated, filled with the light of the Lord, through the sacrament, through his devotion to Sainte Foy and the long vigil he had passed in her presence on the eve of her fête day. During the year of his blindness, while he sang wonder-filled songs and prospered and was loved as a jongleur, he was entertained in castles and sheltered in village houses, and he seemed to have forgotten—as is revealed at the moment in his sleep when, after a year, Sainte Foy appeared to him—that he had been "deprived of Light."

So through this miracle the Light which is the Lord shone on and through the good jongleur, who was known ever after his miraculous healing as Guibert the Illuminé, Guibert the Enlightened, and by the means of the enlightened one, then, God's favor shone on and through Sainte Foy onto Conques and its abbey; for the fame of the miracle of Guibert brought pilgrims to Conques; in greater and greater numbers they came, often, Bernard tells us, as much to see Guibert as to see Sainte Foy. (The monks had given Guibert the job of selling candles by the church door so that he might be better seen by all who came.)

Thus the pilgrims brought with them riches, gold and gemstones; and the miracles of Sainte Foy increased: prisoners were freed from the dungeons; children who might never otherwise have been born were brought into the light of the world; blind eyes were opened to see the earth in all its glory; and those churchmen, clerks and scholars, who came to Conques or dwelled here, steeped like the Abbot Suger in the philosophy of the Heavenly Hierarchies of Dionysius the Areopagite (now known as the Pseudo-Dionysius or as Dionysius the Pseudo-Areopagite) might, like the Abbot Suger in the presence of the Cross of St. Éloy write, "When out of my delight in the beauty of the house of God the loveliness of the many-colored gems has called me away from external cares, and worthy meditation has induced me to reflect, transferring that which is material to that which is immaterial, then it seems to me . . . by the grace of God, I can be transported from this inferior to that higher world in an anagogical manner."

For jewels, with their many varied properties, also functioned, like eyes, as lenses, receiving light, holding light, refracting and reflecting light on all who came to pray among the many embellished reliquaries before the master altar of the Holy Savior and before Sainte Foy, who became more and more in her statue's person adorned with light in all its myriad facets even as her eyes conveyed, and convey to this day, the communicable presence of the eternal Light which is Love.

And so we can in our time behold her, thanks to God and Sainte Foy herself and the jongleur Guibert and the monks who guarded her down through the centuries and the people of Conques who protested and risked their lives to save her during the revolution, and thanks, too, to the magpie (or the white dove) whose very descendants (perhaps) Jack and I see quite often now as we pass by Fonromieu.

The white doves of the farm fly up and around and over the red tile roof of the barn, which is below the road, and at almost the same time, just as often, a magpie soars from the field up ahead, and then another—Mr. and Mrs. Magenpie, Jack and I call them—and off they go. And off we go, following the magpies in their flight, off over the plateau we go, sailing along on our *vélos,* through fields of wheat ripening now into beige, through fields of rye, blue-green, past pastures where drifts of black-and-white Holstein cows arrange themselves on the hillsides in patterns lovely as lace.

The plateau is not completely flat but is made up of long low hills, and the fields in their contours follow the hills and are lined by trees or by long blackberry hedges (*les ronces,* they are called, and barbed wire in French is *ronce artficiel*). There are clumps and squares of woods here and there, and we see them, near and far off beyond the Lot, rising up like islands in the distant waves of green.

Among them there is in particular one that catches at a corner of my awareness each day—a patch of woods on the farthest ridge beyond the crest where the church at Aubepeyre stands, and its length and the way it is cut, gray-blue in the distance against the sky, enters my mind and stirs my emotions, my memories of my long-ago life in the Michigan of my childhood, in the August light of Grand Traverse Bay, bringing back beloved voices lost to me forever now, bringing back the caring of the grown-ups, the beech trees, the merry mornings with the wild strawberry jam Mama made on toast for breakfast in Grandmother Allen's old wood cottage, the long afternoons I spent reading on my cot in the dappled forest light, the green light, the silver light, the "Dreams and Early Memories" I was writing before I first saw Sainte Foy and left all that, for the long time being, as alone and remote yet intact as that particular rectangular patch of woods, which evokes for a moment all my old love and yearning. Just so in New York sometimes on quiet nights in our bedroom on Barrow Street when the drift of air is coming from the west, I can hear a train sound its whistle somewhere beyond the Hudson in New Jersey and it seems to me almost impossible that such a lovely sound, the sound of the trains of my childhood, should come to me like that deep in the city, in my New York life, come to me from beyond the river to the west and bring with it the happy comfort, the feel of space, of distance, of the mystery beyond the hills, of our village in southern Ohio.

"Toot-toot-ta-toot," my father said. "That is the rule when a train approaches a crossing: Toot-toot-ta-toot, that is the rule, except in Georgia." The trains came chugging up the grade from the south, from Cincinnati, chugging slowly toward the crossing. "The heavy freight moves north," my father said. The train whistles bring back from beyond the river to the west the memories of his voice, the feel of our house, the life, the lives, the years of growing up and going off to college in the East and coming home on the Pullman train for vacations, as I go on both in New York and here pursuing the subject and doing the work I was given to do, and receiving with it a deepening, an enrichment, a grace, a whole life I would never have known without Sainte Foy.

.   .   .

We arrive at the ridge where we can see our fir wood down below across a valley, halfway up the next hill. The *fer* wood we sometimes say. Shall we go to the *fer* wood? And we glide off down the hill looking at it ahead, dark, and perfect in shape with its pointy top. The road runs right through it, and the part of the wood to the south is a perfect rectangle, and the part to the north is larger, longer, and hexagonal, the shape of the old hexagonal reliquaries in the Treasure with their patches of Merovingian glasswork and their gemstones glowing and their windows of ancient glass, so that entering into the fragrant twilight of the fir wood, where quiet is defined by birdsong, we feel we are in a holy grove, protected, like spirit bones within a reliquary. The trees in perfect rows form long corridors that open at the end into the pale north sky, and the sun in the needles above us is silvery and refracted like a star.

We climb on then up to the hilltop, to the crossroads called La Croix d'Aussets, where we will turn off to the south for Lunel. A plain wooden cross stands on the corner, where we can see for miles. Far off to the north, very faintly at this season, rise the pointed gray volcanic peaks of Cantal, and to the east in the distance is the high plateau of Aubrac, whose wild and dangerous solitudes the pilgrims had to cross coming from Notre Dame de Puy to Sainte Foy de Conques on their way to Saint Jacques de Compostelle. In winter both the plateau of Aubrac and the high peaks of Cantal are covered with snow, and then they seem to blaze in their lovely snow-white tranquility, far away, high up, close to heaven. Standing here in winter you can smell the distant snow mixed in with the odor of the grassy earth, where now cows—white Charolais and light tan Limousine—are munching grass. We listen to their peaceful ear-tickling sounds. "They're ripping and snorting," Jack says. "They're doing their work. France is the second-largest exporter of milk in the world. And that's a *true* fact." We laugh and head off for Lunel, nine, ten, eleven kilometers, depending on which way you go.

I remembered the first time we saw Lunel, in the summer of 1977, coming from the east, from St. Felix de Lunel. It rose up above the plateau like an Italian hill town and was built, as I had dreamed it would be. Rampart wall, château (now a school), church, and the houses around it in the high village are all built of the same tawny yellow limestone—*rousset* it is called. The *rousset* darkens outside in the weather to become a tawny yellow (its name comes from *roussel,* which means "dark yellow" in the patois) but inside, when the stone has been quarried from underground, and when it is smoothly cut, as the church at Conques, the *rousset* remains luminous and pale as soft sunshine.

"Lunel!" said Jean Sègalat that summer when, as we were setting off on one of our expeditions, we spotted him standing outside his gallery, and we rode up the ramp to greet him.

"Ahh, Lunel," he said, musing for a moment, standing there, as he often does of an afternoon, breathing in the air while he observes the passing scene just below him on the principal street through Conques. He comes out to rest his hand and to escape from the damp chill of his gallery, Monsieur Bousquet's former *cave,* where his lithographs are hung along walls he has draped with black cloth, and where, toward the back, at a small table under bright light, he works creating his ink drawings.

"During the Hundred Years War," he said, "the monks of Conques fled to the château of Lunel for protection."

"What a time of calamity," wrote the Abbot Raimond de Reilhac in 1359. "Our country was prey to so many tribulations and dangers, to invasions and intolerable hardships, that it became impossible to go on with our life as we should, for from hour to hour we thought that the total destruction of the holy monastery was come."

"The monks took with them, of course," Jean Sègalat continued, "the statue of Sainte Foy and the rest of the golden treasure, and they remained at Lunel in the château there, it is said, for four years and four months and four days without ever going out."

"Conques is *dur* . . . Conques is *dur* . . . it had to be strong or it could not have survived," he said, standing in the shade of the linden tree near the trellis where the climbing red roses bloom, next to the sign that says GALERIE EMANUELLE.

"The gallery was going to be for her," he said. *"Mon amie,"* he says, his voice changing when he speaks of her. In Decazeville, where they both lived, she had run away from her husband to be with Jean, and they had come to Conques together. But her husband would not give her a divorce.

Perhaps it was because of that. No one knew why she did it. Not even Jean. She had been drinking, distraught, they say, so perhaps, perhaps, she took the overdose of sleeping pills by accident.

In the early hours of the morning of the fête of Sainte Foy, October 6, 1975, she was found dead in the apartment she and Jean had rented so they could be together—on the other side of the Hôtel Sainte Foy, above the old magnolia tree that grows behind the monument to the War Dead. She was thirty-nine years old.

Jean Sègalat was forty-nine that year. He cannot get over her death. He cannot recover from his grief.

We know him with the beard he has grown since the time of her death, a slight man physically, slim, not very tall—he is, he told me once, exactly an inch taller than Napoleon—a man of charm and gentleness with a beautiful voice and a fine face, fair skin tending toward a faint rosy pink; his beard is silky, neatly trimmed, sandy brown and, like his hair, turning gray; his blue-gray eyes are gentle and old with soul.

He is a real raconteur; and his deep, vibrant voice is wonderfully melodious and strong when he recites, as occasion suggests it, from the vast store of poetry he has by heart. I have heard him intone from his favorite poem, Victor Hugo's "La Conscience," from Villon, and from Apollinaire, and from *Cyrano de Bergerac,* which he adores. Also he can say lines of prose by heart from Montaigne; and late at night when we three have dinner together he comes at last to

Faulkner, for whom he has a passion (in French translation, of course).

Jean Sègalat speaks French clearly and with elegance and wit but, he tells us, with the accent *Aveyronese*. However, he says, he can if he wishes when he is in Paris speak with the Parisian accent; and when he does he is invariably mistaken for a Parisian. I have no doubt of this. He is a marvelous mimic. He can do the Fraysou to perfection, or Charlou, or Monsieur Fabre, the *forgeron,* or Zée-Zée, or Père André in a state, or Père Gilles.

"He has the façade," Jack says, "the wonderful French façade! They may be suffering, but when they greet you they muster up cheer, humor, they go out to you. It is so courteous, so dignified."

"He's a natty dresser," Jack said another time as we observed him in the church after mass, walking, looking up, stopping, his head tipped back. He wears a sweater, a cotton shirt, blue or white, gray wool pants, or khaki cotton in summer, a necktie when he is dressed up, a tweed jacket; he is elegant in a shabby-aristocratic way—his clothes always look just right, and never new.

"We mustn't talk to him: he's working," Jack said. Jean seemed to be wandering around studying the capitals. (And we seemed to be wandering around studying him.) "He looks like Cro-Magnon man," Jack said.

"Jack!" I said.

"I mean he looks so gentle and so civilized," Jack said. "And there's something about the bone structure of his face, his head. Cro-Magnon man was a sweet large-headed man—as Henry Miller saw him—very intelligent and peaceful with a highly developed sense of beauty; driven out by a smaller-headed, nastier, more competitive race of Homo sapiens."

Jack's description of Cro-Magnon man seems to describe Jean Sègalat perfectly; and really, I decide, after some reading, he could be descended from Cro-Magnon man. Cro-Magnon means "Great Hole" in the patois of the country around Les Eyzies de Tayac, where in 1868, as they were cutting through the land to lay the railroad, the workers came upon the three ancient skeletons in the rock shelter, which the archaeologists Édouard Lartet and Henry Christy, later, after study, named Cro-Magnon Man; the name was

applied henceforth to the early people who, it is presumed, fifteen,
twenty, thirty thousand years ago, during the last ice age, lived in
the great peaceful region we call the Dordogne (the French call it
Périgord) and in Quercy, which borders on the Rouergue, and
painted the walls of their sacred caves, of the cave called Lascaux
near Les Eyzies, of the cave at Font de Gaume, and, closer to Conques, the one near Cahors, at Peche-Merle.

There are people in Quercy, I have read, who are descended
from early pre-Celtic inhabitants of that country, and they have a
different skull structure from that of the later Celtic peoples. If
after the last ice age some of the early, gifted Cro-Magnon peoples
had returned northward after generations, if they had migrated,
mating, as they must have to some extent at least, with the invading
Homo sapiens, might not some of their genes have survived and
come down to our time in Quercy, emerging somehow most
strongly in such a rare, highly developed, gifted son of this country
as our Jean Sègalat?

Whether this is anthropologically au courant, I do not know. But
having gone down into the cave at Peche-Merle, where, deep in the
flowing subterranean chambers, the Deity enwraps one still in
awesome wings of breath, and having felt there somehow the spirit-
heart of what these early human beings knew in their sacred caves,
I like to think of Jean Sègalat as being descended from the one who
saw the form of the horse's head projecting from the edge of a
smooth rock wall there and painted the perfect black line to call
forth the body of the mare; and from the one who sometime later,
inspired with the mystery of music and number, painted the spots
just so, both on and above the perfect body of the mare; and from
the one who, after centuries, painted that other piebald horse over-
lapping, standing close as horses do still, their hind parts near for
comfort and protection, as they look out in opposite directions,
grazing, dreaming, watching; and from those who, generations
later still, were among the ones chosen to have the red painted over
and around their hands, reaching, outstretched in prayer, pressed
against the sacred wall above and below the now piebald horses so
that their haloed hands, the negative imprints, were left to cry out
down through the ages in reverential invocation: We are here; we

are mortal; with our beings and our bodies we are striving; our minds reach out as far as they are able; oh, hear us, listen, see: we honor you and we entreat your favor. Now with our hands and with the power of paint, cool, grainy, wet, red, blown over and around our hands, we put our life spirits on the mystic wall in the place where we revere your horses and sing their stories, dancing, in the wonder of their presence here in your holy cave. See, see now the magic of our hands, see their haloes. We leave our signs so that after us the mortal ones who come later will know that here in your sacred cavern we worshiped you who are light and yet resound so darkly in the earth.

And Jean Sègalat also, I imagined descended from the one who went, centuries later still, with her child down into the inner sanctum where the Voice breathed, soft as distant thunder; and they gave themselves up for a time to the stilled ecstasy of knowledge of the world beyond the walls of time, and left their bare footprints in the clay that turned to rock; for that was toward the long winter when the ice pushed forward and closed off all entrance to the cave for the next twelve thousand years and more; and the rains came, and the snows, and the people moved southward and the seas rose, flooding the coastal plains when at last the warmth returned; and yet there were some of a future generation who remembered the stories they had heard from those who came before them of the land of the mild yellow cliffs and the temples under the earth where, in the flickering light of torches, bulls ran and bison and horses; and reindeer swam.

So there he went, late in the twentieth century after Christ, in the stone gloom of Sainte Foy de Conques on a Sunday after mass, our Cro-Magnon friend, with his large intelligent head, and his small body; there he went, deep in study, while we, following along at a distance, not wanting to interrupt, found ourselves continuing our study of him. "You see: he's sketching," Jack said.

He was engaging, rather, in a mysterious form of concentration as he went on walking, stopping, tipping back his bearded head, taking in the images of the capitals, which, then, he would bear in his mind back to his *cave-galerie,* where from his hand, in pen and ink, they would emerge on paper, the capitals and the columns, transformed.

He was preparing to draw them, I later realized, to decorate the book of Conques he was doing with Jean-Claude Fau. Jean-Claude was writing and assembling the text and Jean Sègalat was illustrating it; the capitals and columns would illuminate the wide margins of the French translation of the "Song of Sainte Foy," and the spaces at the chapter ends.

The process was of a piece with his oeuvre altogether, which evokes a kind of shadow-mirror Conques or Decazeville or Rodez or the high bare regions of Aubrac or Lozère, where the past and the present flow together in a vision that is uniquely his—romantic in a way and fantastic, poetic; sometimes grim, sometimes overflowing with humor; filled almost always with people of all kinds from many epochs, including our own, and with tiny, surprising, sometimes naughty details that make you laugh when you find them; and governed overall by the sharp and biting satiric eye that Jack admires so much in him.

I say his oeuvre altogether, but I am speaking actually of his work in pen and ink, his work since the time of his accident, because Jean Sègalat began as a painter. As a young man, after the war, at the end of the forties and in the fifties, when he returned home to Decazeville from his studies in Paris, he achieved a fine reputation here in Aveyron based on his work in oil paints. His *Cruxifixion* hangs in the church at Decazeville—a Christ all white and seemingly filled with light, suffering, hanging on the cross, alone in a field of darkness. Nearby along the wall proceed the Stations of the Cross painted by Gustave Moreau.

He won the Prix Cabrol in 1956, and his work hangs in the Musée Denys Puech in Rodez side by side with that of Aveyronese painters of earlier generations—Eugene Viala (1859–1913), Casimir Serpantié (1855–1949), and Roger Serpantié (1891–1974). (The entire collection of local painters of the nineteenth and twentieth centuries is described in our Knopf *Traveler's Guide to the Art of France* as "appalling.")

Jean painted scenes of the factories at Decazeville. He painted workers coming out of the mine; he painted the house of a miner.

The critic Jacques Bousquet praised the poetry of the work ("*poésie ouvrière*") of this painter from the *bassin houiller* of Decazeville-Aubin, the mining district, "which had no painter before him."

"Oh, you must have been very *engagé*," he told us young Laurent Fau had said to him in awe after he had first seen Jean's *Calvary*—Christ carrying His cross up the bleak and desolate mountain walls of the Découverte at Decazeville—the largest open-air coal mine in Europe—and people in modern dress, Decazeville people, workers and bourgeoisie crowding after him in hate and fury, throwing stones.

"No," Jean Ségalat said he told young Laurent. "No, I wasn't really *engagé*. In every age painters have painted those around Christ in the dress of their time and in the landscape they knew. *C'est normale.*"

In fact, though, Jean told us once that in part this particular painting had risen out of the terrible scenes of brutality he had witnessed after the war, the frenzied, violent persecutions of those who were said, sometimes unjustly, to have been *collaborateurs*.

Jean was productive and successful, a rising star in the arts in Aveyron, when, still in his thirties, he injured his hand. He was cranking up his car to start it, and the crank spun back, hitting his fingers, striking them with tremendous force.

When the injury healed, he could no longer paint. Jack noticed that the index finger on Jean's right hand is a little shorter at the end, and withered just there, but no doctor, no specialist in the hand—and Jean has visited many over the years—can find any reason, when they examine him, why he cannot paint as he painted before. There is no physical reason, and yet he cannot. It is almost as if the blow from the accident, the trauma to his hand, prevented ever after that mysterious flow of vision back and forth from his brain through his hand into the brush and onto the canvas and back.

Jean took up ink drawing, which, Jack points out, demands more minute and intricate skill from that same hand. Jean misses the paint. And as time passes his nostalgia for the oils, the brush, the colors becomes more acute. He thinks about going to see yet another specialist in the hand—one he has heard about in Toulouse—with the dream that there might be an operation, something, that could enable him to paint again as he did in his youth, applying the paint thick on the canvas, heavy and rich.

Sègalat is proud of his paintings, as proud as the red cock that stands so nobly cocksure in its frame on the wall of the dining room of the Hôtel Sainte Foy. But Jack thinks there was something sentimental in Jean Sègalat's work as a painter, that there was nothing in it beyond its content to distinguish it in quality from the work of, say, a thousand other second-rate painters who were graduates of the École des Beaux-Arts in the last one hundred years. Yet when it comes to his ink drawings, Jack thinks that he has carved out his field, and that in it he is unique, first-rate. Jack thinks that his accident was a kind of blessing from God to force his real and unique talent to come forth—the humor, the occasional biting, nasty quality of what he sees and renders so precisely. He is a George Grosz of France, of the Rouergue, of the Chemin de St. Jacques de Compostelle, Jack says.

"Look! Look at the expression on her face!" Jack said when we were in the gallery once studying the series of lithographs Jean had done on the story of the *Bête du Gevaudan*. Jack was stunned by how marvelously and exactly Jean had captured the expression on the face of the woman who stood naked in front of the window where the beast had appeared, the look of knowing in that instant as she stood there unclothed that there was nothing more left between herself and a hideous death.

Pausing then in 1977 with Jean outside his gallery on our way to Lunel, I saw the street below as he portrayed it in one of his ink drawings hanging in the Hôtel Sainte Foy. In the drawing the passage between the Hôtel and the Fallières' *tabac/journaux* is crowded with medieval pilgrims in their robes, with scallop shells upon their hats, their staffs, their scrips, all mingling in a jolly fashion with a few fat, almost naked modern-day August tourists; and in the midst of the milling mass pressing forward up the street, you spot Zée-Zée Cannes, dressed like a Renaissance dandy with puffed silken sleeves and tight silken breeches, a large and elaborately decorated codpiece, ruffed collar and cuffs, Zée-Zée swaggering with smiling aplomb in his coxcombical role, while Victor, the hotel's dachsund—their *valet de chambre*, they call him—is on his leash, pulling out ahead; and above, near the cast-iron sign that says HOSTEL STE FOY, we see the heart-shaped face of Madou (Madame Cannes) with her wavy black hair, peeking out of a little wainscotted window. She is wearing her glasses to spy secretly on the goings-on below. Jeannot, her husband, true to his character, is of course nowhere to be seen.

This humorous vision of Jean Sègalat's flashed before my mind's eye for an instant while he went on talking about Conques, very seriously. "He's didactic, he's pedantic," Jack sometimes complains. "I know, I know, I adore it," I say. "He's doing it for me. He's giving me material for my book."

"The tourists don't see Conques as it really is," Jean said. "There are terrible things . . . harsh . . . cruel . . . there are terrible things in its history. The tourists say, How beautiful! How charming! They don't really see Conques. Conques is *dur,*" Jean Sègalat said. "Look at how narrow this valley is, how deep and precipitous. Think about those rock cliffs. Think of how difficult of access it always was, how difficult to live here. Look at the church. Look at it." Jean Sègalat pointed at it both up and down across the way from his gallery. (To go into the church from here you must walk down a long, steep flight of stairs adjoining the stone embankment.) "Look at how high up the windows are, think of how thick the walls are. The church is a great *châsse!* It is a fortress, built to receive the pilgrims, yes, the masses of pilgrims, but built as a fortress, nonetheless, built to hold and protect the golden statue of Sainte Foy. Conques is *dur:* it had to be or it could not have survived.

"When I was a child, when my parents first brought me here, I was still very little, and I was terrified. You know that rock cliff down near the Dourdou where the marble marker says, 'Here according to tradition, in the sixth century, a thousand Christians died, martyred.' They call that field below the cliff still the Field of the Monks. I thought that a thousand monks had all been forced to go up there, and one by one they had been pushed over the cliff to their deaths. I thought I'd have to go up there and stand on the edge where that huge painted crucifix is. That terrified me. And here, too, in Conques itself, I was afraid I might be pushed over the cliff at the far edge of the cloister. I thought I would be taken to lie in one of those coffins, those stone sarcophagi, you know them? Those

Merovingian sarcophagi piled up there along the abbey wall behind
the church. I thought I'd be made to lie down in one of them and I
wouldn't be able to get out.

"And then, in those days, the Treasure wasn't as it is now. It was
in a lot of little rooms in the abbey, and you couldn't go into the
Treasure then without also seeing the Christ they called the Christ
Made of Human Skin. It is horrible. You have never seen it? You
ought to see it. It is in the abbey somewhere stored in a cupboard
now, I think. Ask Père Gilles. It is horrible. I shudder, I still shudder
when I think of it."

He paused. "But you should be going," he said. "It is a long way to
Lunel.

"*Mon amie,*" he said, his voice changing, "she and I used to drive
up to Lunel from time to time. There is a lovely pietà of the sixteenth century there in the village church. And the stone of the
church, of course, is the stone of Sainte Foy de Conques."

"Ahh, Lunel!" said Jeannot Cannes that same summer afternoon.
He had lifted his finger to indicate he had something to tell us, as he
stepped through an opening in the hedge that separates Monsieur
Bousquet's property from the narrow flagstone walk that leads up
to the *bar/terrasse* entrance to the hotel. He shook our hands, explaining that he had been in the bar arranging things and that he'd
heard us out here with Jean Sègalat and decided to come out for a
moment—a thing he claims, in general, that he never does during
the summer season. He claims that he never goes out of doors all
summer long, that at night when the hotel closes he goes from his
kitchen to their apartment on the third floor of the hotel and drinks
a brandy and reads until two or three in the morning before he
sleeps. Actually, he goes early every Monday and Thursday morning
to the market in Decazeville, and I have seen him backing their Citroën jeep around to pick up sacks of flour down at the Moulin de
Sagnes. And, too, sometimes in the evenings Jeannot comes running over to Rosalie's house after she has come in from her gardens,
and he calls up to her kitchen window from the steep stone passage
below with an order for lettuces, strawberries, leeks, onions,

turnips, Swiss chard, carrots—whatever she might have for the next day.

But it is true that he never goes out in the sense that he is never seen by the tourists or by the guests of the hotel. He doesn't go up to the plateau to walk in the sunlight and breathe, the way his brother, Zée-Zée, does. He is not seen abroad in Conques at all until November after Toussaint, when the first sign that the season of their *vacances* has begun is himself out in the hotel garage-parking, washing their car and pausing in the Conquois way to chat at length with whoever might pass by.

And he is a reader, a reader who has steeped himself in history, the history of Conques and of the region, particularly its ancient castles, many of them now in ruin, this intense, intelligent man, tall for Conques (as tall as I am, about five feet nine), thickly built and strong, not at all fat, with a high forehead and black hair cut very short and deep blue-gray eyes, a long nose, a large cleft chin, and an interesting curling mouth. He speaks in a precise and urgent manner. "The château at Lunel was the granary of the monks of Conques," he told us. "Then, as now, the grains were grown on the plateau, while the vines of the monks of Conques"—he smiled—"were here, as they are to this day, on the broad south-facing slope above the town. The vegetables, too, the herbs and the fruit trees were cultivated here within the abbey grounds or in the gardens of the villagers. Beehives were kept in the abbey, as they are now. At one time the abbey of Conques was rich—very rich—with vast landholdings and many dependencies as far off as Roncevaux; it established free towns, the Villefranche, where freed and escaped serfs could come for safety and find work and training as artisans; and yet it was always self-supporting, a completely self-contained entity—except, of course, in times of war and destruction. So that is another reason the monks of Conques would have fled up to Lunel during the Hundred Years War—not only to protect themselves and the Statue of Sainte Foy and the rest of the Treasure, but also to be sure they would have enough bread to stay alive. The chestnuts were not planted until later, in the fifteenth century. The fields were destroyed by the brigands, and any wagons bringing grain would have been attacked; but the grains that were grown on the plateau were stored there at Lunel as well, and the château was well fortified. The château has been turned into a school in recent years, but you can still see the ancient crenellation of its battlements, you can still see the machicolations. And it is built, of course, of the *rousset,* the limestone from the quarry of Salès near Lunel, the same quarry, it is supposed, that supplied the yellow limestone for Sainte Foy de Conques.

"The monks stayed there at Lunel for four years and four months and four days without ever going out," he said. "The abbot, Raimond de Reilhac, kept a kind of journal."

The telephone was ringing in the hotel and he had to shake hands and dash back through the hedge to get it, but we took our leave of him and of Jean Sègalat well instructed that day.

Well instructed, yes, but it wasn't until somewhat later, when Kalia told us about it, that we learned about the presence of the dolmen there less than a mile west of Lunel on the plain below Mont Kaymard.

"Ah, yes, La Pèira Levada [The raised stone], it is called," Madame Benoit told us—later when we tried to talk about it.

But it was Kalia who had first brought it to our delighted attention in an earlier visit. "Lunel," said Kalia. "Then you know the dolmen of Lunel?

"What? *Pas possible!*" he said, joking, popping his blue eyes in astonishment, and he brought us then and there into his house and leather shop right on the Place de la Basilique (as he calls it, not wanting, I believe, to have the word "church" in his address), and sat us down at the big round table by his fireplace so he could draw a map for us; or, rather, he offered us a drink of wine or of coffee there in that good leathery-smelling room and then he drew the map for us so we could find the dolmen.

Kalia is young, about thirty-five, fine-boned, with blond hair and fair skin (you see the quality of his skin at his throat). There is a kind of beauty and perfection in him, in his body, of which he seems to be completely innocent and careless; he is always in motion, talking, working on the leather, working on the house, making something with his gifted hands—drawings, wood sculptures—comforting, coddling, talking to Serge, his little son, mimicking, acting, playing the comic, instructing. Kalia is brilliant, filled with ideas and enthusiasms. He is generous and sweet as a saint. And he has charm. Though he may be haunted, a dreamer with tragic flaws, he melts our hearts, Jack's and mine, and he has given us whatever he had to give, including the dolmen, which belongs to all the world but which we might never have found without him.

Sitting at the big round table in front of his fireplace, he illustrated the map, with tiny drawings, somewhat as he drew the tympanum for us and sent it to us in New York for a New Year's greeting, designating the straight-up-and-down orderly figures to the right of Christ in the Heavenly Jerusalem "Perrier!" and the wild disorder of the figures to the left of Christ and below Him "Red Wine!"

He showed us how we could reach the dolmen by way of the road that goes up from the valley of the Dourdou to Montignac and through Montignac (he drew the little pre-Romanesque church there) on up to the ridge and all the way to Lunel that way, along the southern edge of the plateau. But that way is too steep for us on our bikes, going up, we objected. So then he showed us how we could go as we usually do up by way of Fonromieu to the Croix d'Aussets, and then to the right, south, toward Lunel, but when we come to the fork, instead of taking the road to Lunel and St. Félix de Lunel, we should bear right on the road that leads from Sénergues to St. Cyprien across the plateau and over the source of the Ouche. (Kalia drew the dam that turns the source into a tiny lake.) And then, where this road crosses the road coming from Montignac just at the edge of the plateau, we turn left toward Lunel, two kilometers. Kalia drew a picture of Mont Kaymard to the south of the road, and then he drew the farmer's fence along the other side of the road and showed how the farmer's fence goes along straight for a ways and then jogs in and up and out again, making room for the dolmen right at the side of the road. He drew the dolmen, in its megalithic grandeur, the stone slab stretched at the angle time has given it across the lower stones embedded in the earth at either end.

As an afterthought Kalia drew another thing. "Very interesting," he said. "I don't know, but perhaps, perhaps, this is where they got the stone to build the church at Conques." He drew the strangely lumpy hole near the crossroads where the plateau falls off. The hole is covered with grass now but it has an unnatural aspect, as if, Kalia thinks, it once had been quarried. "I do not know, I am not sure, but perhaps, this is where they got the stone. *Peut-être, peut-être,*" he emphasized.

(Jean-Claude Fau says, no, this was not the quarry: That stone, the *rousset* of Conques, had to come from much farther underground in order to retain its purity, its subtle color. That quarry is at Salès, farther east, beyond the dolmen, between Lunel and St. Félix de Lunel.)

Kalia has come here from Paris by way of Toulon, where he met
Marie. In Paris he was a sculptor—he has shown us photographs of
his work in an "expo"—and he was working in "*publicité*" (advertis-
ing). He is an idealist, a Marxist. "But the Party would not accept
me as a member," he said. He was at the barricades in 1968; and
after that he was in Toulon, antiestablishment, anticlerical, through
with Paris and all that success in Paris entailed. Marie thought he
was a "*clochard,*" a bum, at first, he told us. But he wooed her—
beautiful, delicate, black-eyed Marie—and she fell in love with
him. She was a nurse. She had completed her training and had her
degree. Now they are at Conques with their baby.

Serge is a beautiful baby, but he cries a lot. He had to have an operation when he was still an infant, so they spoil him with sugary
things to try to comfort him. Serge is "*pénible,*" Maïté, the *percepteur,*
said. Jack says that's how to learn a language. *Pénible* (difficult) is
what Serge is. He'll never forget that word: *pénible.*

In the winter they go south to Toulon with Serge where it's
warmer in the house of Marie's Sicilian-born parents, and they
come back at Eastertime. After Marie leaves Kalia stays on to work
on rebuilding the house they bought as a ruin. And they are building up their business, Kalia and Marie. In summer Kalia works in
leather. He can make anything—belts, sandals, handbags, vests; and
Marie, who also does wonderful work—she may well be better
than Kalia—Marie is a wonderful cook, and the two are very hos-
pitable. Marie can make couscous or spaghetti dinners for any
number of friends, it seems. And they come, the friends, up from
the far corners of southern Rouergue or down from their woodsy
places up in the hills beyond Lunel, where they, too, have fled to set
up new lives as artisans or the owners of restaurants. They are what
the French call *marginaux,* these young alternate-lifestyle entrepre-
neurs.

Kalia's father is Russian. He drives a taxi in Paris. His mother is
French. She divorced Kalia's father and went to live in Morocco
with a new husband and have a new family there, leaving Kalia with
her mother, his French grandmother, who made life very unpleasant for the child, Jean-Pierre Kaliaguine, so unpleasant that Kalia to
this day cannot eat *soupe,* cannot abide it. He apologizes at dinner

when *soupe* is served: he cannot touch it. "My grandmother . . ." he occasionally adds.

I believe he is tormented somehow deep within himself, but except on the subject of *soupe,* Kalia is full of humor and play. The only English he ever voices is a heavily accented "I am joking" when I haven't been able to grasp something he has said. Jack and I laugh and imitate his "I am joking" (and it has saved many a hurt feeling between us).

"Do you notice how Marie always laughs at his jokes?" Jack says. There is something touching in his spirit, his enthusiasms, his generosity. He has a strong feeling for Jack's work. It inspires him. He thinks it is important that Jack is here in Conques. It is Jack's presence here that excites Kalia. It gives Conques meaning as a place for artists to work. He dismisses Sègalat. Wrongly, Jack feels.

Once Kalia has got his leather business well launched and the house is all fixed up and comfortable, he plans to let Marie take over the making of the leather things entirely, and the shop will be hers. He will become a sculptor again. That is his dream. His five-year plan.

Kalia analyzes Conques. He admires the Fau family especially, and Monsieur LaPeyre, and the Garrigues, Rosalie and Charlou, of course, but particularly Charlou's oldest brother, Louisou. "He is very interesting, very interesting politically," Kalia says. "He is not just a Communist, he is very active. He fought in the Civil War in Spain." Kalia is awed. "Those three brothers, there is something formidable about them," he says. "But they have their enemies," he adds.

Most of Conques is on the right politically, Kalia says; and many of the older people in Conques look on Kalia and Marie and the few others like them with disapproval, Kalia tells us. But he is sympathetic with their disapproval because it is mixed with envy and sadness and confusion: the Conquois children had to leave home; leave Conques and the region and go north to Paris or south to Montpellier or west into other departments or to Algeria to find work. Their children left, and then along came these alien children from the north, from Paris, from that life, escaping conventional bourgeois expectations to come here and make their living as artisans. And the Conquois see they are doing well, Kalia and Marie and a few others like them, buying the ruins of houses and fixing them up themselves, having babies, and making enough money to live quite well, selling leather goods, pottery, wood carvings, copper jewelry, and so forth, to the tourists in the summertime.

It is a kind of reversal of the old sad story of this poor country, the story Rosalie sings in a voice so lovely and haunting you almost burst into tears when you hear it.

"They were singing it to give themselves courage when they had to leave," Jack says. "That's why you cry when you hear it—they were singing it to give themselves courage, those young girls who had to go away to Paris to look for jobs as chambermaids in hotels or waitresses in bars or nursemaids in big houses, like Madame Benoit when she was a girl." The young men, too, had to go away to Paris, or farther north into mines and factories or to other big cities, far from the earth and the life they loved, far from the people and the language they loved so dearly, into a life of poverty among strangers—though many, it should be noted, prospered, in the hotel and restaurant business notoriously.

Rosalie sings this song, which her father taught her, she says. She sings it in a lilting voice that makes the song seem to belong to a silken ribbon of music that began a long time before the rippling-forth of this song and will go on when the song is done.

As Rosalie sings, she translates the patois into French as she goes along.

Partir mais pour partir ça nous fait de la peine
Partir mais pour partir ça nous fait de la peine
Partir mais pour partir ça nous fait grand plaisir
Mais avant que de partir embrassons nos maitresses
Mais avant que de partir embrassons nos maitresses
Et puis nous leur dirons que demain nous partirons
Si nous partirons d'ici c'est pour aller rejoindre
Si nous partirons d'ici c'est pour aller voir Paris
De Paris à Lyon
De Lyon à Marseilles
De Marseilles à Toulon
Et puis nous reviendrons!

We must leave, but leaving makes us feel such pain
We must leave, but leaving makes us feel such pain
We must leave but leaving gives us great pleasure
But before we leave let us embrace our mistresses
But before we leave let us embrace our mistresses
And after we will tell them that tomorrow we must leave
If we leave here, we go in order to rejoin them
If we leave here, it is to go to see Paris
From Paris to Lyon
From Lyon to Marseilles
From Marseilles to Toulon
And then we will come back!

Now we take Kalia's way, as we call it, and when we reach the crest
where the road goes in to Calvignac (or Caubignac, cabbage-vine,
as it was originally called), we can see Mont Kaymard rising out of
the plain. It is an ancient volcano, long extinct, rounded at the top
and shaped over all, it seems, to resemble a huge mammoth's head.
It is still a few miles off to the southeast of us.

The road from here runs straight south across the slightly tilted
plain, so that we bike and coast swiftly down the long grade in the
sunlight through pastureland with cows, past a wheatfield, a stand
of birch trees off to the left, past the little village called La Rebey-
rolles to the right, and down into a shady grove of oak and beech,
where a gray dappled mare comes prancing gracefully over to the
fence to greet us and entice us to get off our bikes so we can be
thrilled by her beauty close up, and she can nuzzle us and then try
to horse-bite us.

Then on down we go, down and over the dam that turns the
source of the Ouche into a magic mirror pond with Lunel, a mile
away to the east across the meadows, perfectly reflected upside
down at its far edge.

From there we climb up the grade through more pasture land to
the crossroads, where the plateau falls off abruptly. You could go
straight ahead, south, winding down around the edge of the mountain into the valley to reach St. Cyprien; or you could go right,

west, along the crest toward Montignac; or go left, across the plain eastward to Lunel.

We are close to Mont Kaymard now, not more than a mile or two from its summit. We gaze at it, as Monsieur Denis said we would, at the smooth pastures of its slopes, which are marked off with blackberry hedges. The faint ringing of sheep bells gives the whole mountain an aural shimmer.

We get off our bikes and stand looking off into the south across ridge after ridge into the blue-gray distance in the sweet breathing peace of this vast afternoon; the receding ridges, as far as we can see, are wooded or are high rocky lea land, bare except for the chapel of Saint Jean le Froid perched, tiny and mysterious in its beauty, at the outermost point of a ridge ten miles or so to the south of us in the wash of afternoon light. Given the primordial hush it all appears to be as it must have been from the beginning, or at any rate for a thousand years, ever since the church of Saint Jean le Froid with its bluish tower, its perfect form, was built over some ancient holy stone.

Rodez is higher than any place roundabouts and there is a saying in the patois that goes "Roudás que roudorés / Per oná o Roudés / Toujóur montorés." (Go round, go round as you will / In order to go to Rodez / You always have to climb.) But we are so high that even Rodez, from here some twenty miles off, can be only dimly discerned, a glinting congregation of buildings clustering around the cathedral, all blurring into the mountain distance, which rises higher south of Rodez to the very rim of the Midi on the great Causse du Larzac beyond Millau and the Tarn.

We ride off down the road as if enchanted, the sheep bells ringing faintly all around Mont Kaymard, and we go to pay our obeisance to the dolmen.

The dolmen. La Pèira Levada. It stands at the edge of the road, and the farmer's fence jogs to go round it, just as Kalia drew it. The dolmen appears to be placed on a line between the peak of Mont Kaymard, the source of the Ouche, and the Pole Star.

We get off our bikes to touch it—an altarlike megalith of gray granite with flecks of quartz and mica and feldspar, covered over all

with lichens—bright green and bluish-green lichens stamped like
flowers here and there, and gray lichen like elephant skin, and black
patches of moss laid across lower rocks, rocks that have sunk with
time deeper into the ground, so that the dolmen tilts a bit.

The low chamber beneath the table roof is so filled with brambles and weeds that there is no question of slithering into it, or of going through it, as pilgrims once crawled through the bottom of the throne of Charlemagne at Aachen. There is no way for me to find out whether, if I could crawl in under the dolmen, I would feel telluric current flowing through my body and my mind.

The dolmen remains mute and humble, as if it were a natural object. Once we came on a special expedition to measure it and found that it is 15 feet 4 inches in length on both sides and 7 feet 8 inches in width at one end and 8 feet 5 inches in width at the other.

But still its ancient secret sleeps in the sunbaked, rain-washed granite, and touching it, with its mosses and its lichens, is a pleasant sensual experience. This dolmen has come to have a place of importance in my imagination and to stand as a cornerstone of speculation, a reminder of the vast system of stoneworks that was designed and put into place by a people who were here ten thousand years, at least, before the coming of the Celtic peoples into France.

There was a second dolmen, too, Jean-Claude Fau told me, not far from this one. The farmer who owned the field had it taken down and broken up.

Also there were standing stones, menhirs, that may once have stood in a ring but now stand as part of a wall near the source of the Ouche and, farther north, in the wall along the drive into the farm called Tras le Bosc (Behind the Woods).

It is said that the ancient Celtic peoples regarded these tomb places and stone monuments of the people who were here before them with a special reverence. Here, they believed, the living came into contact with the world of the dead, with the dwelling place of departed gods. They became places of pilgrimage and focal points of religious ritual and rites. (The dolmens were referred to by later writers as Druid altars.) Forces in the heavens converged here at these rocks, by their mysterious composition and formation, with forces within the earth.

We are left to wonder at their origins and to speculate on how they came to be placed exactly where they were (and in a number of cases still are) and why.

Why, for instance, was this slab of granite, which Jean-Claude Fau says does not occur naturally anywhere in the region, why was it brought here to this exact spot, and how was it transported? My green Michelin guide points out that it was considered a marvelous exploit when the Obelisk of Luxor, weighing only 220 tons, was put into place on the Place de la Concorde in Paris in 1836; these rock slabs weigh about 350 tons. Roads had to have been built to transport these stones, and the means of carrying them devised.

Some believe that roads were built along straight lines (the ley lines of England and Ireland), and that such lines both followed and directed a mysterious force like magnetic current, which flowed within the earth along these lines, working in conjunction with celestial influences, to significant points of convergence, where the great stone circles and underground chambers were built, and where we find to this day ancient stone circles or Christian churches or the ruins of churches and pagan temples once built atop potent sites.

These lines of telluric force are known in China as dragon currents, and there the art of divining them and building according to their influence, called *feng shui*, is practiced to this day.

Some surmise that the ancients understood how to use the energy of objects of great weight and could transport them over vast distances as if by magic. How it was done we cannot know, but that it was done there is no doubt. And that these stones were arranged at certain places in accordance with the most precise and intricate mathematical calculations, and in particular relation to celestial occurrences such as the rising of the sun on the winter solstice, is well understood and confirmed at sites in France, England, Ireland, Wales, Scotland, and elsewhere.

The presence of this dolmen here on this exact spot may have something to do with the peak of Mont Kaymard and the source of the Ouche and the Pole Star. In some way, together with the other stoneworks that were here on this high plain, it may have spoken once upon a time from a distance of the sacred valley with its heal-

ing springs hidden down below where the Ouche flows into the
Dourdou. But there is no way for me to understand how. (The
name Dourdou comes from an ancient pre-Celtic tongue and
means, it is thought, Red River, for there is another Dourdou in the
south of the Rouergue which, like ours, runs red when it rains.)

What did come to me one day as a revelation, after a lifetime, it
seemed, of looking out toward the north from every high point on
the plateau and finding always, to my wonder, there on that ridge
beyond the Lot to the north, the white church at Aubepeyre and the
beech tree beside it, was the fact that Aubepeyre means Dawn
Stone. There must then have been in that place a stone or
stonework of sufficient significance to give the place the name it
bears, perhaps because it caught the light of the rising sun on the
day of the winter solstice in a particular way.

Then I found on my map of the Institut Géographique National
that Aubepeyre is directly north on a line with the chapel at Saint
Jean le Froid. The peak of Mont Kaymard is a little distance off this
line and east of it, so the dolmens on the plateau below could have
been arranged facing slightly to the southeast and northwest to
form a triangle that would lead the walker back onto the straight
north-south path, leading toward Aubepeyre at a point on a ridge
where the Dawn Stone would have been visible as the church is
today. And from that Dawn Stone, as I imagine, the path would have
pointed north beyond the present-day Aurillac to the volcanic
peaks of Cantal, which point up to the Pole Star itself.

"All over France the Benedictine monasteries were built according to the lines of telluric force," says Petite Clémence, the copper-
smith. "There is a line of telluric force running right to the heart (*le
choeur,* the choir) of the Church of Sainte Foy."

Petite Clémence has a friend with an instrument that is able to
determine such things by means of vibrations. "A . . . how do you
say it in English—it is a *pendule*." The friend does not live here.
One time when she came, the force ran right into the choir of
Sainte Foy, and then another time, perhaps because of the flooding
under the church, or the scaffolding, the telluric current had
moved to the chapel of Saint Roch (where we find the oldest surviving stonework—the Merovingian—at Conques).

Petite Clémence shrugs. She cannot explain this. "The Romans were astounded when they came to find that the Celts knew how to tap the ground in one place and be heard miles away," she says. "The Celts knew how to use the lines of telluric force for signaling."

Petite Clémence speaks slowly in the excruciatingly halting but correct and interesting English she insists on, even though I beg her every once in a while to please talk to me in French. She does try my patience at times, but then I learn such interesting things from her, and interesting French words, too, when she doesn't know the English equivalent. "*Force tellurique,*" she said when she first spoke of these things. "How do you say it in English? *Force tellurique? Cosmo-tellurique?*" I could grasp the idea of what she was saying, but at the time I had not yet come across the notion of telluric currents in my reading, so I went to my dictionary and found that "telluric" comes, of course, from the Latin and means "of or pertaining to the earth, proceeding from the earth." "Amid these hot, telluric flames," wrote Carlyle. I love the accidental sound associations of the word with words like telegraph and telepathy, deriving from the Greek *tele,* meaning "far off." My dictionary knew nothing of Petite Clémence's cosmo-telluric currents, but I liked them. And though I had felt this emanation from the earth that she called *force tellurique* in several places, and very strongly once in the cathedral at Le Puy, I had understood it in a different way. At Le Puy I interpreted this ineffable resonance as being a manifestation of God the Creator's energy in His creation.

Petite Clémence is so called in Conques not just because of her tiny size but to distinguish her from Clémence Immense, the very large, massive-breasted Clémence, known also as La Femme de Petite Vertu, who works at the Maison de Repos.

Only Père André addresses Petite Clémence by her whole Christian name, Clémence-Isaure, evoking with his voice the august feminine aura of the name of our tiny, roughly dressed, copper-forging, jewel-making artist friend in her old blue jeans and boots and long-tailed men's shirts and thick knitted sweaters, evoking all the glorious Languedocian romance in the name of our patient, stubborn reader of Jung's *Psychology and Alchemy,* our secret Rosicrucian (I believe), who gets at times results of magical beauty at her anvil—mysterious golden bursts in her bracelets and crosses of copper repoussé.

Like Kalia, Petite Clémence came down here fleeing Paris, but her family comes originally from Quercy, from the upland country near Saint Cirq Lapopie, and her father is a distinguished member of the Academy of Nîmes, a passionate scholarly advocate of the Provençal language and of the Félibre Poets, and above all of Frédéric Mistral himself, about whom he has written an excellent biography. He baptized his first four children with the names of heroes and heroines in the poems of Mistral, but on Petite Clémence, his last child, he bestowed the name of the Lady of Toulouse, so goddess-like in her legend that some believe she never existed, but who nonetheless, in the dark years after the Albigensian Crusade and the takeover of the south of France by the north and the deaths or the silencing of the great troubadours and the official death of their language as a written language, became at Toulouse the founder of the Academy of Gai Savoir with its annual poetry contest, the Floral Games, dedicated to the continuing life of poetry in the langue d'oc, became Clémence-Isaure, the beautiful lady, the bountiful, the protector, the muse of the poets of her time and of generations who came after her, down even to the present day. Henry James, in his *Little Tour of France,* comments during his visit to Toulouse that the lady Clémence-Isaure, "is a somewhat mythical personage, not to be found in the *Biographie Universelle.* She is, however, a very graceful myth; and if she never existed, her statue does, at least—a shapeless effigy, transferred to the Capitol from the so-called tomb of Clémence in the old church of La Deurade."

As far as I know, in Conques, only Père André says, "*Bonjour,* Clémence-Isaure," with full awareness of the name she bears—our little friend who hides her fair face with her limp long brown hair and is far more interested in Antonin Artaud than in her own namesake.

Père Gilles, I have noticed, is fond of her as well, and he appreciates her wit, for he has a fine sense of humor himself. "Clémence," he calls out, beaming, when he sees her, if he has something to give her—something to eat, or something to burn in her stove, or something she may want to read or to see. And I have seen the Fraysou smile on her, his eyes sparkling with delight over her repartee.

To the gendarmes, however, she is just another of the suspicious *marginaux,* while to the other so-called *marginaux* she is "a very troubled girl," "neurotic in the extreme," "not comfortable in her skin." But the old villagers see that she has an unusual talent for the creation of copper jewelry, and they worry about her, about whether she gets enough to eat, and how does she live, and how does she keep warm in her rented house in winter with no heat except her little woodstove and no hot water (and no bath). Many of them give her vegetables and other foods to help her out.

"But you live like a young lord," said Clémence-Isaure's old landlady, of whom she is so fond. (She rents the house to her for almost nothing.) "You do not have to work except as you wish," she said to Petite Clémence. "You sleep when you please; you come and go as you wish. You live like a young lord. I wish I had had such a time of freedom in my life before I married."

"She cracks jokes in a voice like Donald Duck," Petite Clémence says. "She speaks French as if she were translating from the Occitan," says our young lord, our Orlando, who will be forty soon, she tells me, and who summer and winter goes putt-putting off on her mobilette to shop in St. Cyprien, to get wood on the plateau, or to visit her grandmother's house in Quercy.

Our Clémence-Isaure credits the early Benedictines with having possessed occult techniques for choosing the sites of their monasteries, their abbey churches. She speaks of the circular pattern of these sites on the map of France, and of the lines connecting them.

But I think it is more likely that the Benedictines chose or adopted these sites because they had been since time immemorial places of pilgrimage and were still frequented by the peoples of the country, who carried their ancient pagan heritage in their blood along with their Christian faith, and in part, too, because there really was and in many cases still is, something in these places that can be felt which makes them sacred. (One doesn't really need an instrument to measure it.)

The megaliths that the ancient people brought over distance often marked sites where this mysterious holy energy came forth from the earth, and the Celtic peoples had been attracted to these places with their waters and had built their round Druidic temples there (as they did at Conques); and when the Romans came, they

took over these ancient holy places frequented by the conquered
peoples, and they built altars and Roman temples to their Roman
gods; and the Christians, in their turn, despite what we read about
the violent and righteous destruction of the pagan gods and altars
in writers like Gregory of Tours, were often drawn to these places,
which came to be sanctified by holy dreams and visions or miracles.

Often these sites, which were ancient places of pilgrimage, were
chosen (in history or in legend) by holy hermits, as Conques was
chosen by Dadon and St. Gilles by Saint Gilles, Rocamadour by
Saint Amadour, St. Guilhem le Desert by Saint Guilliame, and the
place of the tomb of Saint James by the hermit Pellayo. At other
times, according to their legends, these sites for the building of
Christian churches were revealed in dream or vision (as were, frequently, the burial places of the saints, or as the place of the buried
cross of Christ Himself was revealed for Sainte Helena), or they
were pointed out by animals fulfilling mysterious mystical mis-
sions; and these miracles and visions both discovered these places
long venerated by the pagan peoples and sanctified them as Christian, even as the statue of Sainte Foy, so pagan to all appearances,
was sanctified, according to Bernard of Angers, by the miracles
God worked through her (it), as well as by the presence of the holy
relic of the saint's head.

The mystery, the technique, lay in the architecture, the miraculous art, which, though not received by occult means, was most
certainly inspired, the carrying of far older techniques, including
the use of mystical numbers and proportions—geometry—into
the creation of something new in the Romanesque. The choice of
stone (sometimes, as Abbot Suger relates in his book about the
building of Saint Denis, *De Consecrations*, revealed by miracle) and
the education and training of the stonecutters and the builders,
who worked with their hands according to the most precise measurements, all worked in a mysterious way to capture this holy energy of the Ancient of Days within the walls, the volume, of a
church shaped symbolically like the body of Christ with His arms
outstretched on the cross.

As we find all of these elements at Conques, so do we find them
more famously, either hidden or visible, in the history of Chartres
and in the layers and mysteries of its architecture, from Fulbert's

Romanesque crypt and the well beneath, to the light and the stone spaces of the great Gothic cathedral itself; but they are most nakedly visible and sensible in the cathedral at Le Puy and in its legend.

Our Lady of Le Puy is built atop a long-extinct volcano, Mont Anis, the ancient Anicium, which, with two other volcanoes, rises out of a plainlike bowl in the mountains of Velay (adjoining the Auvergne); and there on Mont Anis since time out of mind a dolmen of smooth gray phonolite (so-called because when struck, this rock rings) stood close by a holy well. Around the capstone of this dolmen there grew a legend as magical as a fairy story.

For in the third century after the birth of Christ, when to be a Christian was against the law of the Roman Empire, the Virgin Mary appeared to a woman sick with a malignant fever at a place called Villa near a stream called the Borne. The Blessed Mary told the woman as she lay there dying that if she would have herself carried to the ancient megalith on Mont Anis, and if she would lie down and stretch out on this stone, she would be healed.

It was the month of July and the woman of Villa was taken to Mont Anis, where she stretched out on the stone as the Virgin Mary had instructed her. In that very moment she was healed. When she rose up from the stone, called ever after the Stone of Fevers, the Blessed Virgin Mary appeared a second time, asking that a church be built and dedicated to her, there on Mont Anis; and with that, though it was July, snow began to fall on the mountain.

Not far from there the bishop, Saint George, who had been forewarned in a dream of the miracle to take place on Mont Anis, was coming on foot to bear witness to the holy event, and before him ran a deer.

When the two reached Mont Anis, shining with its cover of snow, the deer, bending down its head, traced with its antlers the outline of a vast church around the stone of the ancients.

Saint George had a hedge of dry thorns placed around the outline of the church miraculously drawn by the deer in the snow, and the following morning, when the snow had melted, the dry thorns had turned into a hedge of eglantine all abloom with fragrant white wild-rose flowers.

There was no way at that time, when Christianity was banned, to build a church of such vast dimensions, but the outline of the Church of Our Lady was preserved by the flowering eglantine, which enclosed the Stone of Fevers; and the holy well remained just outside the walls of this hardy thorny hedge known also in France as the wild rose, the dog rose, the rose of the hedges, and the rose of the Virgin, with its silky five-petaled flowers and its nurturing rose hips.

After a hundred, two hundred, years passed there in that far-off mountain country of Velay, the Virgin Mary appeared again in a vision, this time to a paralyzed woman in the village of Ceyssac. Mary told the paralyzed woman to have herself carried to Mont Anis and laid out on the dolmen there. This was done, and in that same moment the woman sat up, healed. As she was giving thanks, the Blessed Virgin Mary appeared to her once more and asked a second time that a church be built on this spot in thanksgiving and dedicated to her.

Now the bishop, Evodius, who resided then at Reussio (the present-day St. Paulien), decided that he should remove to Mont Anis and build a cathedral there. He went to Rome to ask the advice of the Holy Father in this delicate matter and to request his permission for the move. Bishop Evodius returned not only with the permission of the pope, but with the architect Scutaire, who was also a senator, whom the pope had recommended to help him realize the wishes of the Madonna.

Thus the first cathedral at Le Puy, then called Mont Anis, was built and completed about 497, and the miraculous Stone of Fevers was placed at the foot of the high altar. It was time for Bishop Evodius and the architect Scutaire "to take the road that leads from the banks of the Loire to the shores of Italy," and to proceed from there to Rome to obtain the relics necessary for the consecration of the church. They had reached the village of Corsac and they were not far from the river Loire when they met two old men clothed all in white carrying a casket filled with holy relics.

"There is no need for you to go any farther," the old men said.

"We have with us here all that you need. Go back to the church," they said, "bearing this burden. Take every precaution for its safety. We shall precede you and attend to everything," With that the two old men all clothed in white vanished as if by enchantment. And the bishop Evodius and the architect Scutaire, who would in time succeed him as bishop of Le Puy, retraced their steps, carrying their precious burden.

When they reached Mont Anis the doors of the cathedral were locked, but within there were lights and the sounds of angels singing, and the bells were ringing softly, and the air of the church when they entered was filled with a heavenly perfume. So it was that the cathedral dedicated to Our Lady at Le Puy was consecrated by angels, and its choir was ever after referred to as *la chambre des anges*.

In the chamber of the angels in the early years of pilgrimage to Our Lady of Le Puy it was not a statue of the Virgin that attracted the devotion of the pilgrims, it was the Stone of Fevers itself. In fact, the devotion centered on this smooth gray slab of phonolite placed before the high altar was so fervent that it was deemed excessive. The pilgrims, kneeling and praying, cried out, and the not infrequent healings with accompanying commotions of joy were continually interrupting the celebrations of the mass and the other religious offices.

It was decided that the Stone of Fevers had to be moved outside the church itself, and when the cathedral we know today was built in the eleventh century, the ancient dolmen cap, volcanic rock so different in its composition from the basalt, also volcanic, with which the cathedral is built and on which the cathedral stands, was placed where we find it today—in the great arched porch outside the doors, which one reaches after climbing the hill and the hundreds of stone steps that lead up to the Romanesque cathedral with its multicolored Mozarabic façade and its basaltic stone interior.

You can lie down on the Stone of Fevers if you wish, and Jack and I have each done so, taking turns, surreptitiously, on every visit to Le Puy. No one has yet come by when we were lying there, one looking out for the other, feeling the cold tingly rock beneath us. At first I attributed the feeling to our sense of daring, our sense that

we ought not to be doing this, and to the fact that it really was cold,
especially that May day when we first went to Le Puy and snow fell
so abundantly that it kept us there an extra day.

It was not until several years later, in 1982 when we would make
our third visit to Le Puy, as we were setting off to walk from there
to Conques along the old pilgrim route, that I felt the strength of
the mysterious force like magnetic or electric waves coming up
into the church from below.

We had climbed to the ancient chapel of St. Michel d'Aiguilhe at
the top of the neighboring pinnacle, where the stone altar still
bears its original dedication to Mars. We had stood on Mont Anis in
the cloister considered by Émile Mâle to be the most beautiful in all
of Christendom. We had been drinking in its perfect form and re-
garding the colors and the shapes repeated of its Mozarabic arches,
its slender columns. We had looked carefully at its capitals. (Petite
Clémence has a book I love to borrow by Christian Jacq about the
mystic progression of the symbolism of the capitals of the cloister.)
We had been in the court behind the chevet with the holy well and
the frieze of animals—a lion, a rabbit, a boar, a faun—of antique
Gallo-Roman carving. We had been in the Treasure to look again at
the Bible of Theodulf, at the illuminated purple vellum final page,
where he says, "Remember Theodulf."

"Remember Theodulf." His name rings on down through the
centuries, enchanting me. "Remember Theodulf."

Then, standing in the nave toward the back, we were saying our
farewell in that strange black basaltic church where, through centuries, pilgrims gathered to follow the Via Podiensis (the Way from
Le Puy) that leads to Sainte Foy de Conques and on to Saint Jacques
de Compostelle. Our packs were on our backs.

Mass was being quietly celebrated on a midweek morning near
the high altar, behind and above which the Virgin stood beneath her
baldachin, clothed in layers of white silk and tulle, all glowing with
light—the light of their two faces, mother and child, and of the colors of their crowns, the white light of her gown of glory—when,
the attention of my eyes and heart on her, I felt the chthonic current moving in waves up into the church from (it seemed) deep
within the extinct volcano on which the church was built.

Beneath us the stone remained as still and hard and solid and cold as it must have been for almost a thousand years; and yet in another sense the earth had opened to send this sensation of primordial power—like a voice with sound waves but no sound—up through the stone of the mountain and the flagstones of the church into the very air of the sacred space.

It was not, as we felt it, a pleasant thing to experience: it most certainly did not cause rapture. In fact, it was disturbing. Disorienting. Jack felt it, and Bill Barrette, our friend who had joined us for our pilgrimage, said, very abruptly and urgently (sounding not at all like himself), that we had to get out of there.

One might have decided it was nothing at all; but for me, like a revelation, it led to an understanding that has become central to my thinking. For I realized—gradually, I suppose, in the course of our pilgrimage walking toward Conques—that something was there, some force or power that could be felt and that could affect one whether one willed it so or no, and that this energy had been there at Le Puy since the beginning of the world and had come forth with flames and molten rock when Mont Anis was still a living volcano, and that the waves of this same ineffable presence came from the earth in varying ways at a thousand times ten thousand points around the earth, and that the places where this force was concentrated were the holy places of the earth, some with a long, continuous history as such, others left in the wilderness to speak to whoever might come, others built over and stifled.

As it was because of this power emanating from within the earth that millenniums ago the ancient peoples transported the huge slab of phonolite across miles of mountain country to be the cap of a dolmen on Mont Anis, so it was also because this stone, thus positioned, could receive and pass on a mysterious chthonian pulse to those who stretched out on it, blessed by vision or nurtured by prayer and faith, that the Virgin Mary, Mother of God, had chosen it as a place for miraculous healing, and as the place where a church should be built and dedicated to her; and that the bishop Evodius undertook to see that it was done when, at last, the time was right; and that when the work was done it was said that angels came to consecrate the cathedral: for this place was holy before all worlds.

When, some centuries later, the Stone of Fevers with its thau-maturgic powers was removed to without the portals of the church, the statue of Mary, the Mother of God, the Throne of Wis-dom, holding the Christ child, the Word made flesh, on her lap, came to replace the stone in this holy place, where the force was, metaphorically, like the power of the Incarnation itself in being at once spiritual, heaven-sent, and of the nature of God the Father as Creator, and at the same time physical, physically potent, as was and is God, the progenitor of the Word made Flesh, who is of one substance with the Father, who, nevertheless, needed His Mary even as He needed humankind in order that His Christ child be born. God could not be born except of His mother. And so it was that she, the handmaid of the Lord, was overshadowed by the Holy Ghost.

It is not known when the black image of Mary the Mother of God first came to be placed on or behind the high altar of the cathedral at Le Puy.

The earliest written reference to her statue is dated 1060. It could well have been carved in the Auvergne or Velay before the turn of the millennium, for in addition to Sainte Foy in Majesty, dating from the ninth century, we have recorded in 946 the making of the golden Virgin in Majesty of Clermont-Ferrand, and the men-tion, too, in Bernard of Angers's *Liber Miraculorum Sanctae Fidis,* of the golden majesty of Our Lady of Rodez participating in a synod at Rodez before 1013; but according to tradition and legend, Our Lady of Le Puy was brought back from the East, from Egypt, or from the Sudan, by a crusader, by a king, by Saint Louis. She was said to have been found, carved from ancient cedarwood, by the prophet Jeremiah.

(At Conques when I asked Monsieur Charlou how it felt to carry Sainte Foy on her fête day—he is one of the four to bear her in pro-cession—he replied adamantly, "That is not Sainte Foy. That is a statue brought here from Egypt a long time ago.")

Faujas de Saint-Fond, in the course of his research on the extinct volcanoes of the Auvergne and Velay in the eighteenth century, made the only detailed study of the miraculous statue of Our Lady of Le Puy. He thought that it had been an ancient statue of Isis and Horus, brought back from Egypt by Saint Louis and converted by a jeweled crown and the crosses on the gown of the child into Mary holding Christ.

Faujas de Saint-Fond said in his *Recherches sur les volcans éteints du Vivarais et du Velay* (Paris and Grenoble, 1778) that when he first saw the statue in the cathedral, it was covered with a cloak of golden cloth that enveloped it from neck to toes and gave it a conical shape. The child Jesus, who appeared from a distance to be glued to the stomach of His mother, showed His little black head through an opening in the cloak.

Then, having obtained permission to study the statue without its vestments, he found that the seated figure of Mary was two feet three inches in height; he remarked on the stiff and rigid carving, and described Mary's very long, oval face, which was black, her long nose, and the wild, astonished look in her enamel eyes. He noted the painting on the linen that was wrapped and glued tightly round the statue as if it were a mummy, and that formed the gown of Mary, while the tunic of the Christ child was painted with Greek crosses. Mary's hands protected Christ; one of her hands was on His knee; His little hands were in His lap, and His feet were bare.

Faujas de Saint-Fond's work for his engraving of the statue was done in October and November 1777, less than twenty years before the cathedral at Le Puy was invaded by the troops of the Revolution and turned into a Temple of Reason, and Mary, relieved of her crown and her jewels, was taken to the Hôtel de Ville, where her nose was cut off by the saber of a soldier (and thus was found, by a naturalist who was present, to have been made of cedarwood); then, like the queen of France, she was thrown into a manure cart and carted off to the public square to be burned.

As the flames consumed her, a compartment in her back (hidden from Faujas de Saint-Fond), which contained a parchment scroll— the heart of her origin and mystery—was revealed; and then the scroll was quickly turned into flames while the statue slowly burned.

It was to her that the mother of Joan of Arc, Isabelle Romée, had come, walking several hundred miles in her distress, to pray for her

daughter's safety after Joan left home with the soldiers to have the
dauphin crowned king and drive the God-damns (the English) out of France.

Many years after Isabelle Romée knelt here before this statue of Mary in Majesty, entreating her to protect her daughter, Joan, it had become the custom to clothe the statue in a cloak like that described by Faujas de Saint-Fond. Some credit the origin of this custom to Louis XI, who came on pilgrimage bearing gifts for Notre Dame du Puy in 1476, but it could well have been more than a hundred years later that Mary and Jesus began to be cloaked so that they took on a bell-like shape, with only their two black heads, crowned and mysterious, sticking out of their robe, the mother's directly above the child's. The Virgin Mary appeared therefore to be very short and wide because although she was seated, she seemed to be standing. And for this reason the statue came to create an iconography that manifested, Faujas de Saint-Fond thought, a most barbarous taste.

Yet so they are portrayed being carried in procession to thank the Virgin for averting the plague in 1630; and so they are painted in votive offerings from the seventeenth century on; and so they were copied on medals and sculptures; and so it was that a black Virgin and Child carved in wood and painted to resemble them, cone-shaped like an ancient fertility symbol, in brocaded vestments, woof of silk and warp of gold, was made in the seventeenth century for the chapel of Saint Maurice-du-Refuge. It was this statue which, some fifty years after the ancient miraculous Virgin was consumed by flames, was brought to replace her beneath a baldachin above the high altar of the Cathedral at Le Puy.

These places, where His energy wells up and flows down in such a way as to make them sacred places of the earth and of the spirit, have been in the course of human life on earth marked by stones; have been sacred caves, which were painted; have been reverenced or feared, used for ritual and magic, for healing and worship, for sacrifice, for prophecy; have been thought to be places where spirits were or are, or gods, or the dead, or departed ancestors; have been places where mounds were built; have been considered ground too holy for the hunt; have been called right up to the minute, as Petite Clémence would say, "*Haut lieux,* how do you say it in English? *Haut lieux,* high places *cosmo-telluriques.* Saint Jacques, Le Puy, Conques, and many places that are not even Christian— Stonehenge, Stonehenge is such a place *cosmo-tellurique,*" she says.

And she goes on. "When it is measured with the—how do you say it—with the *pendule,* the *force tellurique* here at Conques in the church is the same as at Chartres. The vibrations are of the same quality . . . and the same strength, almost the same strength."

These thoughts were beginning to form in my mind as a kind of ruminating undercurrent of our pilgrimage through eight days of walking from Le Puy to Conques, following the old Via Podiensis along the trail now called Grande Randonnée 65, the way marked by squares of red and white stripes, on trees, rocks, fenceposts, stone walls. On the surface we were our bodies walking, proceeding slowly, our three selves, experiencing as we walked, the earth, the air, the hardship of it, too.

Jack and Bill and I walked through flowers. Serpolet (wild thyme), blue bells, grasses, wild carnations glowed in the rain. Dark volcanic rock as we climbed out of Le Puy. After the stone village of La Roche we followed along the gorge of the Gazelle through fields filled with small boulders all covered with lichens. The way became rough. We stepped from boulder to boulder, our path fenced in between the fields. "Look! All the rocks have been thrown in here," Jack said. We walked between high walls of gray stones while the rain fell. Jack and Bill ahead of me with their ponchos over their packs looked like camels. Bill with his blue poncho and blue umbrella held over his head looked like a nineteenth-century figure, like a tall Ruskin or Byron in the Alps, as he moved along slowly with his camera equipment and his great hump of a sack. The cows regarded us as a curious species of fellow animal— to be stared at, approached, and, certainly, not feared.

The pain of the pack. We had not counted on that. The weight of the pack was pulling on my neck, my shoulders. Yet even with the pain, which became at times excruciating, I was filled with joy—at the flowers, the light in the flowers, the blue of the harebells, the pink of the sweet william.

At a certain point the earth changed and we were on a road of red earth—so bright it was blinding, Bill said.

After the rock pile where Saint Roux was martyred, the path became impassable, deep in water; we nearly slipped and fell on the wet stones, forgetting the momentum caused by a pack on one's back. Eventually we climbed through barbed wire to traverse the field beside the Chemin de Saint Jacques. (It should be noted that the G. R. 65 does not at every point precisely adhere to the old Chemin de Saint Jacques because the old Chemin used the ancient Roman roads when convenient, and now those ancient roads are often routes or highways with too much traffic to be pleasant for a walker.)

When, at last, we reached a little paved road, we consulted the map and took the shortest way into Bains. It was already five o'clock and we had another seven miles, it looked, to go. We drank a coffee in the café there. Ask if there is a bus, Jack said. And it was settled. The bus to St. Privat would stop here at five forty-five.

I visited the church—twelfth century, bare, and plain, dedicated to Sainte Foy then and still. The portal a Romanesque archivolt of twelve arcs; and in the outermost, the twelfth rim, was a frieze of still figures, tiny, all looking out, facing us—a man, perhaps Adam; a fish; an animal with a tail and very large eyes, smiling; a lion; a snake; a horse's head; Sainte Foy; a lion; Sainte Foy again at the top (I think) or maybe Saint James; and so on down the other side, a lion; Sainte Foy; an owl; a pilgrim; and Eve, perhaps, holding a snake.

The bus ride was a joy. At St. Privat en Allier we were delivered almost right into the Vielle Auberge, where high up, by narrow stairs, Jack and I had a room with white eyelet curtains at a window looking out over the deep gorge and the torrent rushing down to the Allier, and a round table with a white eyelet tablecloth and a nice bed with a white eyelet spread and besides that a hot bath to soak in.

And then came dinner. The wild hilarity of our relief at having gotten there, the red wine, a Haut-Médoc, and the superb food, the caille aux raisins the best quail I ever tasted.

In the morning at St. Privat we bought some boxes at the post office and mailed our boots and most of our books and whatever clothes we could slough off to Conques ahead of us, and from then on we walked the way Carol, our neighbor on Barrow Street who goes trekking in the Himalayas, said we should in the first place, in our Adidas country jogging shoes. (My big toenail turned red, then black and eventually fell off on account of that first day of walking from Le Puy with my pack too heavy and my boots a size too small.)

We bought picnic things, too—a loaf of bread, some slices of ham, tomatoes, cheese, oranges and grapes, a bottle of water; and then off we went, down a little road past fields of sheep—nearly a third of them black sheep—to reach the village of Rochegude with its heavy bare stone houses. Not more than nine houses, some of them in ruin, all built with stone and white mortar. No one around. We saw the sky through the wall belfry of the chapel of Saint Roch out at the edge of the rock promontory, and higher up to the right, over the village, the ruin of a castle tower. Down here a monument to members of the Résistance killed in combat.

Leur Sacrifice
Notre Liberté

Movements Unis de la Résistance

Morts au combat

Roche Auguste
Tourdiat Jean

Victim Civile

Bernard Marcel

It was not always so peaceful here, I thought as we stood on high rocks looking down over meadows into the valley of the Allier far below, shimmering green beneath layers of sunlit atmosphere.

The chapel of basalt looked very old, pre-Romanesque with its bare cylinder of an apse and its small nave. Its only windows were high up and as narrow as the slits for shooting arrows in early medieval town walls. The door was locked. We couldn't go in. Like so many other chapels built and dedicated to Saint Jacques along the Chemin de Saint Jacques, this one was, in the fifteenth century, given over to Saint Roch.

If we could have entered we would have found a statue of the saint above the altar—Saint Roch with his leg bare, his bleeding plague sore exposed on the inside of his left thigh, and at his feet the faithful dog holding a loaf of bread in his mouth; Saint Roch is dressed, partly in deference to Saint Jacques, whom he has supplanted, in the hat with the scallop shells of the pilgrim to Saint James, in the cape, with the staff, the scrip.

I regaled Jack and Bill with these iconographic arcana, and I tried to tell them the story of Saint Roch, whose pilgrimage toward Rome as a very young man became something other—a ministry of healing in the service of the Lord. I followed as closely as I could remember the story as I got it from Mrs. Jameson in her *Sacred and Legendary Art* (London, 1848), for she has the loveliest and most sweetly illuminating way of telling the stories of the saints, her words somehow becoming like the stuff of haloes.

Saint Roch was born in Montpellier to noble parents, most probably in 1295. His mother had prayed to God for a long time, asking that she might bear a child, and Roch came into the world with a small red cross marked on his breast. Because of the sign he bore and because of her prayers, his mother, Libera, considered him consecrated to a religious life, and she watched over his education with care. The boy Roch grew up acting as one called to the service of God. His parents died before he was twenty, and following the counsel the Savior gave to the young man who asked, "How shall I be saved?" Saint Roch sold all his property that the law allowed him to sell and gave the money to the poor and to the hospitals in Montpellier. He left the administration of his estates to his father's brother, and putting on the dress of a pilgrim, he journeyed on foot toward Rome.

When he arrived at Aquapendente the plague was raging, and the sick and dying encumbered the streets. Saint Roch went to the hospital and offered to assist in tending to the sick. Such was the efficacy of his treatment and his tender sympathy that it was said a blessing more than human waited on his ministry. Some were healed merely by his prayers or by the sign of the cross he made as he stood over them, and when the plague ceased shortly afterward, they in their gratitude imputed it solely to the intercession of this benign being who, with his youth, his gentleness, and his fearless devotion, appeared to them to be little less than an angel.

Hearing that the plague was desolating the province of Romagna, Saint Roch hastened there and in the cities of Cesena and Rimini he devoted himself to the service of the sick. Then he went to Rome, where a fearful pestilence had broken out, and he spent three years in Rome, devoting himself always to those who were most miserable and those who were abandoned by all other help.

In this way some years passed as the young Roch traveled from city to city, wherever he heard there was disease and misery; he healed the sick and alleviated the suffering. Finally in the city of Piacenza it pleased God that His servant Roch should himself be struck with the plague.

One night in the hospital there he sank to the ground overpowered by fatigue and want of sleep. On waking he found himself plague-stricken. A fever burned in every limb and a horrible ulcer had broken out on his left thigh. The pain was so insupportable that he shrieked aloud, and fearing that he would disturb the inmates of the hospital, he went almost crawling into the street. But here the officers of the city would not allow him to remain lest he spread infection around.

So, supported only by his pilgrim's staff, he left the city and went into a woods beyond the gates of Piacenza. There he lay down in a secluded place to die. But an angel came to him, the legend says, and a spring began to flow nearby. The little dog who had faithfully attended him through the years of his pilgrimage disappeared as he slept and returned with a loaf of bread for Roch. So it happened every day that Roch would wake to drink the spring water and eat of the bread his little dog brought him, until at last he was well enough to set out for home once more.

The journey was long and when he arrived at the village near Montpellier which was, in fact, his own village, he was so changed by long suffering, so wasted and raggedy, that nobody knew him. The whole country at that time was full of suspicion and danger because of hostilities and insurrections, and Roch was arrested as a spy.

He was brought before the governor and judge at Montpellier, who was his own uncle. But not knowing Roch, his uncle offered to throw him into prison. Roch said nothing, believing it was God's plan that he be tested further; and so he languished in a dungeon, with nothing to sustain him other than a little water and a pittance of bread. At length, near death, he asked that a priest come to administer the last rites, and when the jailer came the next day the dungeon blazed with light. By the side of the dead prisoner was writing that revealed his name and history and contained, moreover, these words: "All those who are stricken by the plague and who pray for aid through the intercession of Roch, the servant of God, shall be healed."

When this writing was carried to his uncle, the governor, he was seized with grief and remorse and wept; he caused his nephew, who bore on his breast the little red cross that was his mark at birth, to be buried honorably, accompanied by the tears and the prayers of the whole city.

Saint Roch died, it is said, at the age of thirty-two in 1327. For nearly a century after his death the devotion to him in his own country, where he was most beloved, and in neighboring regions as well, was fervent. By his intercession the plague was miraculously averted and diseases healed, but he was not known in other places.

Then in 1414 a council of the church was held at Constance (the same council that condemned John Huss) and plague broke out in the city. The council was on the point of dispersing, the prelates in their fear having decided they must flee, when a young German monk who had traveled in the south of France reminded them that there was a saint of that country through whose merits many had been redeemed from the plague. The council had an effigy made of Saint Roch, and they carried it through the city in procession. With that the plague ceased.

It was with this miracle that the fame of Saint Roch began and devotion to him expanded all over Christendom.

"At Venice, you know," I told Jack and Bill, "they hatched a plot in 1485, and a kind of holy alliance was formed to commit a pious robbery. The conspirators sailed to Montpellier disguised as pilgrims, and they carried off the body of Saint Roch and returned with it to Venice, where they were received by the doge, the senate, the clergy, and all the people with inexpressible joy. And so we have the magnificent church of San Rocco in Venice, built to receive the precious relics of the saint. It is a pious theft, a *furtum Sacrum,* like the theft of Sainte Foy's bones, taking place in almost modern times."

As we stood on the rocks at Rochegude above the chapel and below the tower in that lovely late-August midday light, we felt as if we could fly easily over the valley and down. But when we actually started down, the path was so steep and gravelly that we kept slipping nervously. I think I cried out in panic a couple of times; and Jack swore at the path angrily at least once, perhaps more often.

We crossed the river at Monistrol d'Allier, and then partway up the road beyond, seeing that we were not going to come to any cafés, we turned back to the hotel we could see on the other side of the river and had our coffee there on the terrace. Then we set off once more to cross the river and start the climb upward, along the road at first and then off through the woods, past a strange grotto-chapel dedicated to Mary Magdalene and barred, so we could only look in at its lumpy living-rock ceiling, its altar, its saints, and the bare benches for those who would come to worship there. On we went, climbing upward along steep paths. We were not in the best of spirits.

At a certain point, late, and already having climbed a long time and with a long way yet to go, we quarreled, I recall, about whether to take the path, G.R. 65, or the road, but Jack and Bill won and we took the road. I was bitter for a while but forgot it in my joy when at last we reached the crest.

Later, as we walked toward Saugues, evening was coming on the high green hilly plain. The dark fir woods on the hilltops. We were in the Margeride. Sheep were rushing, the beautiful large black sheep of this country, their bells were ringing, green fields, waters rushing, clear streams in the late sunlight rushing, shining, over stones, the animals hurrying, hurrying home; and, at last, over a rise, we descended to Saugues.

The Margeride. Forever after (as long as I live) it will ring in my mind, the Margeride, green and wide and filled with light (like heaven), the Margeride, where at Saugues we saw our first Romanesque Virgin, our first Throne of Wisdom statue.

I wrote in my notebook a translation of what was said about her on a plaque in the church there where you could look at her through protective glass—Notre Dame de Saugues.

> The Virgin is the *Sedes Sapientiae,* the Throne most worthy to hold the Eternal Wisdom, the Son of God.

> No other Romanesque Virgin has the noble elegance of Notre Dame de Saugues.

There was the rapture of this discovery, of her face, her eyes, the look in her eyes compelling one to awe before the central mystery of life as she sits with stiff dignity on her throne holding Him, the Christ child, in her lap, protecting Him with her long-fingered hands, knowing . . .

She is, I would later learn (from Ilene Forsyth's *The Throne of Wisdom*), one of a small group of twelfth-century Majesties of wood and polychrome in which Mary wears ecclesiastical vestments—a chausable and the archiepiscopal pallium. "A dark coat of varnish applied prior to 1904 as a conservation measure was removed shortly after 1960, revealing early polychromy and enhancing the aristocratic elegance of this beautiful work," writes Forsyth.

Our Lady of Saugues carried our pilgrimage upward to the beginning of a new quest, new knowledge. And the next day at Chanaleilles we found another Romanesque Virgin in the early medieval church there—a black Virgin in Majesty with the Christ child, all alone with a little light like a candle burning beside her. We were alone in the church with her. We could have touched her, who is so greatly venerated as a protectress of children at baptism. The wood of her statue was somewhat corroded, but her influence permeated the atmosphere of the whole church and I left very moved.

As we walked on I thought of the Virgin at Le Puy, who was burned to ashes during the Revolution—that though she came from an earlier period by a hundred years, at least, and perhaps from the East where the Holy Land lies, or from Egypt, she must have had the same power to move whosoever beheld her to this awe at once mystical and aesthetic and compassionately human.

We walked on an hour or two beyond Chanaleilles through the wide Margeride, green, sun-bright, and then upward, the land changing, toward Saint Roch—a chapel, not a village, though it is marked on the map, a chapel and spring some hundred yards below it with a rectangular granite basin to catch the waters, and a baroque sort of monument rising above it with a stone cross at the top and an image of Saint Roch standing tall in the niche, holding his pilgrim's staff and showing his plague sore, while his little dog, ears raised, looks out.

LITTLE

Saint Roch himself, it is said, stopped here. He had gone on pilgrimage to Notre Dame de Puy, they say, on his way home from Italy to Montpellier; and here, a century before his time, in 1198, in this deserted place called long ago Dead Man's Pass, the Hospitalet had been built (by Helye de Chanaleilles and Hugues de Thoras) as a refuge for voyagers and pilgrims, and dedicated with its chapel and its spring to Saint James. In later times it was dedicated to Saint James and Saint Roch; still later, after the religious wars, when the Hospitalet fell into ruin and disappeared, the pilgrimages to Saint Roch in this place surged, and successive chapels, which were struck by lightning or destroyed by wind, were always, in time, rebuilt, so that to this day, the day we arrived to find a festival here, there have been great pilgrimages to Saint Roch on the two Sundays following his feast day, August 16.

Here the young Roch, wasted from his suffering and illness, drank from the spring and refreshed himself, and now the chapel was filled with a thousand candles banked upward in rows all around, a thousand candle flames, a thousand prayers of heat and light that filled my throat to a tightness of tears, seeing people waiting to put their limbs in the spring below the chapel. They had taken off their shoes and wooden legs and were waiting bare-legged or bare-armed to bathe their withered and mutilated limbs, their open ulcer sores, in the spring water. *Priez pour nous, Saint Roch.*

Across the road from the chapel the festival was in full swing. Striped blue-and-white and orange-and-white tents had been set up. Games were being played. Sausages were smoking on grills. Under the awning of one tent, among hundreds of religious wares, we were drawn to the photograph of a face in a gold frame, the face of another Romanesque Virgin, we thought, because of her extraordinary beauty, her large, noble polychrome face, and her eyes with that look of tranced contemplative majesty that filled the eyes

of Notre Dame de Saugues. We had to beg the sun-weathered ven-
dor to tell us who she was. He didn't want to say, but finally he told
us she was Notre Dame d'Orcival.

The very next day, walking on from St. Alban toward Conques,
we found a tiny black Virgin, gray-black faces of Mother and Child,
dressed as they were at Le Puy, not more than nine inches high, in
a niche behind the chickenwire over the fountain of the village
lavoir at Chabannes-Planes. After we got back to Conques we went,
by car, to find Notre Dame d'Orcival in her church among the volcanic peaks of the Auvergne.

Beyond Saint Roch our path led us downward through a pine
wood. The odors of pine, the smoky light, the sun like quicksilver
in the pine needles.

Between Le Rouget and St. Alban a bank of bluebells beneath a
rock. Seeds like stars caught in the broom. "It looks like the Milky
Way," Jack said.

Our room at the Hôtel du Centre in St. Alban sur Limagnole was
clean, almost shining white. Four windows looking out on the
clocher-mur (wall belfry) of the church. Jack and I watched the bells
in full ringing at six-thirty. Later, toward eight o'clock, the orange
light of sunset came in through the half-closed shutters. . . . and
we went down to another of our wonderful high-spirited dinners
with Bill.

I don't remember what we ate that night. The next dinner we
will never forget was that at the Hôtel Moderne in Aubrac. Was
there ever *aligot* (cheese and potatoes) as good as that? Not to mention the trout! And the lamb, the *gigot*! But that dinner with the fire
burning in the dining-room fireplace and the Puisséguin-St.-
Emilion 1978 and the silver dishes with the scallop-shell handles
Bill liked so much came at the end of a day in which we almost, like
the pilgrims of history and legend, lost our way into the night trying to reach Aubrac.

We had come from Aumont Aubrac and had left Nasbinals to
walk to Aubrac by the Grande Randonnée 65. The day became
overcast, and several hours after we left Nasbinals we could no
longer find the red-and-white marks of our G.R. 65. The sky was so
thickly overcast we didn't even know where the sun was, and we
hadn't brought a compass, grave omission. We made forays this way

and that, consulting our walking guide, trying to figure out which way to go, and the clouds swirled down and around us and became mist, and we started climbing without really knowing anymore in which direction we were going. At one point it was hailing, at another, strangely, the sun came out for a few minutes, and we realized we were going the wrong way. The only note I made that day is spotted with raindrops. I wrote, "We are in very high country where the grass is cropped short by cows; wild pansies grow here. No trees except the beeches clustered, short and twisted, down in the hollows. Gray rock walls going over the hills, close up dappled

with lichen." I remember that late, toward seven, and very high up, we came upon the top of a ski lift. Jack thought it was an interesting sign of my upbringing as contrasted with his and Bill's that they had stood there trying to figure out what on earth the contraption was, and then I finally showed up and said casually, according to him, "Oh! Look! The top of a ski lift!" We realized that if we followed it, at the bottom we would surely come to something, a road at least. But it seemed too steep and the wrong way; besides, the

Hannah, walking near Le Puy de dome, along the pilgrims' route

cloud we were in had blown away with rain and wind, and exploring our summit, we spotted a truck way down below, and people loading a horse into the truck. When we saw them we began calling out and going toward them as fast as we could, while they, in turn, loaded the horse as fast as they could and drove off through the gates, which they closed behind them, leaving us with the firm conviction that they were stealing the horse, but also the realization that if we followed the way they were going, we would surely come to a road. Bill photographed us with the wind blowing our ponchos into wild shapes near a cross at the top of the mountain, and again, lower down, as we pursued the vanishing truck and the car behind it while members of the huge and beautiful race of Aubrac cattle were advancing on us and getting too close for comfort. Jack remembers the wind whipping the strap from his pack against his cheek so hard it really hurt. (The cross was, we decided later, consulting our map, the Croix des Trois Evêques, for it stands on a peak where the ancient borders of Rouergue, Lozère, and the Auvergne come together; the mountain was the Puy de Gudette, 1,427 meters, or 4,846 feet.) But at last we reached the road and walked a ways in the wrong direction, until we came to a milestone that indicated Aubrac was the other way, five kilometers. And so we arrived marvelously ready to appreciate the story of the bells that used to ring in storms to guide pilgrims through the clouds to the shelter of the hospital-monastery at Aubrac, founded in 1120 by the noble pilgrim Adalard (the romantic Adalard); and, also, by then we well understood the words from the Bible (Deuteronomy 32:10) that were engraved over the western door of the monastery: IN LOCO HORRORIS ET VASTAE SOLITUDINIS (in a place of horror and of vast wilderness).

"Rough white country sheets," I wrote in my notebook. "How wonderful they feel in a bed thick with blankets."

I skip to the last day but one. We had come down into the valley of the Lot from Aubrac, altitude 1,350 meters or 4,429 feet. (When the people of Conques mention Aubrac they always say, "Up there," lifting their chins to indicate that direction, their voices, too, somehow implying the high place of their imaginations.) We had walked from Espalion to Estaing by way of St. Pierre de Bessuéjouls, with the beautiful early Romanesque chapel and altar dedicated to Saint Michael in its tower. Then after spending the night in Estaing, we set off, crossing the Lot once again on the Gothic arched thirteenth-century bridge. We climbed upward and then north somewhat above the river past Castaillac, where the cruel priest Gerald, who gouged out Guibert's eyes, had lived. We saw Castaillac below us and went down to see what it felt like there. Unfriendly. "The sins of the fathers," I said.

We went back to our Grande Route 65, as we called it, and on to Golignac. The stone cross at Golignac with a tiny pilgrim Saint Jacques and scallop shells and the Virgin and Child on one side; Christ crucified on the other. Climbing upward once more toward Espeyrac, we were, toward late afternoon, back in our country, a country of soft earth and the smell of cows, and then heather, light-filled heather. The heather glows, Bill said. And it is true: When it is cloudy, the heather does glow. The broom, rough broom brushing across the skin of my legs. I love it. Beech trees dappled with lichen. The handsome black sheep running ahead of his flock to greet us before we reached Les Albousquies where, I decided, Martha, the mother of the priest Gerald, lived when she took Guibert in and nursed him back to health to make amends to the Lord for her son's vile deed.

We went down then toward Espeyrac, where we spent the night in the Hôtel de la Poste, which is right next to the gray stone church where Guibert, the blinded jongleur, coming out from the celebration of the mass, and standing there before the church doors with his staff, received—as Sainte Foy had promised when she appeared in his sleep—the ten deniers he would need to buy the candle she asked him to light at Conques on the vigil of her fête so that he might be healed by the Lord through her intercession.

Nowadays the village schoolchildren have their lunch in the Hôtel de la Poste, and we come driving over in the evening five or six times in the course of the summer and the fall to dine there. It feels like another world, remote from Conques, when we park the car, walk past the church door where Guibert had stood, and eat a very good dinner—perhaps *omelette aux cèpes* (mushrooms) to start with, and sometimes wild boar Bourgignon or a stewed *lièvre* (hare), and always the salad I crave and cheeses and fruits, all for twenty-five francs, for less than five dollars each, while the village schoolteacher, the *instituteur,* reads his paper, *Humanité*, and his blond daughters do their homework in a corner and their pretty mother runs back and forth with the dishes while her mother cooks out of sight in the kitchen and comes out later to embrace us.

When Jack and Bill and I emerged from the trail we were on the road just below Espeyrac, so we saw it walled and gray and medieval-looking above the smooth green meadows. We were right at the pilgrim's cross with Christ crucified blending into the stone, lichen-mottled, all one, Christ and His cross. The *instituteur* drove by in his car and stopped and got out to greet us. The cross is eight hundred years old, he told us. His daughters came along on foot. They'd been up in the meadows picking flowers, and they stopped to kiss us each three times in the Rouergue way, lovely, graceful girls they are, growing taller, the older of the two must be thirteen by now, I thought, as we admired their flowers and melted, Jack and I, so happy to be greeted this way. Proud, too: We were showing off for Bill, after a week of being strangers along the way where as a species pilgrim walkers were not, we concluded, very popular with the people who lived beside the *chemin,* particularly not with their dogs.

In the morning as we left Espeyrac, cows' breaths were steaming, bells were ringing, dew was shining in the meadow. Past Taulanet (Rosalie's home village) we climbed through a fir wood. An enormous rock like a standing stone at the hilltop against the sky. The château of Sénergues across the green hills. The fragrance of things. The rustle of wind in the cornstalks. The blackberries were ripe. Chestnuts were swelling green on the trees. It was the second of September. Trees apple-laden. The put-put of tractors. Ground was being plowed for planting the winter wheat. Blue cornflowers. Watery lichens. The lower bark of trees like elephant's skin, encrusted with lichens. A lovely stand of birches. Birds twittering. "There were no birches here when I was a boy," Monsieur Charlou said once. "The birds have brought them."

"Beautiful mud—like amber," said Bill. "Look at the shadows. You could make pottery out of this."

We could see the white church at Aubespeyre, and then we were back on our road, walking swiftly, past the Croix de Loubatières, past Font Romieu, and up and down and up to enter St. Marcel, going past Michel's enormous hill of a manure pile and his barn and then the cemetery and the church where two carved stone Merovingian sarcophagi, discovered beneath the flagstones during recent repairs, stand upright now outside the church doors; and on we go past the dogs of St. Marcel, who lifted their heads from the warm blacktop road to look at us, then laid them back again. Chickens scurried across the road in front of us, and we walked on along the crest of our plateau to where the path goes off, down through rocks and heather, into the lovely shade of old oak trees, and down through vineyards until, just before noon, there it was close below us—Conques, Sainte Foy de Conques, solemn, majestic, sweet, and joyous in the great sorrowing stone harmonies of its beauty. As God said to Moses: "Let them make me a sanctuary that I may dwell among them."

The Angelus began to ring out over the valley.

And later, in the darkness of the Treasure, there was Sainte Foy gleaming with her light. "If you look into the crystal balls on her throne, with all the reflections, it is like seeing into infinity," Bill said.

Detail,
Sainte Foy
in the
Treasure

Standing here with our bicycles on this high plain beside our mute old dolmen, Jack and I, touching its warm rough surface, listening to the sweet ringing from the pastures on Mont Kaymard, breathing in the June afternoon, I muse on the difference between this old rock and the Stone of Fevers at Le Puy. For the Stone of Fevers was so placed that it was itself the focal point, the object of pilgrimage, the thaumaturgic vehicle moved by the life energy coming from the innermost depths of the earth; whereas our old dolmen, by contrast, must always have been a way station, even for those who died and were buried here; they were buried on the road by this stone which, together with one other pointed the walker back to the north-south line between Saint Jean le Froid and Aubespeyre, down into the protection of the sanctuary on the warm sunny slope where medicinal waters sprang from the cool subterranean clay and schist rock.

Nor am I the only one to think this dolmen is connected to Conques. There is a legend carried down through the years and told, still, by the old people roundabout Lunel. La Pèira Levada, they say, is a block of stone that the Virgin Mary let fall by the wayside when she was helping to build the church for Sainte Foy at Conques, carrying huge blocks of stone from the quarry at Salès along that way to go down to Conques.

I see her, beautiful and immense, carrying the blocks of stone, so many in her arms at once she hardly noticed the odd one that dropped as she went past, floating as if she were flying, along the Strata Conquesa, as this way was called in the Middle Ages, going from the quarry at Salès past Lunel and past, in fact, La Pèira Levada, which had been there all along. It had been there for millenniums when the cart, heavily charged with blocks of the limestone carefully cut at the quarry, and drawn by the twenty-six pairs of oxen, went by the dolmen on the Strata Conquesa day after day, year in, year out, until at last the church of Sainte Foy was completed.

The story in the *Book of Miracles* is not the stuff of legend; it is
gritty with stone and with the weight of stone and with the agony
of effort of hard and dangerous work; it's got the feel of the earth
and the breath of animals and the cries of human beings trying, caring. You almost hear that heavy wagon rolling along the Strata Conquesa and then starting down toward Conques, descending the
slope through that copse, recently cut, where the accident occurred.

The account of what happened was written down by the anonymous monk (with his Hellenisms) who added to the *Liber Miraculorum Sanctae Fidis* stories of miracles that had occurred since Bernard
of Angers's time and should not, he felt, be lost to posterity. He
wrote down this particular story late in the eleventh century, soon
after the church we know today had been built.

He got the account of what happened from his confrère, the
monk Saluste, "a man held in the highest esteem because of the in-
tegrity of his character and the holiness of his life." Saluste had seen
what happened with his own eyes, and he was still alive when our
author wrote down what he had told him:

> The wagon, heavily loaded as it was, came down the moun-
> tain, and started to pass through a copse of wood, recently cut
> but still covered with sharp trunks, when one of these tree
> trunks got caught in the spokes of a wheel, stopping the cart, the
> men, and the oxen.
>
> The men all got together to push with their arms and their
> shoulders, while one of them, Hugues, who directed the work,
> armed himself with a strong boar spear to use as a lever to dis-
> engage the wheel that was caught. But having succeeded in that,
> Hugues slipped and fell under the cart, so that his leg was
> crushed and he was dragged about six yards down the mountain
> before the others were able to halt the wagon.
>
> The horrified men ran toward him, full of fright and anxiety,
> all invoking with a single voice the help of Sainte Foy. In their
> agony they called out again and again for her help. Once the
> cart had been secured and they found that Hugues was still
> alive, they were able to move him out from under the wheel and
> to take off his shoes and stockings. The bone of his leg was bent
> like a sickle.

In their sorrow and their helplessness the men were crying out to Sainte Foy for help when Hugues himself, sitting up, took his own leg in his hands and straightened it out as easily as if it were soft wax.

At this, affliction turned to joy, and tears of happiness flowed from every eye. The happy Hugues asked all to turn once more merrily to their work. And so the heavy load was delivered, without further incident, to the basilica of the glorious martyr, where they deposited the stone with the most ardent thanks to their powerful benefactress who had saved them from such a terrible danger.

The unnamed author of the continuation of Bernard of Angers's *Book of the Miracles of Sainte Foy* ends this story (which concludes the second and final *Book of Miracles*) with a peroration resplendent with praises of Sainte Foy, but I see Sainte Foy in her church still in the process of being built. I see her praying on her knees, as she prays in the tympanum in "her corner of force." I see her on the dusty flagstones in the gray light in her working nun's robe, her large long-fingered hands pressed together, her sweet worn face sad in the concentration of prayer, her eyes almost tearful but very wide open and aware of the other world in which the hand of God reaches out to almost touch her head that she might know that He has heard. (Her church was oriented by the architect and the builders not directly east-west but at a slight angle to that axis, so that the first beam of sunlight to strike the church on the sixth of October, the day of her martyrdom, would enter the church by the high arched window at the center in the western wall, close beneath the keystone of the barrel vaulting.)

On the sixth of October, her feast day, the first rays of sunlight to enter the valley and strike the church go through an arched window high in the apse and through the church to the western wall, where they shine through another window. This oculus (eye), the perfect circle, the symbol of Eternity, of God, who was in the beginning, is now, and ever shall be, world without end, amen; even as a beam of the rising sun that went through the dolmen at Lunel, once upon a time, would lead the angel smiling in that beam straight from there to the air over Conques.

Petite Clémence speaks of the *compagnons,* of how they cut the stone and built by hand according to the most precise measurements. I think of the builders looking out of the top of their tower on the capital in the cloister with a look of high triumph and joy on their faces. One of them will blow his horn.

Jack and I hold hands and ride off laughing happily down the Strata Conquesa into Lunel.

The people of Conques do not think very often about Le Puy. Le Puy is not on their minds. As the people of Lunel think about Conques, so the people of Conques think of Saint Jacques de Compostelle.

Saint Jacques is there, his image; Compostelle is there, far off to the west, as a kind of dream, a conscious dream, which is in their blood—a destination at the end of the Milky Way, the Chemin de Saint Jacques, where it dips down into the west at that Finis-terre, that end of earth where their Celtic ancestors went, both literally and symbolically to die. The feel for that farthest western place beyond which the earth blends into the sea and the sky when the sun goes down into night has come to them through the wild centuries; and Conques is on the way to there, to Saint Jacques de Compostelle.

So living out one's life here in this bowl, this *conque* in the mountains, one is living out one's life on the way to Compostelle, Starryfield. The words, "Saint Jacques de Compostelle," spoken, escape into the air of Conques continually like so many golden birds or bees, like so many glimmering moments of thought or prayer heading out into the heavens to join the stars.

"Again and again," says Madame Fau, "my husband and I were planning to make the trip to Saint Jacques de Compostelle. But always, for one reason or another, we put if off. . . . Now I will probably never see it," she says sadly. But brightening, for it is her way, she says, "Jean-Claude tells me that although the cathedral at Saint Jacques has a baroque façade, inside it is *tout à fait* Conques; it is exactly like Conques! Only much bigger!"

There is a fine, straight, blue-eyed old woman, Madame Dissac, who passes by Rosalie's house going up the Rue du Château and back several times a day at least; she is going to visit her daughter and her family on the far side of the Place du Château, but Rosalie and Charlou refer to her as Saint Jacques de Compostelle—because she is always walking, walking, walking, like a pilgrim, they explain. (She is Monsieur Fabre's older sister, but neither they nor their families have spoken for many years.)

"Life is an envelope," said Madame Benoit. "We come from the unknown and we are going toward we know not where in this envelope we call our life." She was sitting in the evening, knitting, on a little wall by a cousin's house above a garden terrace on the narrow Rue du Château. "Perhaps living in a place of pilgrimage, people in Conques understand this more easily than others," she said. (I think of the Venerable Bede's bird flying in from the winter night to the light and the warmth of the banquet hall and out again into the darkness.) "This was once the principal street of Conques," said Madame Benoit, tapping her cane on its stones. "People came in here by the Porte du Barry to go on down the Rue Charlemagne and over the Pont Romain and so on toward Saint Jacques de Compostelle. Or else they went up there and left by the Porte de Vinzelles to go on to Sainte Anne and Grand Vabre and to take the ferry over the Lot, going on from there, perhaps, to Our Lady of Rocamadour. Some people think this explains the mark like an upside-down Y below the scallop shell on Conques's escutcheon."

When we finally reach Lunel we turn south at the crossroads to go up the short, surprisingly steep hill to the church and the château in the high village. First we stop for a coffee at the café along the road, just at the top of the hill, where you turn into the village to go to the church.

The woman who serves us has a cousin who has lived in the United States, she tells us. He is a journalist. He comes from here. He has a house in Conques, but has not been here in a long time. He lives in Spain now. (We take in this seemingly improbable information, and years will pass before we meet him, one evening at the house of Monsieur LaPeyre, and have an absolutely marvelous time

with him, chattering away in English, while Roger LaPeyre, a host
to his very bones, beams on us with delight over the meeting he has
brought off, even though he can't understand a word we are saying.
François Pellou tells us that yes, he used to live in New York. He
still owns a house on Bank Street. He promised his parents he
would never sell the house in Conques. But he has been spoiled by
American standards of indoor heating and lighting, not to mention
plumbing, he tells us. He is trying to get his Conques house fixed
up enough so that he can visit and stay in it. Workers had been there
all through the spring, electricity had been put in, electric heating,
too, but the wires had never been connected to the outside! In-
credible! Typical! Absolutely typical! Unless you are here, nothing
gets done. Everyone knows that, but what can one do?

He spoke of the poverty of this region, of the extreme hardship
of the life in which his parents grew up. He spent the night in his little trailer up on the road above his house, and he drove off in the
morning. To this day we have not seen him again—the most charming of journalists, François Pellou.)

When we leave the Lunel café, high on the coffee and the story
of this cousin who has lived in the United States, we go to the
church, but it is locked. We wheel our bikes over and stare up at the
crenellated battlements of the yellow stone château, now a school.
We look about helplessly, still wanting to go into the church, and a
woman comes along, plump and rosy and pretty in her farm dress
and apron. She is forty-five perhaps, or fifty; she has brown hair and
a warm smile. She is happy we want to visit her church. We go over
to the door with her and she pulls the key from its hiding place and
proudly opens the door for us to reveal the little church, painted
white and full of light within, the ribbing of *rousset* luminous and
pale as soft sunshine. She talks of the pietà, the statue of the Virgin
holding the dead Christ in her lap. "Her nose is broken off," she
says. "But she is beautiful in her sorrow."

It is already after seven when Jack and I bike through St. Marcel
coming home the other way, along the crest of the plateau. We
speed along the slight downhill grade in the still-warm sunlight,

breathing in the June fragrance of the fields and the high pasture-land; we come to the farm Bourrious, where the other Madame Garrigue, we used to call her—Rosalie's sister-in-law—is bent over in her field, harvesting some new potatoes.

"*Bonsoir,* Madame Maria!" I call as I speed by. "*Bonsoir,* Madame Maria," calls Jack. And she rises up to wave, a bulky rosy-faced, apple-cheeked woman of sixty years or more. ("No, not *toujours gai,*" Monsieur Charlou, her brother-in-law, asserted firmly when Jack, a while ago, suggested that she was.) "*Bonsoir,* Madame Anna. *Bonsoir,* Monsieur Jacques." She waves.

"*Ça va?*" I call out, coming to a stop.

"*Oui, ça va,*" she says. There is a hint of sadness in her voice.

"*Et Monsieur Louis?*"

"*Ça va,*" she says.

He must be off somewhere in a lower pasture with his sheep and their dog, Mirka.

"*Bonne soirée,*" calls Jack, and we go on, slowly now, for as we approach the old farmhouse and the sheepfold, there are ducks and ducks, soft feathery ducks, moving about in the grass on their big webbed feet. (Madame Maria makes a superb *fois gras de canard.*) This is Madame Maria's farm, since her old mother died two years ago. This is where she grew up, above Conques on this high ridge where, looking out, you can see for miles across the plateaus in every direction. Bourrious was once the watchman's house for the abbey. She and Monsieur Louis come down still to their house in Conques every night, but each day at some point they drive back up to Bourrious in their little white car.

"She drinks," whispered Rosalie once, distressed. "Almost as much as Monsieur sometimes." Rosalie pointed up the hill; she meant Monsieur Fabres, the *forgeron* (blacksmith). "She harvests only enough potatoes each day for the family dinner the next," said Rosalie. And she and Charlou call her Alouette (skylark). I could not figure that out until I found in my dictionary the saying "She waits until the *alouettes* shall fall all roasted from the sky."

But when we come upon Madame Maria up here she is always outdoors, bent over, working at something or other. I think of her as she was one day when I passed here alone. She had on bright pink gloves; and with the gloves and her straw hat she looked, as I drew

near, as if she were dressed for a garden party somewhere. I saw her
bend over then; I saw she had a pair of scissors. The gloves were
rubber, and she was picking nettles.

"For a *soupe?*" I asked, when I drew up beside her.

"No, for the ducks," she said.

And when I told her how pretty she looked—as if she were set
for a party in her pink gloves—she rose to the occasion, drawing up
her bulk into a graceful, mincing, little dance-walk, and said, "Ah,
yes, I am playing the lady."

I think of her that way, at that moment "playing the lady"; and I
think of her eyes—large, sad eyes, tawny yellow, the most mysterious eyes I ever saw, almost the color of the stones of Sainte Foy de
Conques.

A noble brown rooster crosses before us, and we are gone, coast-
ing along the heather-covered crest to the point where we can see
below us.

We stop and pull our bikes over to the edge of the road and look
straight down and there it is—Conques—some six or seven hundred feet below us and less than a quarter of a mile away, a compact
pinkish fairy-tale city, solidly there with its towers, its castle, its
yellow stone church rising tall and massive above the old stone
houses gathered around it, all slate roofs (from here), roofs and
glimpses of walls with their old wooden beams, their mortar and
stucco pinkish-beige from the red sand of the Dourdou valley, the
whole town contained and girdled round with portions of its thick
old rampart walls still standing and there improbably in this green
gorge, magically shaped like the conch shell from which the town
got, indirectly, its name.

For into the hollow in the broad, steep, south-facing hillside that
rises above the Ouche, Conques is built, rounded, peaked, and
wide at the top, and tapering into the narrow Rue Charlemagne,
which, below the church, drops down along the cliff edge, houses
on both sides, into the Dourdou valley. "Old houses of the Middle
Ages," writes Conques's poet, Émile Roudié, "Lined up like pilgrims in procession, going toward the church." ("No more," said
Père André, shaking his head at this line when he showed me the
copy he had typed of his friend's poem. Père André meant, sadly,
"We don't have the processions anymore."

"The same houses live on/Resounding with new steps," writes Émile Roudié. "Émile Roudié, Médecin Colonel, en retraite. Poète Rouergat, 12 Fevrier 1877–26 Fevrier 1953. Officier de la Légion d'Honneur," it says on his gravestone down in the cemetery.

> All things are born and all things die;
> But, you, Conques, my dear little village,
> Perched like a nest in the depths of a wild conque,
> you don't change.

For Conques was not named Conques because of the lovely conch-shell shape of the town, which, indeed, did not exist as such when it was named. When the young King Louis named it, he chose its name not from his own Germanic tongue, nor from the Latin in which Ermold Le Noir would address him in verse, but from the language of the people he had come to govern—a language he had learned after riding into his kingdom in 781 on horseback at the age of three in full military dress. In their language, the ancient langue d'oc, *conques, conquas, conchas* (deriving from the Latin, which came in turn from the Greek meaning "shell" and "shell-like cavity," and which designated too, in Latin, a deep vessel used for holding oil and salt, as well as the conch shell, Triton's horn) came to mean also a deep and sheltered place in the mountains. This is the way Saint Columban used it about the year 600 when, after some of his monks were massacred by thieves in the colony he had established at Bregenz on Lake Constance, he wrote in Latin, "We had found a *conques* of gold, but it was full of serpents." This is the way Louis used it when in the year 801 he baptized Conques (Conchas). The prose account of the Furtive Translation, or the Pious Robbery, written down in the eleventh century, explains it saying, "The monastery of Conques, surrounded on all sides by abrupt mountains, takes its name from the conformation of the place—*ad instar conchae*—in the form of a *conque*."

This is how Émile Roudié used it in his poem, and this is the way I hear it used every so often when I pass an old woman, one or another, standing on her porch, or standing at a window, looking out in the evening at the view, and seeing me, she cups her hands, lovingly forming the shape of the valley, and says tenderly at the same moment, "A *conque*! A *conque*! A beautiful *conque*."

"This is a *conque!* This is a *conque!*" said Monsieur Charlou, pointing to a deep, hammered-copper vessel on the wall in Rosalie's kitchen. There are copper cooking pans as well and a large open copper kettle all glowing on the walls of Rosalie's beautiful kitchen.

"This is a *conque.*" M. Charlou says a third time, and, taking it off of the nail where it hangs on the wall high up over the polished wooden cabinet he bought for Rosalie before they married in 1952, he lets me touch it and look into it. He is a good and careful teacher. The hammered copper *conque* is oval in shape, about a foot deep, rounded at the bottom, and it glows within and without. "You see, it is not flat," says M. Charlou. "It is not used in cooking. Look at these handles. It is used for carrying. It is used in the *vendange* [the vintage]." When the baskets of grapes are brought in from the vineyards, the grapes are put, bunch by bunch, into the *conques* and carried by this means up to the high oaken vat in the *cave* where they will undergo their first fermentation.

The wonder that we, Jack and I, should actually be here, living in Conques, sleeping at night in our funky bedroom that feels like a room in a little beach house somewhere, that we should breathe in all night the fragrance of the roses that bloom along the steps outside our window, and wake in the morning and open our shutters to air filled with the warm sounds of clucking hens, to mists that fill the deep valley and burn off, even as we watch, to reveal the airy front towers of the church.

"Conques!" says Jack—this tall, wide-shouldered, gentle, blue-eyed man to whom I am married.

"He is good to you, isn't he," said Rosalie when we were first becoming friends, as we sat talking, she and I, in her kitchen in the evening late while Monsieur Charlou finished putting the cows to bed (so to speak) and Jack was up at our house in his atelier painting. "He is good to you?" Rosalie asked because she had been praising Jack. Monsieur Jacques, she calls him. Later I understood that this is the first question one woman asks another at the point of becoming intimate.

"Oh, yes," I said.

"*Mon Charlou aussi,*" she said. "*Nous avons bien choisi!*" (My Charlou,

too," she said. "We have chosen well!" In the patois, the *ou* ending is
the diminutive.)

She smiled triumphantly, my lovely girlish friend. In October
1978 she would have been married twenty-five years. And I in December only seven. They spoil us, both of them, we discovered, by
making our coffee in the morning.

"Conques!" I say now, echoing Jack, and we laugh in simple joy.
He gets out his binoculars to spy on it.

He pretends he is going to find something astonishing down in
Conques, that, for instance, he will see Madame Fabre bending
over in her garden. Monsieur Charlou likes to tell us that Madame
Fabre has an amazing *derrière*, Beautiful *fesses*! *Shum* is a word he also
uses from time to time, admiring her. I thought at first it was a
word in the patois, but it is German, perhaps dialect or slang, the
equivalent of our word "ass," as I hear it.

During the war, he was taken to Danzig, no, to near the city of
Danzig, for forced labor. He worked in a factory. "It was terrible, it
was horrible, the things I saw there . . . the things I saw there." He
is not specific, but when the subject comes up, he is likely to pale,
to become very serious, to say "the things I saw there . . ." and then
stop. You only know that what he saw filled him with horror and
marked his life since, marked his view of the world and his soul, as
the scar he shows marks his body. He pulls up his sleeve and opens
his palm and you see the white scar that runs from the center of his
hand inside his arm to above where his elbow is. "When that happened they sent me home," he says. "I was useless then.

"The things I saw there . . . the things I saw," he says. "That is
why I did not want to have children. I did not want to have children
only to bring them up to be ready for another war. No. No.

"My brother was a prisoner of war, he was imprisoned in the
country near Frankfort. Things were not so bad there. But where I
was, the things I saw . . ."

Sometimes at lunchtime he laughs, telling of those years. "Once,
after we were bombed, the British flew over and dropped chocolate with leaflets all over the town," he says. "Propaganda. And the
authorities forbade the people to eat the chocolate. They didn't
want us to eat it either. They said it was poison. But we, the de-

tainees, we were so hungry, we didn't care, we ran out and got the chocolate and we ate it. Good chocolate! Then when the people saw that we didn't die, they began to eat it, too." He laughs. "We weren't allowed to have anything to do with the local girls," he says. "But we did." He laughs. "*Mein Liebling*," he says, laughing, his eyes shining. And he gets a little drunk on wine at lunchtime, the wine of his own vineyard so carefully cultivated, so carefully made, and he talks of Madame Fabre's gorgeous *shum,* outlining its shape admiringly with his hands.

Rosalie ignores him when he does this. Or sometimes she says, "*Pas serieux!*"

And he goes on. He goes on. "Obsessed!" roared Janine, once when she was here and we were all having *dîner* together at noontime. "Obsessed," she roared, laughing her head off, for Monsieur Charlou is one of the gentlest, kindest men in the world, with a deep and sensitive soul—you can't be near him without feeling this. "Obsessed with sex!" Janine cried out. For he is irrepressible when he gets going.

"Do you see," Jack asked me, "how sometimes when he gets going, with those thick black eyebrows, and that long nose and his wild half-toothless grin, Charlou looks like Satan—no, not Satan, because you always see how kind he is—but he looks like Satan's benign brother."

Once when we were outdoors in the Place du Château after lunch, Charlou said, pointing up to the *forgeron's* house, "*Il s'ébranche tous les matins*" (which translated literally means "He trims his branch every morning"). "And that's why she walks around like this," Monsieur Charlou said. And he imitated Madame Fabre's mincing little walk, moving along as she does, always seeming to hurry, but holding her super-ample little bottom as if she favors it, yet wiggling it flirtatiously as she goes, just the same. For there is no doubt about it: a little woman, a bit over fifty, pert and well formed and capable, Madame Fabre is a coquette. The coquettishness is in her blood, as strong in her nature as is her sadness, her anger, her grieving for a life that should have been finer, her burden, which, however, she keeps concealed. She puts up a good front and she makes the best of what is, and she has, contrary to what

Rosalie believes, a heart. It is only that she is . . . you don't say, you rub your index finger against your thumb. It means she cares too much about money, that she is not above a few little tricks, a little dishonesty, to get a bit of extra money or give out a bit less when she sees the opportunity.

Jack moves his binoculars. He cannot find Madame Fabre (of whom he is quite fond, as is she of him). He cannot find her bending over in her garden. But maybe, he says, he'll spot Monsieur Fabre, the *forgeron,* leaning out of the window of their house, blowing his whistle to call her to the telephone.

For her vegetable garden is beyond the wide terraced hillside flower garden that divides our house, the tiny house we rent from them, from theirs. Her vegetable patch is a deep, flat garden, carved out of the hillside above the former convent and on the level with its roof, and she could be deep in that garden (cut off from our view from here), fending off the banter of two or three of the old men from the Maison de Repos (rest home) who come out there in the evening to hang around the fence above her garden and admire her while she works, or perhaps she could be engaged in conversation with the other Madame Fabre (not related), who might for a moment be pausing there with her little boy, Thomas (one of the most beautiful children on earth).

By this time of night Monsieur Fabre is always a little . . . you don't say "drunk," you twist your nose with your fist and make a kind of Donald Duck quack. In fact, he has been a little bit that way since noon. Or before. He is a tall-seeming, thin, dark-haired man of fifty-three with an old, still-boyish face, something puckish about him, charming, this blue-eyed, sensitive, unshaven, once-handsome man with a lump in his jaw. He has the skilled hands of an artist, a blacksmith, and he has a bawdy, witty tongue. When he gets one of his outrageous thoughts, he closes his mouth a second, holds his breath, it seems, and his eyes rest in a suspended dance while the wheels go round in his agile wicked mind, and then out he comes with something naughty; Simone, his daughter, or Madame Fabre, whichever one is nearer, starts beating on his back or his arms in hopeless attempts to try to stop him.

Even Madame Benoit cannot stop him. *"Fermes ta geule!"* she

snapped in anger once when we were having lunch there. ("Shut
your monster jaws.") But on he went laughingly. Madame Fabre had
made a cheese soufflé for our first course, and then she served a
rabbit stewed with tomatoes and onions. Excellent, all of it. He
tried to put more wine in Madame Benoit's glass. She covered it
with her hand. "I want to preserve the whiteness of my face,"
Madame Benoit said proudly.

Once he went too far and their house was quiet for days.
Madame Benoit did not go there and no laughter came through the
windows at noontime, nor did it later in the afternoon, toward five,
when she used to drop by. Occasionally Simone, who was still in
high school then, would scream furiously at her father. I asked Rosalie what had happened. "He spoke against the Virgin Mary," Rosalie
said, trying as hard as she could to suppress a smile.

The *forgeron*. He stands outside his forge (outside the walls of
Conques just beyond the Arch of Vinzelles) of an afternoon under a
raggedy old blue beach umbrella, welding a piece of machinery, and
every few days he makes a terrific racket driving up and down the
narrow cobblestone streets of Conques in his tractor wagon, delivering long tanks of gas. Monsieur Fabre is a plumber as well as a
blacksmith and the owner of the gas-tank consignment of Conques.

"*Il est bête*," Madame Fabre said once. "He's crude, he's stupid."
Then she laughed, embarrassed by her vehemence. She had been
praising Jack, saying how gentle he is and fine, and I had tried in my
awkward French to say something praising Monsieur Fabre.

Mademoiselle Fau praises Monsieur Fabre's extraordinary skill
with his hands, and his wit. "It is a pity you cannot understand him,"
she said. "It's a pity. He is really very witty." Then she added, as
everyone knows, "Of course, you must see him in the morning before eleven if you want him to do anything."

"*Il est bête*," Madame Fabre said, and then laughed as if she'd startled herself.

It is her father she is proud of (her father and her mother, dead,
the two of them, these many years); it is her son, her beautiful son,
Jean-Pierre, who is her pride and joy now. He works in construction in Montpellier, but he comes here on special weekends and to
spend his vacation in the little apartment they have made for him

above the garage at the back of the house we rent from them, and he is as fine as she thinks him to be. All of Conques admires him, this extraordinarily handsome young man with his clear blue eyes, clear but not hard, dreaming eyes, and he is cordial, that is it, he is cordial with everyone and he loves his parents, he honors them, pities them (I sense) for the hardship of their isolated life here in this little village, and he looks out for his sister, eases her loneliness, and, while he is here, includes her in everything he does.

Madame Fabre once showed us a picture he painted—"Oh, a long time ago," she said. It is framed and hanging in their kitchen–living room with its long table and its fireplace and chairs to sit in near the fire. Madame Fabre is proud of his painting, a charming watercolor, a "*naïf*" scene of Conques, the rooftops, the houses, the western façade of the church, more or less the view you see from their windows looking out toward the east. "He doesn't paint anymore," Madame Fabre said sadly.

"My father was an artist," she said. "A sculptor. A stonecutter. He made nineteen monuments for the war dead. After the First World War. Nineteen monuments. He made the monument here in Conques. You know it?"

"Oh, yes," I nodded. "It is very fine."

"He could never get the war out of his mind," Madame Fabre said. "He could never forget the trenches, his companions, dying around him, wounded, bleeding, arms shot off, heads shot off, night and day, in the rain, the cold, he couldn't get the thought of it out of his mind; it all stayed crawling around in his head like the lice he got in the trenches." She brought her hands up to her hair and rubbed them around wildly with anguish as if trying to scratch away the lice, the memories that tormented her father.

"You know the Moulin de Sagnes, don't you?" she asked.

I nodded.

"Originally, you know, it was built by the monks of Conques when they cut through the rock there to drain the swamp that was in the plain of what is now St. Cyprien; they made the waterfall of the Dourdou there, and it was natural to build a mill as well. When my father bought it, it had fallen into ruin. It was his dream to rebuild it,

and to make a home for his family there. He did all the work himself,
he rebuilt it stone by stone. It was not easy. My mother loved him, she
made many sacrifices for his sake. Many sacrifices. She had to take a
path up the hill, to walk three kilometers to the spring for water each
day. And there were five of us. She made many sacrifices for him. The
way Madame de Gaulle did for her husband." (This was at the time of
Madame de Gaulle's death, and we were reading of her life and his in
all the magazines.) "My mother was proud of my father, proud of
him. And she loved him. There are things he made still at the Moulin
de Sanges. I will take you there and show it to you in the fall. In the
fall when the tourists are gone I will have more time." (She works
mornings in the Hôtel Sainte Foy through the summer, cleaning the
rooms and making the beds when the guests have left.)

Madame Fabre speaks with the clarity of the well educated—unlike Monsieur Fabre, whose voice is so slurred it is hard to make
out a word he says, and when I do, I often have to pretend that I
haven't. It is easy for me to understand Madame Fabre. And she
writes clearly and correctly as well.

"She was going to be a nun," Monsieur Charlou told me. "She was
educated in the convent at Rodez."

He paused. "But she could not take the vow of chastity," he said,
hee-hawing with delight. "Nor of poverty," he said, significantly.
And he rubbed his index finger and his thumb together.

"Les jeunes amoreux," said Monsieur Fabre, showing us a snapshot
of them thirty years ago, after the war, before they were married.
"The young lovers." And Madame Fabre blushed. How beautiful
they were!

"My brother," said Monsieur Fabre, pointing up to a framed photograph hanging on the wall. The young man in the photograph was
slim, very fine, handsome, standing at his anvil with his hammer
raised; his sleeves were rolled up, his arms were smooth and muscular, his eyes were extraordinary eyes, blue and dreamy, the eyes
of Jean-Pierre. Monsieur Fabre stood there wheezing with sup-
pressed laughter. For a moment, looking at the beautiful young
blacksmith, I did not get the joke. Then I saw it was himself.

· · ·

Jack cannot find anything interesting down in Conques. "I see our roof," he says. We laugh. He puts his arms around my waist and we and our bikes start to lose balance. We are in a state of happy foolishness from the long exercise, the air, the sun, green June, golden June, and Conques below us—home!

The town bell rings once. "Seven-thirty," we both say at the same time. The sun is still warm on the skin of our arms and our faces. Jack trains his binoculars to the western mountain that rises above the Dourdou, almost straight up in places, a thousand feet, wooded and green, save for the rock cliffs that jut forth and for the high, heather-covered humps. Beyond, that plateau, like this one, goes on for ten or fifteen miles with fields of grain and hay, of cattle, of sheep, and tiny farm villages, clusters of five or ten houses and barns, here and there. Jack is looking for the chapel of Saint Roch up there, then for the barn we can just see on the high green crest from the table on our terrace when we eat, then for the yellow farmhouse we love. "That's just where I'd like to live," Jack says, because it seems to be airy and sunny and full of light and large white rooms. A new house, it is, built at a little distance from the old gray stone farmhouse.

From here we can see through the cut of the Dourdou Gorge southward into the green bowl of St. Cyprien and beyond, rounded plateau, hill after hill, down the long valley into the distance, where, on top of the farthest ridge, gray and barely distinguishable, rises the cathedral at Rodez with its famous bell tower.

Now Jack directs his binoculars from the western plateau down through the woods to the place where the little chapel of Sainte Foy looks out, a peach-colored white like the moon on a hot summer night; looking out from that wooded mountain gorge, it is as small as the moon in the sky and as lovely. Soon the shadow of the mountain will slide over it, and as the woods darken the chapel will retain its light until the last of day has faded.

There on that spot, Aronisde, the pious robber, laid down his precious burden for a moment. It was about 866 and, exhausted from his journey, safe at last in his own country, he drifted off to sleep. "He was hungry, he was dying of thirst," says Monsieur Charlou when he tells the story.

Beyond the Dourdou at Conques a joyous procession was forming to welcome the holy relics. The ivory horns were sounding. The cross and the relics in the golden *A* brought here by Charlemagne were carried forth from the abbey church. The smoke from the censers rose in the air. (In that age when kings fell down weeping before the relics of the saints, the ceremony for the welcoming of a saint's relics was modeled after the *adventus,* the ceremony for welcoming the emperor.)

Ten years had passed since, as the ancient account says, "for the well-being and the preservation of their country, the monks of Conques decided they must obtain the relics of Sainte Foy, holy martyr of Agen, and for this mission wisely chose the monk Aronisde—for the holiness of his character, for his austerity, for the sweetness of his manners and his amiable disposition, and above all for his prudence and the shrewdness and quickness of his mind." He was the priest of a parish dependent on the abbey of Conques and he had acquired "a consummate skill in the commerce of life."

Disguised as a pilgrim priest, Aronisde had set off for Agen with a confrère as a guide; he had returned with the miraculous body of the saint, and, safe in his country at last, he fell into sleep, where, as if in a dream, a young girl of incomparable grace and beauty, still almost a child, appeared to him. Her aspect was angelic and perfectly serene, her face white, but with the nuance of the rose, and the expression of her face such that no beauty here below can give an idea of it. Her dress appeared to be woven of thread of pure gold, and her veil was wound around her head in the form of a crown, with four pearls of extraordinary radiance. She spoke with a voice of indescribable sweetness.

"You have worked hard and well, my father," she said. "For my sake you have exposed yourself to the most cruel perils, and in doing so you have pleased my Lord Jesus Christ. He has asked that I reward you with a sign. Tell me, Father Aronisde, which you would prefer: From the rock above where you sleep now, when you awake, a spring will gush forth. Would you have that it gush forth wine for a day or water forever?"

And the prudent Aronisde replied that water forever would do more good.

"With that," says Monsieur Charlou when he tells this story, "Sainte Foy put her white hand into the rock. And when she drew out her hand, the waters began to flow. You can still see the trails her fingers made in the rock there. You can *feel* the trails of her fingers drawing out the water, if you put your hand into the water there.

"And from that day to this," Monsieur Charlou concludes, "the water that flows from that source cures maladies of the eyes."

And in that place on the mountain, just above the rock where the spring gushed forth, a little chapel was built, and there the pilgrims in after years would stop as they left Conques and toiled up the mountain on their way from Sainte Foy de Conques to Saint Jacques de Compostelle. There they stopped to drink the water that flowed from the sacred source, and to bathe their eyes and faces. There they stopped to pray in the chapel and to look back for the last time at Conques. "They prayed for their safety," Père André said. "Often they stopped a time to work while they were at Conques, and the monks gave them money, so when they left, they were the prey of bandits. Did you ever think of that?"

And there the people of Conques go even to this day. Rosalie and Père André, both of them, send us there with bottles when we go, to fill them with the healing water. "It is good for your eyes," Rosalie says. "And if you drink the water of Sainte Foy when you're sick, you will get well. Also, if you smooth it onto your face, it is good for your skin."

Let's go, let's take our picnic lunch there tomorrow, we decide, and we set off on our bikes, holding our brakes tightly, downward into Conques, where, in the Treasure, Sainte Foy sits, her arms uplifted, in her holy trance, alone, thinking of God.

Toward the bottom of the hill, at the place called L'Estoulène, just above the rocade, we hear Rosalie from somewhere below us—"Ehhh! Ehhh! *Bonsoir!*" she calls, and finally we see her down through the walnut trees and the high grasses in her lower garden. She is wearing her orange flowered dress and she is waving wildly with a trowel in one hand, her hair shining, her fair face rosy. "Hey," we call back. *"Bonsoir, bonsoir! À tout à l'heure!"* See you later!

"*À tout à l'heure!"* she calls back, content.

Later, around ten, as dark comes on, we'll find her and Monsieur Charlou and walk back into town with them and the two massive cows, Fleurou and Parisii.

III

Evening: Voyage Around Conques

Jack and I are drinking the black-red wine of Cahors. The town bells have rung nine times, and repeated: nine. Here at our table on the tiny terrace, like a landing on the stairs of the *ruelle* that goes past our house, we have dined on veal rubbed with lemon and broiled with oil and garlic, new potatoes from Rosalie's garden, and asparagus she gave me last night, for an omelette, she said, but I made it for our vegetable this evening. We have eaten a salad of *frisé* (curly endive), and a goat cheese, a *cabecou,* from the flock of brown goats (with bells!) at Montarnal, where we love to go swimming in the Lot, the icy black river there flowing swiftly beneath green mountains and the round tower of the ancient castle. Now we are eating Rosalie's strawberries, the best strawberries in the world—ripe, red, fragrant, juicy strawberries; day after day they come, and they keep coming, from Rosalie's gardens.

"Have you ever in your life before had enough strawberries?" I ask Jack.

"Don't gush," he says, his mouth full, and we both laugh.

June at Conques in the mountains of the Rouergue. I could sail out of my head from the joy of it into the air and the light—the long clear light of the first hours after the sun has gone down behind the western mountain, whose shadow has risen slowly through the golden-green light in the chestnut leaves on the mountain. The sunlight has glowed a last minute on the smooth old tree, the cross up there, against the sky, and then left our valley, our *conque,* a bowl of pure shade, all still.

But high up beyond the Dourdou to the southwest the sun is still shining softly in the green meadow on the rim of the plateau, where seven cows are grazing—distant, black, four-legged figures in the last slant of evening sunshine. An eighth figure appears. Jack lifts his binoculars. It is the farmer from the yellow house come to take them in for the night. Then we see them moving single file, winding slowly along the ridge against the sky. And they are gone.

Old Madame Delbes (*delbes* means "of the birch tree") passes by, going up the stairs to her garden near the *boules* court with her basket. She wears a heavy black cotton dress and a blue-and-white garden apron. *"Bonsoir, monsieur . . . dame!"* she says. *"Bon appétit!"* She pauses a moment on our landing and looks out across the valley. She comments on the view, the weather. She chatters on a bit as we smile up at her. *"Et voilà!"* she concludes with a sorrowing, sighing breath. She continues on up the stairs.

"Look at her calves!" Jack says. "Look how strong they are!"

Once, on her way back down again, she stepped into our kitchen and sold me half a basket of string beans. Friends who were visiting were wowed by this. "She's medieval! Medieval!" one of them said when she was gone. She is an old farm woman, a widow, very plain, and she has long since given up her animals and sold most of her land. But she keeps her garden with its apple tree up by the *boules* court and another with several walnut trees below the path near the *capellette,* and she keeps her beloved dog, Markizou, and her house on the Place du Château with its beautiful sixteenth-century doorway with flowerpots of geraniums and begonias all around it, and its old grayed wood staircase, preserved like a fossil, all the way up the front. Every tourist with a camera photographs her house, and I have seen Jean Sègalat out in front of it in the evening lecturing on it informally to two friends (Conques, he says, its character, was saved by its poverty), but she seems to be lonely here.

I noticed that neither Rosalie nor Madame Benoit ever seems to talk to her, and I asked Rosalie if there was something bad about her. "No, no, there is nothing bad about her," Rosalie said. "It is just that she is *bête . . . et curieuse.*"

This is a quality I have noticed in several women here—they try to find out things about you or others, and it is different from friendly interest, and different certainly from what we call curiosity; it seems to go with a certain aggressive lack of charm and applies to all those Rosalie describes as *curieuse.*

Madame Delbes seems different from the others though, perhaps because she is so sorrowful and alone except for Markizou. And then Markizou is such a strange, mangy mongrel—a descendent of generations of stray-dog mixtures of boxer and schnauzer

and black poodle, we think, from his looks. It's hard to tell. "Markizou had an almost human face," Jack said of him later. "And his hair
was parted."

Once Jack gave him a piece of bread when Madame Delbes
wasn't there, and he buried it. "It was the oddest thing I ever saw a
dog do," Jack said. "It was as if he were saying, 'Thank you, I don't
know quite what to do with this now, but thank you. I'll look into
it later.' "

And later when we returned one year, we didn't see Markizou.
When we asked after him, Madame Delbes burst into tears. "He
died," she said. "He was all the family I had left at home."

In August Madame Delbes's son comes to visit her, but only for a
few days or a week or so, and once I met her granddaughter, who
grew up in the *banlieue*, the outskirts, of Paris and teaches English
in a *lycée* there now. When she, the granddaughter, heard I was
writing a book about Sainte Foy, she asked me if I believed in the
miracles. "Oh, not I, not I," she said in the course of our conversation, "but my grandmother, she still believes in the miracles of
Sainte Foy." I like knowing this about Madame Delbes.

"Bonne soirée!" Jack calls out to her now in the Provençal and
Rouergat way, when she turns at the top of the stairs to summon
mangy Markizou, who would otherwise have preferred, perhaps,
to hang around and dine with us.

All the while down below in the side yard that adjoins the Geneste house, little Lucie has been going round and round the apple
tree with her wheelbarrow; this plump, golden child, large for her
age—she is only three—all soft in her pajamas, is moving her head,
with its thick, straight blond hair, this way and that (she has, too,
the bluest eyes), and she is talking and murmuring in a sing-song as
she plays happily, going round and round the apple tree, where the
rope swing that Monsieur Denis, her grandfather, made for her
about two weeks ago hangs quite harmless for the time being.

Ever since the morning that Monsieur Denis came out with his
ladder and climbed up to hang the swing, that thing has caused
Lucie no end of misery and terror. For it was made entirely for *her*
pleasure, and everyone assumes that if she would only try it once,
she would find out what a wonderful thing a swing is. But from the

very start it filled her with fear, and each time someone tries once again to persuade her to try it she sets up a great crying howl of distress.

Dany, her grandmother, her Mama-Dany, has swung in it. Rosalie has swung in it. Her aunt Claudine and her uncle Bernard have swung in it. Even Madame Benoit swung in it. And I swung in it with Madame Benoit pushing me. But not that sight nor all our joys, our oohs and ahhs, combined have yet persuaded this child that she would like to swing in the swing. Now she appeases it, circling round the tree, where it hangs like a snake, keeping a wide berth of it, she and her friendly wheelbarrow with a little doll that's bumping along inside it, while Lucie sing-songs and chatters and murmurs, and heaven knows what she's saying.

The town bell rings once. It is nine-thirty.

Now, as with the sudden silent throb of afterglow, the color of the western faces of Conques's houses turns an even richer, warmer rose-brown. The houses glow. We can see them from here, the near houses of the Quartier du Palais, and the far houses one after the other rising up the long Rue Émile Roudié. And the church, too, glows—its deep yellow *rousset*.

It never seems quite believable that this happens, but at the same time, too, at this hour in this light, the figures in the great tympanum over the western doors of the church come forward somehow, their presence more clearly defined. When you look up at them they seem to be closer, to be looking out and down at you directly, some of them. The colors that still cling to the stone in places grow—the blue on the robe of Christ the Judge in Heaven seated in His almond-shaped glory, His mandorla; the yellow and light orange on the wings of the angels above Him; the different blue on the mantle of Mary, who stands near Him to the right at the head of the procession of the elect, her hands held together in prayer; the reddish-purple and the black and ochre casts of hell and of the sinners trapped there forever with demons and devils and flames and Satan himself, king with seven horns like a crown; the rose in the seven arches of the Heavenly Jerusalem where Abraham gathers his children to his bosom; the blue on the robe of Sainte Foy who, "in her corner of force," Père André says, is represented not in

Heaven, but here, here at Conques. She has come down off her throne, empty now, before the altar with the chalice that holds the Blood of Christ; she has fallen on her knees on the floor of her church, where above hang the manacles of prisoners she freed through years of time by her prayerful intercession with the Lord; she is praying for all her people now, praying for the souls of the dead. On the last day in time, the hand of Jesus reaches down through the cloud waves of heaven which, mottled with blue, seem to form His sleeve. His finger, as noted, does not touch her head. Rather, the orb of the halo of His hand continues to overlap the halo of her head—there on the great tympanum in "the corner of force" of her long afterlife here at Conques.

It is time to clear the table, to stack the dishes and hurry down while the light lasts to look at it—this Last Judgment of the twelfth century, a work of art, perfectly preserved. "One of the four marvels of the world!" Rosalie said once, face shining.

Detail,
Tympanum

("Ah-ha-ha," laughs Monsieur Charlou knowingly, for he has had the tympanum there to edify him all his life, "have you noticed the devil's *queue*"—his tail, literally translated, but it is a euphemism for penis, I've gathered; and this one belonging to the devil on the tympanum at Conques is indeed extraordinary. Besides, he's got a horrible long snake for a tail.)

Qué n'a pas bist	Who has not seen
Clouquié de Roudès,	The bell tower of Rodez
Pourtal de Counquos,	The tympanum of Conques
Gléiso d'Albi	The church at Albi
Campana de Mendé	The bell of Mende
N'a pas res bist.	Has never seen anything.

When I found this wonderful old patois saying in my big Bouillet and Servières, *Sainte Foy, Vierge et Martyre d'Agen*, I copied it out so that I could ask Rosalie how to pronounce it.

I went down with it when she and Monsieur Charlou would be finishing their lunch, as she always has time to relax then if no one comes in to buy something. She read it to herself and seemed to fill with pleasure and then she read it aloud, mouthing it in that warm tender furry-fuzzy way of the patois. She repeated the last line, changing the order of the last two words to make it sound more natural. *"N'a pas bist res!"* she said, shaking her head, and smiling. "Now you read it!" she commanded. I tried and she corrected me. I tried again and finished, *"N'a pas bist res,"* as she had done. She laughed, pleased. I was getting it, but it sounded so funny to her. She took my arm in her teeth, a kind of mother animal love bite she gives from time to time when she's feeling playful. She took me over to Dany Geneste, and I read it to Dany, and Dany doubled over, her hands deep in her apron, laughing, and the two of them began chattering at me in the patois. Dany comes from the village of Longueviale up on the plateau, not far from Rosalie's village of Taulanet; they come from the country of Senergues, the two of them, and they began trying to get me to repeat things after them that they told me to say, and then they would be bent over laughing, both of them. Some of the things they were telling me to say were quite naughty, I believe (for I couldn't get them to tell me in French

what it was they were saying at certain moments), but generally, I
think, it just sounded hilarious to hear a foreigner trying to learn
their mother tongue—the way the words sounded coming from
my mouth was so funny, it being absolutely unheard of that someone who did not know this language from infancy should ever learn
to speak it.

It was from this time that Rosalie, who would never correct my
French, never help me at all, except that very occasionally, when
the matter was desperate, she might supply the word I was trying
to come out with—it was from this time that she began teaching
me a few words and phrases in the patois—how to say "goodnight"
(*buene nuèch*), "to bed" (*au lièch*), how to say "until tomorrow" (*à dé-
mose*), "the wine" (*lou bis*), and things a little more complex. She
would become stern, commanding, taking on the authoritative role
of teacher, but warmly, lovingly, for this is the language of families
and villages, this is the language one speaks to one's children, to animals, and to the old people one loves, this is the language of flowers and herbs and foods, growing foods, and trees, the language of
proverbs about the weather, the language of love and sex and tenderness, the language one's mother and grandmother lavished on
the beloved child, this is the mother tongue, the language of songs
and dancing, and this is a secret language, too, that the authorities
sent down from Paris cannot understand, nor, for the most part,
the bourgeoisie of the towns removed from the soil for more than
a generation; nor can the foreigners who come here understand it,
no matter how good their French may be. This is the language one
speaks with one's friends, fellow farmers and compatriots who
come from the villages on the plateau. One starts off, perhaps, in
French, but as soon as things get relaxed one is off with verve and
relief, chattering away in the beloved patois.

"She doesn't understand the patois, does she," said Fraysou once
to Monsieur Charlou when he wanted to tell him something he
didn't want me to hear; and, well satisfied that I did not, Fraysou
proceeded to regale Monsieur Charlou with what was on his mind.

"It is *not* a patois," says Janine, who, coming down from Paris on
holiday, tends to know everything. "Not a *patois*," she says a bit
testily. "Knowing French you cannot possibly understand what they

insist on calling the *patois* here. It is another language. It is the Occitan language."

She is quite right, too. Their mother tongue, is indeed the ancient Occitan language, as it is called now—traditionally it was called the langue d'oc or Provençal; and in the Middle Ages it was known as Limousine. *La langue romane,* Père André calls it in what he is writing about the "Song of Sainte Foy"; and Claude Fauriel in his *History of Provençal Poetry* calls it also the *langue romane.* It is a language as different from French as Spanish and Portuguese are, and though it is now dying out and efforts are being made to revive it, in the 1940s and 1950s, when Charlou and Rosalie came of age, it was, in spite of centuries of what Saint-Beuve called its misfortunes, still spoken in Europe by more people than spoke Portuguese.

Babet told me that in the old days (the 1940s and 1950s) the people who came to see her husband, Doctor Fau, would always ask for the doctor in the patois when they came to the door. She pronounced the way they asked for him and told us how she replied as she led them down to his office, where he, in his turn, spoke the patois, which had been lost to him for the most part in his childhood growing up in Rodez, but which he had made a point of learning when, after the army was demobilized (like Émile Roudié he had become an army officer doctor), they came to live in Conques with Babet's parents. When Doctor Fau was preparing to retire during the year before his sudden death, she told us, it was very important to him that he find a young doctor who spoke the patois to replace him in Conques and the countryside roundabouts.

The "Song of Sainte Foy" is considered one of the earliest, most subtle, and loveliest monuments in this language, which reached its great flowering in the poetry of the troubadours in the twelfth century and was then wiped out abruptly and almost completely as a literary language by the Albigensian Crusade (1209–1229) and the subsequent takeover of the south by the north of France.

"Kill them, kill them all: God will know his own," Simon de Montfort said, directing his soldiers to kill all the people of Béziers, the Christians and Cathars alike, who had fled into their church for

protection from his brutal army, which was razing and plundering
the south on its crusade to wipe out heresy. "Kill them, kill them
all: God will know his own." His words have stayed alive like the
blazon of the Midi, conquered by the north, that it might never forget.

For though the great troubadours ceased with the horrors of that
war to sing, and the literature of the south seemed to die, it did not
do so completely, for the language remained alive, their treasure,
beloved and fragile and yet enduring and strong, for it could belong
to anyone, no matter how poor, and to everyone; and though the
language suffered from the fact that although for centuries those
who spoke it in their childhood, when they were educated, wrote
for the most part in French, and the language broke down into hundreds of local dialects, all subject to incursions from the French.
Nevertheless this beloved language went on being transmitted
from grandmother and grandfather and mother and father to
daughter and son, and when in the nineteenth century, at Font-
Ségugne near Avignon, Frédéric Mistral and his friends founded
their movement of the Félibrige, dedicated to the idea that their
poetry was derived from the people and should be addressed to
them in a classic langue d'oc, a language that could be understood
by all the peoples of the Midi, they said that their movement was
born of a mother's tear—the tear of the mother of Joseph
Roumanille, who had given up so much for the education of her
dear son and then could not understand the language, French, in
which he wrote his first poems; and he saw her tear as he was reading them, and it moved him so much that he, the oldest of the Félibres, determined that from then on he would write in the
Provençal that she would hear and know.

Nor were they alone—Mistral and Roumanille and the others of
the seven Félibres, for even as they founded their movement in high
spirits in 1854 at Font-Ségugne (meaning continuous spring), Jas-
min, the barber at Agen, was writing his songs, his curl-papers, he
called them, and he had a tremendous following, this poet who had
been so poor in his boyhood that the church at Agen (the Church of
Sainte Foy and Saint Caprais) had fed him and clothed him; and
Gelu was writing his bitter poems at Marseille, while all along in

Toulouse the Academie des Jeux Floreaux, which had been founded in 1323 by the legendary Clémence Isaure and seven young troubadours anxious to maintain their language, continued to exist. The seven young troubadours of Toulouse called themselves the Compagnie de Gai-Savoir and their muse and patroness, Clémence Isaure, presided over the Floral Games, where their songs were sung or recited.

Closer to home, in the time of our earliest long bike rides here, those first weeks we spent in Madame Fabre's house, Jack and I had become fascinated by the mysterious black château we'd seen from the ridge above Bourrious in the green mountain hills beyond the Lot. Jack had found the château in his binoculars and at the same time found a village with a church a little to the east and below the château. We located them on our maps and figured out that the château was called Selves and the village La Vinzelle, and we had gone on an afternoon trip to visit them.

Then, later, I read somewhere that the Château of Selves was "a little bit the Font-Ségugne of the Rouergat poets who wrote in the Occitan tongue."

I was trying to find out about this, about what had happened there, who had met there, how the Château of Selves had become the Font-Ségugne of the Rouergue. No one could tell me. Finally I found the answer in a book of the Châteaux of Aveyron that Jeannot Cannes regularly takes out of the library in Rodez. The history of the châteaux all around is his special, passionate interest, and he wanted me to see this slender book. I found out that at Selves the idea of founding the "Grelh Roergat" was born and that the idea was realized at Rodez on March 6, 1921, and that the Grelh Roergat has never ceased to work to safeguard the Occitan tongue. Henri Mouli, a poet and schoolteacher, and his poet friends, I learned from further reading, gathered round Zélia Poujade, the daughter of the castle, and so it was there that they used to meet and that, in high spirits, their movement was born.

And yet, even as these movements to bring about the reflowering of their literature continued, the efforts to wipe out their language became, with the establishment of universal, free, and compulsory education at the end of the nineteenth century, gradually more successful.

At the time that Rosalie and Charlou went to school, in the 1930s, the ancient language of the people of the south of France was literally being beaten out of them. In their households and their villages these children, Rosalie at Taulanet and Charlou here at Conques, like Père André at Bobosc to the east in the Auvergne in the 1920s, spoke the patois and only the patois until the age of six, when they were sent off to school. Then, from that first day in school, they had to begin learning French, and not just studying French but learning everything they were taught in French. If they were caught using even a word of the patois, in the playground at recess or at lunchtime, they were whipped across their hands with a ruler or a switch.

"It was hard! It was *hard!*" Rosalie said with a cry of pain still closely recalled. It hurt so much to have to give up her language, her mother tongue, and to try to learn in the foreign tongue, in French. It must have hurt her, hampered her acutely, physically; and this beautiful, lively, extremely intelligent woman never did learn French very well. When she writes letters in French—and her letters are as alive and natural as her talk—her spelling is often phonetic. When she has to write something official she turns to Monsieur Charlou for help with spelling and grammar.

One day at the fête of Sainte Foy, she said, she saw the nun who was her teacher in Senergues. She had come out from the convent in Rodez with some other nuns for the solemn mass. "I couldn't speak to her," Rosalie said. "She is old now, so it isn't very nice of me, but I can't speak to her, I am not going to speak to her ever. She was *mean!* She was *mean!*" And she said it with the same cry of pain.

Monsieur Charlou, who speaks, according to Mademoiselle Fau, three dialects of the patois, recalls his schooling here at Conques more philosophically. "The schoolmaster struck us across the backs of our hands if we were caught speaking the patois—*even in the playground,*" he said. "He used a ruler or a switch. And it hurt, oh yes, you can be sure, it hurt."

"But that is horrible," I said. "How could he do that? He could not have come from around here."

"Oh, he was *Aveyronnais, sans doute,*" said Charlou, "but he had his orders. He did what he was told to do: he did what he was supposed to do. His orders came from Paris. He had no choice. It is the same thing with the gendarmes. No matter how much they might like you personally, if they received orders from Paris to arrest you, they would have to do so. They would have no choice."

Monsieur Charlou said, "He had no choice" in the same way, adamant, definite, as when he spoke of Monsieur Martin. Monsieur Martin is Spanish, a refugee from Franco's Spain, living at the Maison de Repos, but he has some money. He receives a pension because he worked for the Germans during the war, Monsieur Charlou explained to me. I didn't understand how a refugee from Franco's Spain could work for the Germans. "He had no choice. We were an occupied country," Monsieur Charlou said.

(Monsieur Martin often came to sit at the little table in Rosalie's kitchen by the window. He would sit there drinking a glass of wine as if their kitchen were a café. They would be eating their lunch and Monsieur Martin, having already had his lunch at the Maison, would be drinking. Once he got out an envelope and opened it and showed us a picture of the girl he loved, years ago, before the war. Tears were running down his face. Rosalie twisted her nose when he wasn't looking. Another time he was pounding the table angrily and saying: "When Franco dies . . . when Franco dies . . .")

"Imagine being criticized and punished," Jack says, "for that dear language you learned at your mother's knee."

I will never forget the joy that went through the church on the fête of Sainte Foy when Archbishop Cardinal Marty, who came down from Paris for the day, switched, after a few minutes, as he delivered his sermon, from French into the patois and gave the rest of his sermon in the patois, just as a friend from this country would have if he were talking with them, for he came from Villefranche de Rouergue, and the patois was his mother tongue, too. The delight of these country people—for on the fête day of their saint they come down from the plateau in great numbers, not just from Montignac and St. Marcel, but from all the villages roundabout as far as Sénergues and Espeyrac and Lunel and St. Félix de Lunel, and up from the valley of the Dourdou, from Grand Vabre, from St. Cyprien, and Nauviale, and from La Vinzelle beyond the Lot, and from Viellevie, and Montarnal deep in the valley of the Lot, the old men in their Sunday suits, with their deep-colored, almost purple, weathered faces, and the children, sitting on the stone stairs all the way up to the present-day choir loft in the back of the church as high as the triforium—the delight that emanated from these country people as they listened to the sermon about their holy martyr, Sainte Foy (Sancta Fé) in their village language was expressed in utter stillness and yet was as audible, I imagined, as the rustling of the silken skirts of the Holy Virgin Mary when she appeared first to Saint Catherine Labouré on the night of July 18, 1830, in the church in the Rue du Bac where Madame Benoit went, quite by chance, when as a girl she first went up to Paris to work. (Madame Benoit has told me several times, for it has a special significance for her, how the first church she went into after she arrived in Paris— she was not yet eighteen—was, without her knowing beforehand, that very church in the Rue du Bac where the Blessed Virgin Mary had appeared several times only seventy-five years before.) I was sitting next to Madame Benoit, who had specially brought us as her guests to the mass, *la grande messe* for Sainte Foy, and I could feel her response to Archbishop Marty very warmly and closely. I could feel her delight, her proud satisfaction with every word the archbishop spoke; and her delight, her proud joy and that of the others, filled the air of the church as high as the tribune, as high as the vaulted ceiling arching over. Thinking of Madame Benoit as a child playing the part of an angel in the passion play, descending from the tribune on a rope, bringing the cup to Jesus, and ascending again as Jesus would, too, ascend to heaven in the tribune, I thought the joy Archbishop Cardinal Marty brought them might lift us all as high as the tribune if we hadn't held on to the benches.

For this was their ancient language, the language of a conquered people who had remained conquered and poor, but strong and rich in their culture, their language; this was the language that all authority had endeavored for centuries to wipe out, so it was the language of a kind of natural conspiracy, for it had gone on being transmitted with love, spoken, always spoken, the mother tongue, learned, but never taught in school, and there it was now on the eve of its perhaps dying out (for the young people now and their children no longer speak it), there it was coming from the pulpit at Conques in the year 1979, coming from their archbishop at Paris, their cardinal at Rome. There was their archbishop at Paris, speaking from the pulpit in their own ancient language. Their cardinal was speaking the personal ancient language, which they had been punished for speaking, punished so that they did not, in part for the pain it caused and in part because times had changed, pass on to their children. There was the archbishop, their cardinal, nourished like Père André on the milk of the patois, proudly talking with them in their language here in their abbey church, talking in their language which is the only language other than Latin that is inscribed in their church—on the wall of the sacristy are two rows of frescoes that tell the story of the arrest of Sancta Fé, and her trial by Dacien and her passion and her martyr-death, and her elevation a hundred years after her death by Saint Dulcidius, and accompanying these largely obliterated frescoes there are lines of verse nearly obliterated but clearly written in the patois, the *langue romane,* of the fifteenth century.*

---

*My great authority on this subject, Charles Claude Fauriel, points out in his *History of Provençal Poetry* that Caesar did not realize that two of these languages, those of the Belgae, as Caesar called them, who occupied the land north of the Seine, and those Caesar called the Celts or Gauls, who occupied the land between the Garonne and the Seine, were in fact very closely related languages, whereas the language of the Aquitani, who occupied then the land between the Garonne and the Pyrenees, which we now call Basque, was completely different from the two related Celtic languages and from any other language now surviving on earth. Yet Fauriel found a great many words in the old Provençal that derived from the Aquitani and are exactly the same as certain Basque words to this day, as well as many words that are the same as those in the present-day Breton and Welsh. But the greatest number of words not of Latin origin came into the Romansch, as Fauriel calls it, from the Celtic tongue, which disappeared completely in France but is still spoken in parts of Ireland and Scotland.

It is not known exactly when the original languages of Gaul, amalgamated into the Latin of the Conquerors, dissolved along with the Latin into the Romansch, which would come to be a language of such genius, but it *is* known, by an accidental reference in the Dialogues of Sulpicus Severus on Saint Martin, that at the end of the fourth century the Gallic (or Belgic) and Celtic languages were still spoken by the people of Gaul. "Certainly," replies Postumanius to the man of Gaul who has apologized for his speech, presumably because he does not believe his Latin is sufficiently polished, "speak to us in Celtic or in Gallic, if you prefer it, provided only that you speak of Martin."

And it is known that by the year 813 the *langue romane* of Père André was spoken all over Gaul (or France), for in that year Charlemagne convoked councils of the church,

It is commonly understood that with its harmonious substratum derived from the Latin, this ancient language is the purest, the closest to Latin, of the Romance languages. But it is not so commonly known that whereas the majority of its words derive from the Latin, nevertheless it has preserved thousands of words from the original languages of the people of Gaul, from the Greek of the Phocaeans and those from the Isle of Samos who had settled at Masillia (Marseilles) six hundred years before the Romans conquered Gaul (and whose alphabet was in use in Gaul long before the Romans came), and from the three languages Caesar found when he conquered Gaul.

"And what Caesar says of the people of Gaul still fits us exactly," Jean Sègalat instructs. And then with pleasure he carefully elaborates. "Caesar says that the Gauls are an intelligent and courageous people even though they are braggarts. But they are always ready to make a good meal." Jean Sègalat says this last sentence with enjoyment. "And it's true, too, about the way we brag." He goes along mimicking the way the French brag, all puffed up, boasting.

———

five in all, at Arles, at Mainz, at Rheims, at Châlons on the Saône, and at Tours, for the purpose of reform, and one of the outcomes of these councils was the decision that sermons first composed in Latin be translated into the languages of the people—in some cases into the Frankish language, and in others into the lingua romana of the masses of the ancient inhabitants of these cities. On the death of Charlemagne, in 8 1 4, a poem was written in Latin by a priest or monk, exhorting the people of Gaul to share in his grief and to celebrate the dead monarch in Latin or in the *langue romane*.

The people of Gaul were known by the Romans for their eloquence, and this they brought to the pure Latin tongue, and also, it seems, to the adaptation of the Latin tongue to their own, to the amalgamation that resulted in the Romansch, as Fauriel calls it. He believes that Romansch most probably began to develop in the province of Gallia Narbonesis, which had been under Roman control long before Caesar conquered the rest of Gaul—that a language like the Romansch may have begun to develop among the mass of people there even as the higher classes were still being educated in the schools of rhetoric and grammar and spoke a perfect Latin. This process of taking Latin into their own languages must have spread and been firmly established all over Gaul by the time of the Frankish invasions in the fifth and sixth centuries, for these invasions ended the Latin culture, destroyed the cities and the schools and civilization as it was then known. It is a fact worth noticing that the *langue romane* took almost no words from the Teutonic conquerors. The two languages remained separate, and for the most part those who came deep into Gaul abandoned their own language for the *langue romane* of the people of Gaul.

We are just pushing back our chairs to get up from the table and go off into the evening to see the tympanum when Laurent, one of the most delightful children of the earth, appears at the top of the stairs of the *ruelle* that descends by the wall of our house and jogs to the right at our terrace for a few feet before it turns to continue down by steps.

His tall, sturdy mother has him by the hand, and he is tugging away contrariwise, but nevertheless proceeding step by step down the stone stairs. Even though he is trying with all his infant might to distract or obstruct their steady progress, his face remains the face of a happy cherub—rosy, milky-white, with wavy brownish hair, and large blue eyes with long thick eyelashes.

His mother and he are going down to Rosalie's house to take their bottle of milk from the coffer outside Rosalie's kitchen door. (Each family supplies its own particular bottles to receive the milk of Fleurou and Parisii.)

Laurent has his pacifier in his mouth. His mother, who is quite lovely herself in a sensible natural way—strongly built, olive-skinned, brown-eyed, with short, thick, brown hair—does not intend to pause as she goes by our table, but Laurent pulls out his pacifier and lets out an ebullient roar of greeting.

He knows Jack's secret.

One day when Jack was working, sitting at his table concentrating on painting a black outline, he heard soft footsteps on the stairs and felt someone enter the room behind him. He thought it was me, and that I was waiting for him to finish before I interrupted.

When he finished the line, he turned. And instead of me, there was Laurent standing very still, looking up, his pacifier in his mouth. He must have been awed, I imagine, by the jars of paint, the colors, the mysterious concentration of this big man, taller even than his father, who is the tallest man in Conques.

At the same moment that Jack found Laurent there, he saw the boy's mother out the window beneath the old walnut tree in the Place du Palais. She looked frantic. Jack swooped Laurent up into his arms and went to the window and called out to her.

When I told Rosalie this story, she laughed. "He escapes and he comes down here and walks into the kitchen and says *Ça va?* as if it were perfectly normal for him to be out on his own at his age, going calling."

As we sail off ourselves down the stairs in a state of euphoria we pass, first, the Geneste house, where Dany has caught Lucie up into her glowing olive arms. It is Lucie's bedtime.

At first we thought that Dany and Monsieur Denis were the slightly older parents of this splendid child, but then Rosalie told me, no, they were Lucie's grandparents. Lucie's father is Francis, the youngest son of Denis and Dany, and Lucie's mother, Sylvie was only thirteen when she was born. She was not well. She had tuberculosis and she had to go to stay in the hospital.

We had seen the young people visiting there on vacations. They played with Lucie. "There is one she really grooves with," Jack said. That was Sylvie, Lucie's mother. When the young people went out in the evening they used to crawl by under the window so that Lucie in the kitchen having supper would not see them leaving and set up a howl.

As we go by Dany says to Lucie in her pink pajamas, "Say goodnight to Madame Ahnnah and Monsieur Jacques."

But Lucie won't.

"I wish Dany wouldn't try to make Lucie speak to us," I say when we have passed. "It only makes it worse."

"Little xenophobe," Jack mutters.

The green doors of Rosalie's house are lustrous: she keeps them clean and gives them a fresh coat of green enamel when necessary. Flowering begonias, rose-orange and pink and white, flow out over the brims of their pots on the ledge above the door. A little sign says, "*Chambres à louer,*" rooms for rent.

Only the other day Rosalie was acting up in front of her door, pulling her *casquette,* the front-brimmed soft beige cotton cap to which she is so attached, down over her forehead and doing a dance; and Madame Benoit was calling from her window with the utmost affection for Rosalie and delight in her antics, *"Gamine! Gamine!"* Rosalie was standing right where Clémence Immense, La Femme de Petite Vertu, was standing that day with her skirt lifted in a fetching manner when, according to Rosalie, Madame Benoit called her *"Putain!"* whore, and told her in no uncertain terms to move on.

Now just as we are passing under Madame Benoit's window she leans out with her arms outstretched to catch hold of her shutters and close them for the night.

"Bonsoir, Ahnnah, bonsoir, Jacques, bonne nuit," she says. "I am going to bed now. I will be up at six to prepare myself to go to the early mass. I do the same thing in Paris. I go to bed early, and I rise at six to go to mass. And when I come home in the evening, my son prepares our dinner for us."

"He is a good boy," she said to me another time. "He is very good to me." He was a baker, specializing in *confiserie;* and he is retired now. He writes poems, which he sends to her, and when autumn comes he begins to write letters telling her how much he misses her and how he hopes that she will come home soon to Paris. "My dear little Mama," he writes.

His letters move and delight Madame Benoit. (They are filled with real feeling and they are written with rhetorical flourish.) She is proud of them, and of his poems, but she stays on here yet a little longer—for Sainte Foy, and for her annual pilgrimage to the Virgin at San Damiano, and after her return here, for La Toussaint. Then, one day, when Saint Martin's summer has blown away with the yellow leaves and the cold settles in, she boards the train once more for the warmth of her son's apartment in Paris.

The man who owns the old convent does not live in Conques, and no one lives in the convent now except for Madame Benoit, in the two rooms he lends to her, up one flight of narrow rickety spiral stairs from her door on the street. "Be careful on the stairs," she calls down from her window if I am coming up to visit. Her stairs are as difficult to climb as the narrow stairs in the round tower that lead up to the tribune in the church; and just as one arrives in the tribune to a place of glory, so, in another way, one arrives in her

apartment to a place of calm and wonder which she has permeated
with her spirit.

Her apartment is furnished with the barest of necessities—in
one room a stove, a sink, a kitchen table and a few chairs; in the
other her bed is toward the back, and in the front of the room,
close to the window, is an old walnut desk of the convent, where
she keeps her beloved photographs and pictures and the little white
ivory-like statue of Our Lady of the Roses. Across from the desk
near the window, where she can sit and read her devotions and
think about Our Lady or look on the face of Jesus as it was miraculously preserved on the veil of Saint Veronica, is her *fauteuil,* arm-
chair, as she calls it, with a certain pleased irony.

She bought it one day when we took her to Marcillac with us.
She went to visit an old friend of hers, a nun in the convent at Marcillac, and we went on all the way into Rodez and picked her up on
our return. She was waiting for us at the *quincaillerie,* hardware
store, on the road through Marcillac, and the man who owned the
store had given her a canvas chair to sit in while she waited. She
liked the chair so much that when we got there, she bought it, and
we took it home to Conques in the car.

"It was agreeable and so she bought it!" said the man who owned
the *quincaillerie,* all wreathed in smiles of delight over the event, ex-
pressing the wonder and surprise of it with his hands, his arms.

Madame Benoit lined it with soft white pillows, which she has put
into clean white pillow slips with lacy edges, and she sits in it, sometimes with her feet up on a cushioned footstool, and her electric
heater glowing red to keep herself warm; but if I come in, she insists
that I sit in her *fauteuil,* and she sits in a straight chair next to me.
Then her *fauteuil* seems to me to be the softest, most comforting
place on earth to be sitting. I feel a rush of warmth and the sweetness of her breath as she tells me things in her low, intimate voice,
talking very rapidly. "We are talking like good friends," she says.

When Madame Benoit was seventeen, she went up to Paris to
work, to be the maid and the nurse for a boy named Étienne in the
house of a *notaire.* She stayed there two years, and when she came
home to Conques Étienne was looking for her everywhere, running in his garden calling, "Émilie, Émilie."

Madame Benoit laughed and imitated Étienne's childish voice, "Émilie, Émilie," and she showed how he looked under a bench, behind a tree, behind a curtain in the house.

A young man, Antoine Benoit, who had come up from the Auvergne to study with the *notaire* and work to become a *notaire* himself, wrote to Madame Benoit when she was gone.* (In his heart Antoine Benoit must have missed her just as much as Étienne.) "And I replied to his letter," Madame Benoit said. "I told him that if he thought I was just a peasant girl he could play around with, that he should not write to me again. 'But if you are interested in marriage,' I said, 'we may correspond.' He replied that he wanted to marry me. We were married here in the church. The three main events of my life all will have taken place in the abbey church Sainte Foy de Conques—my baptism, my marriage, and in the end my funeral.

"We were married here at Conques and exactly nine months and ten days after our wedding, my first daughter, Germaine Foy, was born. My husband loved her. He loved her so much. He escaped death in the war, the First World War," she said. "But afterwards, during the time he was studying to pass his exams to become a *notaire,* he contracted tuberculosis. He passed his exams, he would have had a fine career, I nursed him, I did everything I could, but he died in 1921. There were five children by that time. I was thirty-three. My youngest child, a baby boy, died that same year of the same illness, and later my oldest daughter, Germaine Foy. She too had tuberculosis. Her father loved her so much. I thought she had a chance, that she might pull through, but when she said one evening, 'Papa was here just now, Mama, Papa was here,' I knew then that she would die. 'Papa came in the door, Mama. He took my hand,' she said. Two days later she was dead. She was just fifteen." Tears

_____

*"He would have been a *notaire,*" Madame Fabre said to me once, emphasizing *notaire* with reverence. It should be noted that in France *notaires* are very powerful and respected people. In rural communities, as Laurence Wylie points out in *Village in the Vaucluse,* they stand next to the mayor in rank. They are lawyers, but they are more than lawyers; they are officials who are lawyer, broker, banker, and recorder of deeds. They preside over every exchange of property, representing both the seller and the buyer, and they receive a percentage of the price of each sale. They are thus extremely well off. They are addressed and referred to as *Maître,* Master.

were running down Madame Benoit's face. "Her father loved her so," she said. "I gave her up to the Lord to be with her father in heaven.

"It hasn't been an easy life," she said. "People thought that with so much grief and tragedy I would lose my faith. But *au contraire,*" she said proudly. "I had to strengthen my faith. I went to work in the Bureau of the Archives of Paris, and I became head, eventually, of the Office of Information. I had many offers of marriage, very good offers, too, but I preferred my independence. I had three children to bring up. I worked. And Sundays I devoted to my family and to the Virgin Mary.

"There she is," Madame Benoit said, pointing to the photograph of her daughter, Germaine Foy. "There she is in her First Communion dress. And there is her father." She pointed to the photographs of the clear-eyed young man with his dark mustache, handsome and grave, looking out from across the years.

"And the Virgin Mary appeared to you in a vision!" I asked Madame Benoit on another visit.

"How did you know?" she asked.

"You told me," I said, "but I wanted to hear again how it was."

"It was at San Damiano when I went there the first time," she said. "The Virgin Mary was in the garden, sitting on a bench, her head like this." Madame Benoit showed me how the Blessed Virgin Mary had been sitting, her head slightly bowed. "She did not speak, her head remained bowed slightly that way. Her lips were moving in prayer. At first I thought she was old, but then coming closer I saw how young she was—eighteen or nineteen years, and of a beauty that is indescribable. She had delicate, very fine features, a thin mouth, a perfect nose. She was a little like this statue." Madame Benoit picked up the small ivory statue of the Virgin of San Damiano, the Madonna of the Roses; she kissed it and set it down again. "She was a little like that around the mouth and chin. And yet not . . . Her eyes were cast down in prayer. And she was dressed . . . I have never seen anything like it . . . she wore a hat"—Madame Benoit circled its shape on her head—"and the hat was wrapped round with a veil of cloth, the cloth that covered her head . . . it was as if it were a cloth of blue woven through with gold, and yet the richness was such it is impossible to describe . . . not something such as you or I have ever seen . . . like that of a noblewoman of another time, another place. Her skin was pale and very beautiful. Her eyes remained cast down; she continued her prayers all the while. Standing beside her was a man. He was big. Big and strong. Like Hercules. His head was enormous. It was like a ball and very dark. He had hair like this." Madame Benoit put her hands up to her head and moved them very rapidly. "Frizzy! Frizzy! Frizzy!" she said. "They say it was probably Saint Michael I saw with her."

"France is under the protection of Saint Michael," she added in parenthesis, in the same way that she once said, "France is consecrated to the Virgin Mary. May is her month."

One afternoon I met Madame Benoit when our gas had run out. I was going down to Francis's café for a coffee and she invited me to come up to her apartment instead. Not thinking, I walked faster than she. "Your legs are longer than mine," she said. I am five feet nine. She can't be more than five feet tall.

She had a passport-sized photograph of a nun tucked into the corner of her framed portrait of Jesus, not the holy image from the veil of Saint Veronica, but a conventional portrait. She said it was her niece who is a nun in Africa, in the Ivory Coast. "My darling niece, Jacqueline," Madame Benoit said. "Like me she is an *Esclave de Marie.*"

Madame Benoit dusted out some lovely china cups with a towel and warmed the coffee in one of the heavy enameled pans that Rosalie sells. She brought out the lumps of sugar she keeps in a tin box to protect them from the ants, and then the bread of St. Cyprien, which she dunked in her coffee. She told me to do the same. The Conquois all agree that the bread of St. Cyprien is superior to that of Conques, but they conceal their rare purchases of that bread from the bakery here.

"All my life I have been dedicated to the Virgin Mary," Madame Benoit said. "My daughter Ginette—her name was Geneviève but we called her Ginette, my daughter Ginette was like me in this. We were equal in our faith, my Ginette and I. Oh, she was lovely, and she was good. And then when she was only thirty she died. . . . Her husband was still young, too—and he did not marry again for a very long time. There were the little children, and after a long time, I don't remember, but it must have been four or five years, I told him that I thought he ought to remarry. He said, 'I know that I should, but I will never be able to find a wife like my Ginette.'

"Oh, she was so lovely, and she was so good, my Ginette," said Madame Benoit. "Finally he did remarry, and it was a good thing. It worked out very well. After all, there were the children."

The first time Jack and I came to visit Madame Benoit in her apartment, she invited us to come for tea. She served us vervain tea and offered us cookies. After a while she gave us some *vin de noix*— sweet, black-brown *vin de noix*.

Charlou's hands are black in July when he makes the *vin de noix*. The walnuts are picked between the first and the tenth of July when they are still green, Rosalie explained to me. You take forty walnuts and remove the outer shells and cut them into four or six pieces and put them into a large crockery jar with four liters of red wine and one liter of *eau de vie* and half a kilo of sugar. You let this mixture remain in the jar for forty days.

The picking of the green nuts should be timed so that the moon will be old at the end of forty days, when you throw out the nuts and pour the mixture through a filter into bottles, for if the moon is waning, the mixture will become clear more quickly. You should let the bottles stand in darkness for six months. Wait until Christmas to taste it. If you wait several years before you drink it, it will be better still. It is good for the digestion—as an aperitif or as a digestif—and also you can use it to season melons. *Melon au vin de noix* is what you find in Aveyron in place of *melon au Porto*.

The *vin de noix* that Madame Benoit offered us was in an old bottle. I asked her if Madame Fabre had made it. "Oh, no, not Madame Fabre," she said. "Rosalie gave me this *vin de noix*."

And, she added after a moment, "Madame Fabre was ruined by the war."

Later I asked Rosalie what Madame Benoit had meant by that remark. Rosalie's reply was "*Attention!* They are cousins."

Madame Benoit said, "When the Germans came to occupy Aveyron they went right by Conques on the road down there by the Dourdou. They stopped. They looked up here. Then they decided not to try it. They went on down the road to Rodez." She fell silent, thinking. At length she said, "They are different in Rodez, different from us . . . they are bourgeois."

In Rodez on that afternoon Madame Cannes was a girl of nine. She was taking her violin lesson, which she hated. "I hated my violin, I hated my violin teacher," she said. When the Germans came to take over the hotel her father owned right there on the Place d'Armes in the center of town, one soldier took her violin and broke it in half, then smashed it. "Secretly," she said, "at this moment, I thought happily: No more violin lessons.

"Another soldier in his big heavy boots got up on the piano and walked on it, and smashed all the keys." She was very frightened and at the same moment, happy, she said, because again she thought it would be the end of her violin lessons. But she and her mother were kept in the hotel as hostages because the Germans knew that if women and children were there, the Maquis would not try to blow it up. And not more than a week later her violin teacher showed up with another violin.

Mademoiselle Fau (who was a young woman in her thirties then) had gone out with her mother. There had been no warning. November 11, 1942, between two and three o'clock. They saw the Germans coming, the tanks and the armored vehicles, the red flags with the black swastikas, coming up the Rue Breteuil. "The terror, the horror," she said. There was no escaping this time.

There was an Israelite family, she told us, who lived in the old bishop's palace behind the cathedral. She told us this when she took us with her for a walk one winter day in Rodez. "The Germans came and battered down the gate, this gate," she said, walking up to it. "The Germans took them, throwing the mother into one truck, and her baby into another . . . the horror of it," she said, wailing as she spoke.

Here at Conques two Jewish families from Belgium lived in the Hôtel Sainte Foy, protected all through the war.

But the Germans were not unaware of the Treasure and the statue of Sainte Foy. Count von Metternich came to Conques and quietly advised the curé to hide everything away as safely and as quickly as he could, deep in the underground recesses of the abbey; at the same time, von Metternich reported to Hitler that the Treasure was in such a pitiful state of deterioration that there was no reason to bother about it. For his efforts to save Sainte Foy, and no doubt, for other similar noble acts of bravery, Count von Metternich died in a concentration camp before the war was ended. But he had saved Sainte Foy.

And she, in turn, helped to save the member of the Resistance who was denounced by Madame Coué. Madame Coué went all the way into Rodez to the office of the *préfet* to denounce him. No one has ever explained to me what was behind her act.

"Monsieur Coste, he was not from here," Monsieur Charlou said. "He was Toulousian. An educated man. An engineer. He was in charge of road building for the department. He was in the Resistance, the Maquis. He was . . . he wasn't setting off bombs or anything like that."

But Madame Coué made a special trip into Rodez to report on him. By good fortune there was someone working in the office of the *préfet* who was himself a member of the Resistance, and he was able to get word quickly to Monsieur Coste. By the time the soldiers arrived, he was hidden in the attic of a cousin of Monsieur Charlou's, a woman no one would ever have suspected. He had to remain there in the *grenier,* hidden, for more than two years. He couldn't go out. He couldn't be seen. The house was almost directly across from Madame Coué's. Once something was suspected. A window was seen open. But the danger passed.

After the war Madame Coué went to prison for a time for her treachery and Monsieur Coste bought a house in Conques hanging out over the valley of the Ouche, high above the church, and with his wife and family, he spent his summers here. He was a good friend of Monsieur Lapeyre's from the war, and that is how Monsieur Lapeyre came to buy his ruin on the Rue Charlemagne and rebuild it after the war for his family's holidays.

"And Monsieur Coste had his revenge," Rosalie said. "When the rocade was built after the war, and the road that went up to Fontromieu by way of *les rochers,* the road ran right through the Coué family vineyard!"

Now from her window Madame Benoit says once more, *"Bonne nuit, mes enfants,"* and as she catches hold of the shutters and begins to close them, her arms and hands look like wings. With her round face and her blue eyes and her soft wavy hair, she looks like one of the winged cherubim in the reredos above the altar of Sainte Foy, except that she in her nineties is all white and blue.

Her shutters close, and in the shadows of her room, the face of her young husband looks out, and her daughter Germaine Foy stands dim in her First Communion dress. The holy image of Jesus from the veil of Saint Veronica retains its mysterious presence as she picks up the statue of Our Lady and kisses it, her lips young and soft and childlike, and then she goes over to her bed and kneels down to pray.

In the morning before she goes into the church she will pause as she always does, and take out a scarf to cover her head. "I believe in the old discipline," she told me once, as she did this. "The Virgin Mary always appears with her head covered."

When mass is ended and Père André has gone to pray in the chapel of Sainte Foy, Madame Benoit and the women of Conques will linger in the chapel of the Virgin Mary and begin to say their rosaries aloud together as the Virgin Mary requested. They pray, saying their *Pater Nosters* and their *Ave Marias,* their *Glorias* and their *Ave Marias* again and again, moving their fingers along their beads in decades as, their voices all in unison, they meditate on the mysteries, the joyful, the sorrowful, and the glorious.

The Church may not approve of their doing this, but then Madame Benoit's favorite miracle is the Miracle of the Open Doors. I have heard her cite this miracle a number of times with pride because of the point it makes. She tells the story in her low voice in her intimate way, getting swiftly to its triumphant moral— from her point of view, which is wholeheartedly that of her forebears who came thronging to the doors of the church on the night of the vigil of the Fête of Sainte Foy a thousand years ago, only to find themselves barred from entering on account of the scruples of the learned monks, who had decided (quite mistakenly as it turned out) that the behavior of the country people in the church on these occasions was a profanation of the holy vigils.

Bernard of Angers tells the story charmingly too, but from his
point of view, which is that of the learned churchman who learned
something about God and His feeling for His people from the miracle He worked that night. For Bernard the Miracle of the Open
Doors is an occasion for meditation. And artfully, too, he includes
details that describe aspects of life peculiar to Conques, and by im-
plication, to this whole remote region of the Rouergue and of the
neighboring countries of the Auvergne and of Toulouse, details that
needed to be explained to his readers in the north: Bishop Fulbert
at Chartres and his former fellow students there at Chartres, as
well as his colleagues at Angers and elsewhere.

It is the twelfth chapter of the second *Book of the Miracles of Sainte
Foy,* and it goes this way:

> Following an ancient custom, the pilgrims come well sup-
> plied with candles and with torches to celebrate the vigils in the
> church of Sainte Foy. During this time the clerks and men of let-
> ters sing the psalms and the offices of the vigil, while the unlet-
> tered people, on their side, sing their country ballads and engage
> in other frivolities of this sort to fight off fatigue and while away
> the long night hours.
>
> This behavior seemed to me to be a shocking profanation of
> the holy vigils, and I did not miss the chance to stand up and
> speak very strongly against this absurd and intolerable practice at
> the chapter meeting of the monks. I even went on to use all sorts
> of arguments to prove that it should be repressed without hesi-
> tation.
>
> To my great surprise, when I had finished, the monks
> protested. They said that this custom was both legitimate and
> praiseworthy; and they said that it had indeed been sanctioned
> by the approval of heaven: to attempt to abolish it would be
> against the will of God.
>
> Then the Abbot [Adalgerius] himself spoke, explaining: "From
> the time of the valiant Gimon, of whom you have already heard,
> the superiors of the monastery tried many times and with great
> strictness to forbid these tumultuous songs, these plaintive bal-
> lads, and the shrill wild cries of the peasants, for they were
> thought unworthy of a holy place. Yet they were unable to suc-
> ceed in putting a stop to this behavior. Finally, according to the

unanimous decision of the monks, it was resolved that the doors of the church should be closed in the evening and that the people would no longer be admitted to the holy vigils. This measure was adopted. The command was executed. The doors of the church were locked and barred; no one was admitted into the church during the night.

"For a time the interdiction was successful. But then, one evening after supper, a multitude of pilgrims, more numerous than was customary, all well supplied with candles and *flambeaux,* came to besiege the very portals of the church. They pushed at the doors and made a great clamor, shouting and demanding entrance into the holy shrine. We refused absolutely, according to our firmly established principles, to open the church to them.

"However, a little later on, while we slept, all of a sudden, without any impulsion on their part—the pilgrims had retired a little distance from the doors themselves—to their amazement, the bars that held the doors shut and locked fell, and the doors rolled open on their hinges of their own accord. Then even the interior gates of iron, which are always locked for the greater security of the relics in the sanctuary, even these gates opened by themselves. These gates, which protect the relics, are never opened except by a single guardian, and no one is ever admitted save those persons considered worthy of this favor.

"At midnight when we arose to chant the matins, we found the church filled with such a multitude of pilgrims celebrating the holy vigil that we could only with great difficulty make our way through the throng to our places. We were in a state of the most extreme astonishment, for we had all the keys in our hands. We asked them what violent means they had employed to gain their entrance, and then they told us of the miracle that had occurred. The miracle was attested to unanimously by the whole multitude of pilgrims. We could not refuse our compliance, for surely it was the will of God that the doors of the church be opened to the people, and the fervent desire of Sainte Foy.

"This miracle occurred before that of Guibert the Illuminé," the abbot concluded. "I bore witness to it as a child in the abbey school, and today, advanced as I am in age, I admire it still."

"I see now most certainly how this miracle can be considered a manifestation of the divine will," I responded. "On reflecting on all this, I see too that one can tolerate these lays, rustic but innocent, which the peasants sing with such naive simplicity. Perhaps if one were to repress this custom one would carry out a grave attack against pilgrimage itself. I do not want to say that God is worthily honored by these plaintive ballads but that what honors Him is the penitence of the holy vigils and the honesty of these simple souls. It is thus that long ago the Israelites were permitted by God to burn animals in sacrifice in imitation of the idolaters; it was necessary only that their sacrifice be offered to the true God and not to any false divinity, and that their hearts, cleansed by God, sing forth His praises. God tolerated these uncouth rites and ceremonies provided they were addressed to Him. If there are those who consider themselves wiser than I, and do not hold to this opinion, I advise them to be on their guard that in the lofty speculations of their superior knowledge, they do not find themselves in opposition to the feeling of God Himself. It is not that God asks for these simple songs to be sung to honor Him, it is rather that He is an understanding father filled with pity for the weakness and the ignorance of his children. He knows the fragility of their nature, and far from looking for something to condemn in them, He searches in the heart of the sinner to find the root of salvation."

This answer, which had no merit other than the simplicity of my feeble knowledge, contributed, however, most effectively to reassure those among the monks who still felt some scruples about tolerating this practice. Thus the roles were changed. I had begun with words against this: it was I who went into combat with my own arms and I was vanquished in the combat. Incensed as I had been, I had the temerity to appreciate the goodness of God and the limits of the human intellect.

As we go down the steep narrow passageway beside Rosalie's house, I remember climbing up through here once with Madame Benoit in the evening after a concert. It was raining and Jack and I were holding our huge umbrella over her. She moved to the side so her feet could catch onto the rough schist-rock stones. She stopped and tapped them with her cane. "Those are the original stones of the pavement," she said. The narrow slabs of schist rock had been set deep on their edges so the surface is ridged and rough and gives the feet something to grab on to in wet or icy weather. "These are the original stones of Conques. Not these." She tapped the smooth flat stones in the center. "And not those." She pointed with her cane to the rounded rocks in the Place du Château. "The Beaux-Arts had those installed," she said. (They are much too slippery to walk down when it rains.) "Those stones come from the Lot," she said. "They are not as good as these. These are the rock of Conques." She tapped them with proud satisfaction. When we reached her door she said, "I am saved!" The rain dripped down around us as we each kissed her good-night beneath our umbrella.

Now on this June evening Jack and I have come right down the steep smooth rocks in the center of the *ruelle;* and as we emerge on the lower part of the Place du Château, our eyes are caught for a moment by the vine-covered balcony of the apartment Madame Castelbou rents out—opposite Charlou's *cave* on the Place du Château. No one is there; the balcony is empty, the kitchen behind it with its glass French doors is not lit.

We turn left and continue our descent more gradually. Then, where the glossy thick-leaved branches of the magnolia tree behind the Monument to the War Dead stretch out over us, we stop, arrested by the empty window looking out from the apartment just above us, where Jean Sègalat lived with his beloved Emanuelle that summertime, those autumn weeks, when they were together here in Conques.

It is almost unconsciously that we are compelled to stop here beneath their window, to look up and think of our friend and to feel the cold and dusty emptiness of the room within, for no one has come to live here since Emanuelle's suicide.

"She was *folle,*" said the wife of an old friend of Jean's, a friend since the days of his childhood in Decazeville. She repeated that Emanuelle was mad; "She was not the woman for him."

And yet she *was* the woman for him—the last, the only, the one he would die for.

She had been rash, others said. She had burned her bridges. She had run off to be with Jean, but still her husband would not give her a divorce. Perhaps it was that . . . she was distraught. . . . There was a certain amount of scandal, of course, so perhaps it was that . . . unhappiness . . . anger . . . confusion . . .

Should she have? Despair was eating at her heart when there should have been the pure summer bliss of love. He loved her well, she knew, but she felt empty, detached; she began to think that living with Jean Sègalat, loving him, wasn't what she wanted after all.

She was impulsive . . . impetuous. She had been drinking, so perhaps she hadn't intended . . . like a child playing with fire . . . perhaps . . .

She stood before the mirror in the bathroom stuffing the pills into her pretty mouth and swallowing them, drunk and sad and all alone, hating God the Father.

"He nurtures his sorrow," Mademoiselle Fau said. "He cannot forgive himself."

"She never would tell me," Jean said when we three had become close. "She never would tell me what she wished for when we lit our candles together at the altar of Sainte Foy."

The summer after Emanuelle's death, Jean came back to Conques, and he opened the gallery that was going to be for her. He gave the gallery her name, and day after day, as he does still, he sat there in the dim *cave* of Monsieur Bousquet's house, the Galerie Emanuelle, working at his ink drawings, and minding the gallery as well.

The two Cannes brothers and Madame Cannes took him in. They gave him a room up the street in the annex of the hotel where he could sleep; and he used to eat with them at the hotel, in the kitchen with the staff, and then he'd help out around the bar a bit in the evening. He was doing that still the first summer we came to stay in Conques.

"Madame Cannes was so kind to her, *mon amie*," he told me once, his voice changing into that tender breaking tone it took on whenever he mentioned her, always calling her *mon amie*.

Then around ten or ten-thirty that first summer of his bereavement, when the hotel closed and nearly all the households in Conques had closed their shutters and gone to bed, Jean would leave the hotel and go down to look at the tympanum before he went home to the annex for the night.

We know this from Sandra and William, our Australian friends, who had rented Madame Castelbou's apartment that year. They used to see him each night from the shadows of the balcony where, the children put to bed, they sat talking quietly outside their kitchen on the Place du Château. They said that always on his way down to the tympanum Jean came up the cobblestone street by the Monument to the War Dead; he advanced a few steps and then stood there under the branches of the magnolia tree looking up at the window of the apartment where he and Emanuelle had lived the summer before.

(The window was not shuttered in the summer, then as now, and inside, beyond the glass, in the dark, the furniture stood, the lamps and the mirrors, arranged exactly as they had been ten months before when, in the night, while he slept so near, his beloved Emanuelle, was dead by her own hand of her own will.)

Every night, we were told, Jean would stand there a long time, looking up at that window, and then he would turn and go down to the tympanum.

But one night after he had stood there a spell in silence he went suddenly up the stairs to the door of their apartment and he knocked at the door.

He knocked at the door again.

For an instant, I imagined, it had seemed to him he had seen the light of her face inside beyond the window. Then she seemed to be moving away deeper into the room in the direction of the door. He went up. He knocked at the door. He tried the handle. He knocked again. He would have gone like Orpheus into the other world, the underworld, to reach her if he could have, to bring her back or stay with her there. But the earth was closed, the door was locked. He knocked wildly one last time and turned and rushed blindly down to the parvis before the church.

As Jean looked up through his tears into the face of Jesus Christ, all the manifold beauties of the tympanum, its myriad details and persons under the one arc of heaven and earth and hell, swirled, blurring around the Christ enthroned, who seemed to come forward closer, looking deep into his eyes.

"Blessed are they that mourn: for they shall be comforted."

It was after this, I believe, that Jean Sègalat formulated his vow.
In the chapel of Sainte Foy as his candle burned with other ex-votos
on the forged iron candlestand, he vowed that he would pray for
Emanuelle's soul, that he would offer a mass for her soul each
month in honor of Sainte Foy; he vowed that he would remain faithful to her, Emanuelle, unto death, and devote himself monastically
to Sainte Foy, to Conques, to his work, his art, and to the memory
of the woman he had loved unto death. And he promised in prayer
that his beard, which he would grow when winter came, would be
the sign of this vow: he would do his work and bide his time and live
out the years that would be left to him as best he could—which, as
it turned out, he would do very well because of his faith, his talent,
his self-control, his work, his art, which occupied him always, continually, intensely, intricately, with his varying subjects, his inter-
ests, his intellect, his love of reading, of poetry, of literature, of
Conques, of Sainte Foy. And though he nurtured his grief so that it
flowed into his art and gave the distinctive flavor to his life on earth
during his last years, he had an innate zest for life, a delight in all
sorts of things, love for his friends and for a good meal, and for the
charm and femininity of certain women, to whom his attentions
should remain courtly, not more, and most of all, love for his
daughter, "ma Jeanne," for she always had a special place in his
heart. And then he took such pride in his little grandson, who
would in time be born, little Jean-Baptiste, who by the age of
four, when he was asked who the great artists were, would reply,
"Well, there is Michelangelo, and there is Picasso, and then there
is Grand-Père," the Grand-Père would report with bemused
pleasure.

Before the altar of Sainte Foy Jean Sègalat formulated his vow,
and said, So be it. And so it would be, for his heart would never
heal, though he would go bravely on, a gentleman, riding like a
knight on his high horse, bearing his inflicted wound of love, which
no one but his beloved could heal.

Once when we came back one year, I thought that Jean was bet-
ter. I told that to old Madame Toux, the retired schoolteacher from
Grenoble who came to stay each summer in the house on the Rue
Charlemagne that Madame La Combe rented out to her.

Madame Toux said, wailing, "No, no, he is not better. Not better," she repeated, wailing in her pained sympathy.

Jack saw that moment when Jean went up to knock at the door differently than I had (more movingly and touchingly, I think), but both of us thought that his beard, his decision to grow it, came from his shocked awareness of the hopeless irrationality of that knocking at the door, of its pathetic futility, and that his beard was the sign of his resignation, of his commitment—to fate, to the will of God.

Jack thought that as Jean stood before the door on that night it seemed to him suddenly that it had not happened, that it had all been like a bad dream, that time had rolled back and it was still the previous summer, when they were together; and that if he went up to knock, she would answer and let him in, and she would be there as she always was, and their evening of endearments would begin; and they would have a late supper, and he would look on her dear face, as he always had, and hear the things she had to say, this enchanting creature he had come to love—so appealing, so feminine, so charming, impulsive (though, it was true, not sensible, not stable, not strong), but she was mysterious, and between their bodies there was that sweet passion, that white fire of love, that flesh moisture more fragrant than dew on flowers. She was soft and slight of build, as warm as gold and smooth as silver; and her face, her face with the high rounded forehead, the thin lips, the eyes all modest when they were downcast, the long nose—she looked, Emanuelle did, like Sainte Foy, like the fifteenth-century statuette of Sainte Foy in silver and gilded silver that stands in the Treasure.

He knocked on the door. But it was not last summer. Ten months had passed since she lay dead in their sheets. She was buried in her family's vault in the cemetery of Saint Roch, over on the mountain above the bridge that spans the Lot at Livinhac, near Decazeville.

"She had a very distinctive face, you know," said Mademoiselle Fau. "You see it emerge again and again in his work, white amid the tones of gray. He even wanted to put her in Jean-Claude's book." The very thought of this seemed to make Mademoiselle Fau angry. "He is limited," she said.

I had assumed it was simply Sainte Foy in Jean's ink drawings and lithographs until the first time we went to his house in Decazeville,

and I saw the photograph of Emanuelle on his desk there—
Emanuelle standing by the rose trellis just outside their gallery,
three roses blooming beside her. With a shock of recognition I saw
that her face was the face of the statuette of Sainte Foy in silver and
gilded silver made by the brothers Huc and Lanfranc at Villefranche
de Rouergue in 1495.

She had the same high, wide forehead, the same long nose, lips,
and full cheeks. She had inherited the features of that young girl
who had stood as a model for the statuette in 1495 with her long
fragrant hair and her eyes downcast, holding the grill, the instrument of Sainte Foy's torture, the sword with which Sainte Foy was
beheaded, and the palm of her victorious martyrdom; she stood in
rich robes, that young girl, to be modeled, and she lent her loveliness as well to the figure of Sainte Foy on the reverse face of the
great processional cross made at Villefranche de Rouergue in those
same years. In time she would have grown to womanhood and married and had children; and those genes that came to form her face
and character were passed on down through the centuries to
emerge in the face of our Jean Sègalat's Emanuelle, even as our
Charlou has so clearly the face of the Virgin Mary in the tympanum;
and the young mason Jerome Florent, who went off to Paris to
study at the École des Beaux-Arts but then returned here to be a
mason (with a gift for painting), has the face of Jesus in the tympanum, he has his nose; clearly he descends from that young man who
in the twelfth century was chosen to sit for Jesus as He would be
when He would come again on the last day in time.

I did not know it for a long time, but it turns out that it is a big
joke in Conques that holier-than-thou Madame Norlorgue looks
exactly like the adulteress in the tympanum, standing in hell, her
breasts exposed, with her lover the monk, the two of them still
bathed in pleasure, absolutely unaware of their whereabouts and
that the snake of the devil's penis is about to get them, and that her
lover's hands are already bound with handcuffs.

How wonderful to live in a place where the artists of past centuries shaped and preserved in their art, in both noble and ignoble
roles, the faces we see still engaged in the tasks and pleasures of
everyday life, passing into the church for mass on Sunday, for a fu-

neral or a wedding or a baptism, under the eyes of the Christ, who looked down from His mandorla in Heaven on their ancestors in the twelfth century and from then through the generations.

"She is a daughter of *chez-nous*," said the guardian at the Musée Fenaille looking with love and awe at the fifteenth-century Virgin of the Pietà. And at Albi, on their way to see us, friends who stopped off there to visit the cathedral saw the faces of the angels in the cathedral in the train station afterward. Angels, angels everywhere, walking hither and thither and waiting in the train station at Albi.

So Jean Sègalat, in putting the dear, remembered face of his beloved, which was as well the face of the Sainte Foy of the late fifteenth century, into his work, and in dressing her in the fringed tunic, the ribboned slippers, the little crown of the wax figure of Sainte Foy that lies beneath the altar in her chapel, hidden from view for most of the year, and giving his Sainte Foy, too, the little wand that the wax figure of Sainte Foy holds in her death-sleep, is only, in his distinctive way, carrying on the artistic tradition of this country. Even if he blended in his mind the virgin martyr and the lady who with her dying broke his heart, is that not a natural part of the mystery of creation—with a gallant sort of troubadour twist?

As Peter Dronke writes in *Medieval Latin and the Rise of the European Love Lyric*: "This more than human, angelic or divine power always had that relation to the human mind which the beloved has to her lover in the courtly experience—to be above him, to shed her light upon him, thereby actualizing his innate potential virtue, to raise him towards herself and thereby to perfect him, granting him a share, as far as he is capable of it, in her immortal and blessed state, to allow him to apprehend the divine through her—this is the paradigm, whether the language is metaphysics or love."

In the evening air we proceed past the war monument to the children of Conques who died for France, and we go up the main street, rue Père Marie-Bernard, between the Hôtel Sainte Foy and the Fallières' *journaux-tabac* to the Fallières' gum-ball machine at the corner of their building.

It is part of our evening ritual. Jack puts in a twenty-centime piece and out comes a ball of gum. The question is which color will it be. If Rosalie were with us she would say, "Green! *Jaloux!* Jealous, *Jaloux,* Monsieur Jack!" Or she would say, "Yellow, *l'amour. L'amour.*"

Tonight Jack is just pushing in the coin when Zée-Zée comes running full tilt down the path from the bar entrance to the hotel and out into the street. "Ahh, *souffle, souffle,*" he says, breathing in and looking up at the sky with his arms held out.

He shakes his head, laughing. *"Comme un gosse!"* Like a kid, he says.

Jack loves to imitate Zée-Zée doing "Ahh, *souffle, ahh, souffle.*" Zée-Zée is a real out-of-doors man, and the tension of being trapped indoors in the hotel for any length of time is too much for him. He escapes like this from time to time in the course of the evening, walks up the hill for a minute or two, breathing, breathing, and then he goes back in. During the mornings he is in and out, carrying the wet laundry in baskets up to the drying barn and hanging it up and returning for more. In the afternoon, even if he just has an hour free, he drives the hotel jeep up to the plateau and parks it near Bourrious and then he walks along the plateau in his shorts, barefoot and with his shirt off, suntanning himself, and breathing.

Like Jean Sègalat he had tuberculosis when he was young (I do not know if, like Jean, he had to have a lung taken out), and it may have made him particularly conscious of breathing. Both he and Jean must have been exempted from *travail obligatoire* in Germany because of their TB. When people ask Zée-Zée what he did during the war he says, "Oh, I did a little the Maquis." Jean has never been strong physically, I think, but Zée-Zée seems to have rebuilt his physical health. With his deep voice and his lean, graceful body, walking, looking out and up, breathing in the air and the fields and the woods and the sky, he is the very picture of health. He waits during the "season," when the hotel is open and very busy, for the fall, when it closes, for November, his favorite month, when he walks, walks all day, he says, from here up to Lunel, and back by way of Montigac. *"Belle saison,"* he says rapturously when November comes and he can go out all day into the autumn air among the yellow leaves.

Belle saison!

Zée-Zée walks on up the street. Sègalat's gallery is closed for the evening, and he is, no doubt, off somewhere dining. Jack is chewing a red gum ball. Before we start down the stairs to the church, we look up at the tall witch's hat of a slate roof that crowns the fourteenth-century octagonal bell tower with its two tiers of Romanesque arched windows, the upper tier of hooded latticed windows protecting the bells, and the lower the stained-glass windows that filter golden light into the lantern tower within the church.

"You see how really close to the bells Jean is when he's in his gallery," I say to Jack. "And to the town bell, too." We can see the town bell as well from here in its open ironwork tower on top of Maité the *percepteur's* house.

It was because of the bells and their effect on Jean that our friendship took a wonderful swing upward to a new level of intimacy.

One day toward the end of one summer I went by to see him at the gallery and found him in a state of terrible exasperation with the bells, the bells, the bells, and the continual interruptions of the tourists who came into his gallery. He told me he had had it up to here. He made a violent gesture across his neck as if to cut off his head. He said he was looking forward to the fall, to tranquillity, to time for his work. "The tourists are the *fléau,* the pests, of Conques," he said.

He asked me if I realized exactly how many times the bells rang each and every day. He gave me the figure and added that the figure, of course, did not include the bells that ring for the *grande messe* on Sunday, the bells that ring for weddings and baptisms and funerals, and the bells that toll, when someone has died, after each Angelus, morning, noontime, and evening, from the hour of death until the hour of burial.

He had given me the exact figure of the daily ringing of the bells, but I had not written it down, and so I came back to ask him because I wanted to have it right, but also because, as he began to suspect in the course of my visit, I wanted to hear him tell it all to me again.

"Count them," he said somewhat sternly when I asked him to tell me again how many times the bells ring each day. He spoke as if I should have to work a little to get the figure he had arrived at with such pain and irritation.

"The town bells ring each hour twice, and ring once on the half hour," he said.

"Then the town bells ring 336 times each day," I figured.

"There is the call to mass at seven-fifteen," he said. "And then at seven-thirty the Angelus. The Angelus has nine blows of call, three times repeated; there are ninety-five rings for each Angelus, and the Angelus rings three times each day."

He did not give me the figure, but left it for me to calculate. "Thus far," I told him, "counting the town bells, it comes to 621 rings, not counting the number of times the church bell rings at seven-fifteen to call the people to the early mass."

Suddenly Jean looked at me smiling. "Ahh, Anne, are you putting me in your book?"

I smiled. It was a revelation that I could tell delighted him, not because of personal vanity, though clearly, as time went on, I realized, he very much liked making himself a character in my book, but because at that moment he understood in a flash of intuitive perception that what I was writing was in no sense detached history or art history or hagiography or a romance set in the Middle Ages, but something more like a novel, a literary work, drawing on details that, I hoped, would bring present-day Conques, including himself, to life as the work revolved around its mysterious central presence: Sainte Foy. He seemed to have understood the exact nature of what I was doing, and from that day on he began to tell me things, things about Conques, about himself, about Sainte Foy, about the tympanum; he began giving me details, glimpses, illuminations, *aperçus*, confidences, that he knew I could shape for my book. When he heard I had not yet gone into the house of Monsieur Rémy Montourcy, the Devil, he said very firmly, "Anna, it is your duty as a writer to go in and see his house."

Just then, that day, when he first understood that he was going to be in my book, and the kind of book it would be, he said, sounding like Mister Nabokov: "It is the details, Anna, the divine details that make a work of literature.

"Oh, I will tell you a delightful little detail," he said. "There is a constant dispute between Père André and Frère Isidore—they do not like each other, you know—and one of the *frissons* of their quarrel is over how many times the first bells, the call to mass should ring. Père André thinks it should be very brief. Everyone who is going to come to mass is already up, in any case: they know what time it is. It is he who says the first mass, you know. And he sets the bells to ring accordingly. But Frère Isidore wants to wake the whole town, and when he has his way, the first call will ring for five minutes. People in the hotel are wakened needlessly. The bells will ring 125 times when Frère Isidore has set them, and about 15 times when Père André does."

"So depending on which one of them has his way, the bells of Conques will ring between 746 and 636 times every single day, summer, winter, all the time," I said.

"Except," Jean said, "between Holy Thursday and Holy Saturday evening, when the Angelus is silenced and the Fraysou leans out of his window at the top of the Rue Émile Roudié to blow his conch shell to call the people to church.

"All these bells are automatic, you know," he said. "But then the bells of the call to the *grande messe* on Sunday, the bells ringing out musically, those are played by Le Fraysou, those and the bells for the marriages, the baptisms, the deaths, Le Fraysou plays those as well."

"Madame Benoit told me that before the soldiers took them away during the Revolution, there were eight bells in Conques, and they all had names," I told him. "The largest was called Le Saint Sauveur (Holy Savior), and the smallest was La Manderelle."

"Very good, Anna," said my new professor.

"I will be there at Estoulène above the Croix de Fer," Rosalie told me earlier. Estoulène or L'Estoulène is the name both of a place where at the end of the last century traces of the old Roman road (or of a road older still) were found, and of the spring that is piped from there down to the reservoir above the town and provides the water for Conques; but Rosalie always designates in which of her gardens she will be working in the evening at Estoulène by its position in relation not to the road to Saint Marcel nor to the *source captée* itself but to the lovely wrought-iron cross on its base of red sandstone in the V where the road from Saint Marcel comes into the *rocade*. The cross stands there for Rosalie and Charlou as the sign of their land, stands tall, its Jesus in proportion tiny: His magnificent body hangs on the cross within a sunburst; His head has fallen to one side; far below at the base two angels, no larger than the dying Christ, stand with folded wings, the back of their wings almost touching, their heads bowed, their hands pressed together and raised in prayer.

"I will be above the Cross of Iron," she said. And now as we climb the road, its grassy bank above us to the right, we hear Rosalie's voice. She is carrying on a conversation with Monsieur Charlou, who is somewhere off in the meadow with the two massive cows, Fleurou and Parisii—Fleurou, the Hollandaise, a black-and-white Holstein; and Parisii, the Brune des Alpes, with her smooth beige-brown fur.

We cannot see any of them but I know that in the last light Rosalie is bent over, pulling up weeds and cultivating the earth with her trowel, and that Charlou is off at the far edge of the meadow beyond, cutting hay with his scythe while he minds what Fleurou and Parisii are eating. From her bent-over position, rising up from time to time, to look around and breathe the evening in (beautiful woman!), Rosalie is singing out her chatter for Charlou in the patois, so Jack and I can't make out what she is saying.

"That voice! That voice! That marvelous voice!" says Jack. He claims that Rosalie's voice comes from the generations of girls who did their courting watching their sheep or their cows on one mountain while they carried on a conversation with the cowherd or the shepherd on the mountain across the valley. And who later minded their children, I was thinking, with their voices, making sure the little ones didn't go in their play beyond the reach of those strong, protective, and enchanting voices, while they went on in the kitchen preparing the noon meal for the men who would come in from the fields; and who, when the children were grown would talk to the woman in the next house or the house across the way, as Rosalie does with Madame Benoit.

Sweeping the kitchen floor after breakfast before her first *clients* come in to buy their fruits and vegetables, Rosalie will call out, "Ehhh, Madame Benoit." And Madame Benoit will come to her window across the Rue du Château and the chitchat will begin. Or if Rosalie is upstairs in her house, running her dust mop around the floor of one of the rooms, and she hears something interesting going on out in the Place du Château, she'll stop everything for a moment, open the window, and call down, and gaily, gaily—that's the way Rosalie is—she'll throw her bit into the conversation.

"Rosalie, *bonsoir!*" we call out as we begin to mount the steep path that leads up the bank from the road to her garden.

"*Attention!* Be careful not to fall!" she calls out, and then we are there at the highest of her gardens, which was also planted last. A vegetable patch it is, a big, squarish vegetable patch, plowed up in the meadowland.

"Ahh! There you are," she says. "Ahnnah! Monsieur Jacques! At last! You brought your *lampe électrique?*" She comes to greet us, stepping carefully down the rows of her garden, walking toward us in her pretty dress, her garden apron, her comfortable body—not slender, but comfortably full—laughing; she is speaking of this and that, in French now, in her voice with its wonderful strength and its girlishness, in her voice that seems to have many chords in it, so that when she is joyous it sounds as if it were rained through with tears—the tears of laughter, of submission to life, to giving it her all.

The hay is not yet cut and the evening smell, rich and fragrant, is rising from the newly turned black garden earth. The mountain

wall beyond the Dourdou seems immense, rounded against the
clear sky, which is still light and pale except to the northwest beyond the Lot, where it is a deep red, as rich and velvety as the petals
of the rose Rosalie has entwined in the iron cross.

We kiss, touching Rosalie's soft cheeks on the right, the left, the
right again, as if it had been days since we had seen her. Her eyes,
her face, her smile, and the pearls around her neck catch the light
of the western sky and reflect it in the darkening evening.

"*Regarde! L'étoile de bergère,*" she says pointing, and as I look to see
the evening star, what she calls the shepherd's star, she reaches out
to try to grab my flashlight and steal it from me. I play and hang on
to it.

"Shine it!" she commands. "Shine it! Look!" she points to a row of
shoots. "These are the leeks coming up!" she tells us. "And in this
row cabbages! Here are onions! Ahh, *regarde!* These will be
turnips." It is not quite night yet, but without the flashlight none of
these shoots and leaves would be visible against the black earth.

"Now," she says, taking my hand in her warm roughened hand
and pointing the flashlight at the row of young ash trees that have
been cut and stripped of their leaves and branches, stuck into the
earth at intervals, and tied in pointed arches. "Look at the beans!
See, they are beginning to climb. See!" Then we walk along the narrow path beside the lower border of the garden, where the land
falls off abruptly down to the road. "These are gladiolas," she says
proudly of the shoots, tulip-like, coming up along the border.
"Here are marigolds and marguerites. Marguerites for innocence,"
she says. "And up there! Shine it! Beside the stakes. Those will be
tomatoes. And, *regarde,* there are the potatoes. And over there"—
she moves my hand—"sunflowers! Sunflowers will grow up, they'll
grow up to be taller than you, Ahnnah, they'll grow to be as tall as
Monsieur Jacques, perhaps.

"And here," she says tenderly, "here are my lettuces." She stares in
the light of the *lampe électrique* into the leaves that will become the
lettuces.

Rosalie loves lettuces and she loves a lettuce salad. "Full of vitamins," she always says, and she serves a salad at lunch and at supper
as well with a little chopped garlic and a simple vinaigrette, with oil
and the red wine vinegar she makes in the huge earthen jar behind

her woodstove. (When the moon is old, she says, that is the time the vinegar makes, that is when it becomes clear; and Rosalie always keeps a stick of elderberry bush in her vinegar because one of her uncles told her to do that.) She uses olive oil or, on special occasions, as long as it is plentiful, walnut oil, their own walnut oil, rich and fragrant.

On winter evenings in January and February, night after night in their warm kitchen with the fire burning in the woodstove, after supper and before their nightly tisane (*infusion* or tea), Rosalie and Charlou sit at their kitchen table shelling walnuts. Perhaps Charlou's brother, Ricou, comes over to help and talk, or Dany and Denis Geneste. The shells are saved to light the fire in the woodstove, and the walnuts are put in special baskets to take early in March to the mill on the stream that leads into Espeyrac, to be pressed there.

First a wood fire is built under the *pressoir* and the walnuts are cooked, Monsieur Charlou explained once. Then after the first pressing they are cooked again before the final pressing. This oil is kept in two immense jars in a cool closet in their basement and poured off with a funnel into bottles as they use it or as it is bought. It is the best walnut oil in the world, and it makes a wonderful salad, as Rosalie makes it, or as you get it at the Hôtel Sainte Foy, mixed with walnuts and Roquefort cheese and tossed in with tender *frisé*.

"How many walnut trees do you have?" I have asked Monsieur Charlou more than once. "Oh, I have not counted them," he always says. "Two hundred, perhaps." Walnuts are his principal cash crop. Some of the trees are thirty-five years old and were already planted when he bought his land. Others are young, striplings tied to stakes at the edge of Rosalie's garden.

It is a delight to look down the steep hill at Estoulène through the slender smooth gray trunks of Monsieur Charlou's walnut grove, especially in autumn, before the walnuts fall and after he and Michel and his uncle from Saint Marcel have finished cutting and clearing and raking the grass in wide circles under each of the trees.

(I have observed that when Michel and his uncle from Saint Marcel came to help Charlou clear the ground under the walnut trees,

Michel's uncle, who is a landless working man, is paid in cash by
Charlou at the end of the week, after their last lunch at Rosalie's,
but the arrangement between Michel and Rosalie and Charlou is
one of those mysterious exchanges referred to by Laurence Wylie
in *Village in the Vaucluse:* Michel helps with clearing the land under
the walnuts in the fall, and at haying time he brings his machine
down from the plateau and pitches in to help Charlou with the haying, and in return for this, Rosalie has his two children, Jerome and
little Arnaud, to lunch every day during the school year, providing
them with marvelous mothering, a civilizing influence, and much
gaiety, not to mention the most nourishing and delicious of foods.)

"One year I had only two kilos of walnuts," Charlou said. "A frost
early in May when the walnuts were flowering killed all the walnuts
at Estoulène for that year. Higher up at Bourrious the walnuts were
not touched by frost, and down in the valley of the Dourdou they
were protected by the fog. Other years I've had as many as two
hundred kilos," he said.

"My lettuces," Rosalie says now, bending down to look in the
light of the *lampe* at the tender shoots coming up through the black
earth. She brings her hands together, half clapping, half praying in
her rapture.

Once in springtime when Madame Benoit came back from Paris
tired and depressed, Rosalie, trying to help, said, "I cannot be sad,
no, I cannot be sad when I see my daffodils begin to bloom."

And I remember Rosalie's pleasure once when I was with her in
her magic garden beyond the walls of town. (I call it a magic garden
because you enter it through a tall wooden door in the stone wall,
and a cherry tree spreads out its branches over the door; and within
the garden there are four walnut trees and an abundance of parsley
and chervil and sorrel and flowers and all the other things Rosalie
grows, and the garden seems to hang suspended on a ledge over
Conques and the valley; but Rosalie refers to it as her garden by the
capellette, little chapel-shrine.) We were in her magic garden by the
capellette in autumn at the end of an afternoon, and Rosalie was
picking up walnuts here and there in the last light, pulling up carrots, going down a little farther to get some turnips for our soups,
and there she found among her turnip leaves a *coulemelle!* A

coulemelle growing there, of all places, among her turnips! A beautiful mushroom it is, with an oval cap when young, and as it grows,
it opens like a little paper Japanese parasol to reveal soft, feathery,
fluted white undersides, its cap a lovely mottled brown, leathery
like the back of an old man's hand. (Usually it is Monsieur Charlou
who finds the *coulemelles* in the meadows when he is out there with
Fleurou and Parisii.) "Oh, my garden," said Rosalie, "how darling it
is!" And she had in her voice all the rapturous delirious ecstasy of a
child as she picked the magic *coulemelle* and insisted on giving it to
me, and then parsley, too, and a garlic clove, so I could cook it up
in oil for Monsieur Jacques for supper.

Rosalie is an artist in so many ways, and one of them is the way
she has remained a child, loving her gardens in innocence with all
their wonders and surprises, and how, for all the work they need
from her, her skill and knowledge, there they are—her gardens,
filled with a profusion of beauty, seven of them in addition to her
kitchen garden on the Place du Château.

Three of her seven gardens outside the walls of town are at Estoulène, a kilometer away from the Porte de La Vinzelles by the
cowpath, as Jack and I call it—the old road to Sainte Anne, Grand
Vabre, to the ferry at the Bac (which means ferry), and on to La
Vinzelles beyond the Lot. The three gardens at L'Estoulène are the
garden *above* the iron cross; and the one where we saw Rosalie
working earlier this evening down through the walnut trees, the
garden *below* the iron cross; and the garden *at* the Croix de Fer, in
the V, in the prow of the ship that is their property, as I feel it to be
here in this high steep place where we are somehow partly spinning
off into the sky and moving along through it smoothly like a great
ocean liner cutting through the sea.

Farther on to the northwest another half a kilometer or so and
slightly down the mountain, above the old road to Ste. Anne at La
Crosette where an old pink stone house stands falling into ruin
among the fruit trees—pears, peaches, apples, and plums of several kinds including the golden Mirabelle, La Reine Claude, and a
small pale lavender plum called Sainte Foy (for it ripens for the
sixth of October)—there Rosalie has a fourth garden, near the
stream where Charlou grows his watercress. Beyond La Crosette

on the steep west-facing hillside (*côte*) their vineyards begin. Some of the grapes are white but most are the black *mançois,* the *cépage* (vinestock) brought here by the monks of Conques centuries ago.

These are the grapes of the wine of Conques and also of the wine of Marcillac, which occasions at times the uproarious and somewhat naughty song that Monsieur Charlou loves to sing and conduct: "*Lou bis de Marcillac*" (the wine of Marcillac). He sings it with a number of suggestive gestures and hump-hum-hums until he and everyone else break off finally into helpless laughter.

Rosalie has three more gardens—her magic garden by the *capellette;* a garden she calls the garden *below* the *atelier du forgeron* (where I have never found her); and her garden across the way from the cow barn, the garden she calls the garden *above* the *atelier du forgeron.* I have found her there many times, for when she is up in it, in the late afternoon, she sees everyone coming through the Porte and she calls out, if she chooses, to engage whomever in conversation. (There are a number of people in Conques, I notice, to whom she simply does not speak, even when they pass within a foot or two of her outside her house.) This is the steepest and most perilous of her gardens, for if you fell off the path climbing up to enter it, you could fall twenty or thirty feet down to the road; and the garden itself is cultivated right up to the edge of this clifflike drop. "*Attention!* Be careful not to fall!" Rosalie calls out when she lures me up there to get a leek or a lettuce or some strawberries or flowers. And up I go into the high world of her garden, where I feel myself to be for that moment the most privileged person on earth.

Rosalie claims that the *forgeron,* Monsieur Fabre, crosses the road and stands below the garden when she is working near the edge and engages her in conversation solely for the purpose of trying to look up her skirts. She has overheard him more than once telling one person and then another how *white* her thighs are. Rosalie tells this as if she were outraged. Then she laughs and pulls up her skirt so you can see he was speaking the truth. Her thighs are indeed very white.

"*White!* White the way Charlou's *feet* are white," Jack said when I told him this story.

We both recall one October afternoon when we found Charlou barefoot in one of his walnut trees near the road. He had climbed up into the tree to shake it so that the walnuts that were ready would fall into the circle of clean, raked grass below to be gathered. He had climbed up barefoot, we understood at once, in order not to damage the bark of the tree; and the whiteness of his feet, of his "aristocratic long-toed feet," Jack said, the whiteness and smoothness of his skin came to us both as a revelation about this man, whom we see usually in his rough work clothes, his fine-boned, weathered, sunbrowned face frequently unshaven ("*Ça pic! Ça pic!*" cries young Jerome, Michel's son, in pain when the time has come to kiss Monsieur Charlou before he goes back to school after lunch). His strong and skillful hands are earthworn, blackened by walnuts or purpled by grapes, toughened and callused by work with his knife, his scythe, his shovel, his pitchfork. This strong, hardworking farmer with his broad brow, wide cheeks, large nose, and the long, thin mouth of his ancestress Mary, standing in the paradise of the great tympanum—this man is slim, sensitive, slight in build, aristocratic in form, in the shape of his feet, his hands, his brow, and in the perfect smooth whiteness of his body we have never seen.

And so is it with Rosalie, though she does not go out into the sun to work until late in the afternoon, and then in a straw hat to shield her fair face, still, when you see her, though you see the full-blown beauty of her face, her blue eyes, her thick, shining, wavy hair, still, when you see her, it is always somehow her work-worn hands you see, for though she scrubs them and scrubs them, she can never quite get the black earth, the walnut stain, out of the webbing of the lines that cover her hands, and she is forever getting a finger cut by a thorny bramble or a weed, or she gets a splinter or a burr, and these injuries she shows like a child, pained but proud, when we get back to the light of her kitchen at night; so you see this woman with her radiant beauty and you see at the same time the scratches on her legs, and you feel and see the warm rough work-worn hands of one who, lying down at last at night in her flowered nightgown in the clean and fragrant sun-dried sheets of their marriage bed, reaches out, her thighs glowing white, to touch the smooth white body of her husband.

"Now *that* is what a marriage should be," says Madame Benoit in her proud, authoritative way. "Look at the way they work together,

the way they help each other, the way they take care of one another."

"Ah, ha-ha-ha!" says Charlou, laughing, in the season when the
mushrooms grow in the woods. "You know," he says (not in
Madame Benoit's presence), "what is the best mushroom of all?" He
laughs. "The best mushrooms," says Charlou, "the best mushrooms
of all are, ha-ha-ha, the mushrooms that sprout up under the sheets
in bed."

"They speak of country matters," Jack whispers in my ear later as
we laugh together in our joy in our life here.

"Lettuces! Lettuces! Lettuces!" Rosalie sings once more,
whirling the beam of the flashlight round and round in the patch
that will grow up into lettuces. "I'm a rabbit!" she says. "You, Aan-
nah, you are a rabbit. And Monsieur Jacques is a rabbit." She
touches him playfully. "We are all three rabbits!" she says. But it is
the chickens who get most of the lettuce she grows, all of the outer
leaves of every head and whatever may be left over each day after
they and we and her *clients,* as she calls them, have taken their fill.

Rosalie speaks proudly of her customers who come to her
kitchen in the mornings to talk and to buy the produce of her gardens. It's not so much a shop as a *salon* Rosalie holds in her kitchen,
but nevertheless, all the while, she is weighing this and that with the
old iron scale she holds up with her hand to measure out a kilo, two
kilos, of beans, potatoes, leeks, spinach, whatever is in season. Or
she'll be running downstairs and up, calling out, keeping the conversation going all the while; she'll be in the apple-fragrant downstairs closet where she keeps bunches of pearly brown onions tied
with rope, all hanging in rows (in these closets it is cool and the
temperature even, for they are below ground level on the Rue du
Château), or she'll be in the room above the *cave* where the apples
are stored with elderberry flowers gathered early in June and dried
in the shade, to conserve them; or she'll be in the closet where she
stores the jars of the various pâtés she makes, and the *cornichons,* the
jams and jellies, the *confit de canard,* the green beans, the conserved
cèpes and the *escargots.* Not all these things are for sale by any
means—they are made and saved for the grand fête days of the
year—but honey she sells, their own honey and the honey of the
Rouergue, very good too, brought by a honey merchant, and wal-

nuts she has ready by the bagful; and occasionally, too, she sells a rabbit, specially ordered in advance. Also, if you ask her, she'll open the door of the *frigo* in her kitchen and get out one of the round quivering fresh white cheeses she makes in molds from the milk that's left over after Fleurou and Parisii have given to Conques each day all the creamy milk it needs.

Now in the near night we hear their hooves as they come slowly, swaying, down the steep road. We hear their breath and then their munching as they stop to eat delectable clover growing by the side of the road. "Fleurou! Parisii! *Ven! Ven!*" Charlou is following them, his *sabots* clopping on the pavement. "Ahhhhhh," he groans in mock exasperation, this patient, loving man.

He has had Parisii for eighteen years, and Fleurou for almost as long. He keeps them in their barn during the heat of the day in summer so that they will not be bothered by flies, and he brings them out to L'Estoulène late in the afternoon.

"*Attention!* Be careful not to fall," Rosalie calls as we descend the path to the road to join Monsieur Charlou and follow the slow majestic progress of the cows back into Conques, to their barn.

Hidden in the grass by the edge of the road outside the garden down at the *croix de fer* are baskets filled with strawberries, lettuces, asparagus, which we will carry into town with us. Jack insists on carrying two of the baskets so Rosalie and I each take one, and as we cross the *rocade,* Rosalie catches hold of my hand, both woman-motherly and childlike, trusting; we hold hands, we are girlfriends, smiling and laughing as we walk along the path with Jack, following Monsieur Charlou with his scythe in his right hand and a bundle of hay on his back, neatly balanced across his shoulders on his rumpled blue cotton-canvas work jacket.

Charlou does everything just exactly so—gently, skillfully, and perfectly. Nothing is ever hurt—no potato or apple is bruised—and nothing is ever wasted, not the time he spends minding the cows nor the space on his back when he walks them in at night. In July, after the hay has been mown, he will begin to cut the broom that grows wild higher up where the meadows end, and he'll carry a bundle of broom on his back into Conques each night. The broom is dried and used through the winter to light the fire in the woodstove in their kitchen each morning. And some of it, too, is tied into brooms, excellent for sweeping, especially in the barns and out of doors in the stone streets.

In May, when the fragrance of broom flowers fills the air and the hillsides are yellow where the broom is thick, Rosalie and Monsieur Charlou go up with their baskets and fill them with the plump yellow butterfly blossoms, which they then dry in the shade. An *infusion* of broom flowers is good for stomach troubles, Rosalie says.

As we follow along after Monsieur Charlou, he occasionally taps the huge flanks of his cows with his scythe to keep them moving and to keep them from straying from the path. "Fleurou! Ahhh! Ahhh! Parisii! Ahhhhhhh!" His ankles are naked, his feet bare in his *sabots,* made by the *sabot* maker down in Grand Vabre. (The best *sabots* are made of walnut wood, Monsieur Charlou told me. "Always the wood from the base, the lowest part of the tree trunk, because it is the strongest. Walnut wood is the best—it is harder, stronger, and lighter. But walnut wood is rarer and rarer now. Most *sabots* are made of beech wood nowadays." He always rubs a new pair of *sabots* well with garlic before he wears them to keep the wood from cracking.)

"Fleurou! Ahhh! Parisii! Ven! Ahhhh!" They have stopped once again to eat something delectable.

Jack loves to imitate the sounds Charlou makes talking to his cows when he's trying to get them home to bed. The "Ahhhs" of different tones, each one different, louder, progressively more mock-exasperated, as if he were telling them he cannot *believe* their greed when they stop yet again to eat something. It's as if he were saying, "Ahhh, Ahhh, Ahhh, it is too much, too much, I can't believe you can be doing this yet again. Ahh! Ahhh. Fleurou. Parisii. *No!* It can't be true. No! Not again!"

Once, in the fall, when we were proceeding along this way and they stopped, both of them, to pick up apples in their enormous mouths, he turned and looked back at us. *"Gourmandes!"* he said, grinning wildly, his partly toothless grin.

Fleurou, the black-and-white Holstein, who is a *coquine,* a rascal, has wandered on ahead a bit, and Parisii, who is more bovine and trustworthy, is quietly eating. Charlou strokes her beige-brown fur.

"Feel her! Come feel her!" he says to us. "Come here." He invites us to do the same. "Caress her," he insists. He laughs, his mouth spread wide in a momentary look of insane delight. "Feel how warm and soft she is," he says. Gingerly we touch the warm silky side of Parisii, sensing the large fragile frame of her bones, the delicate way her skin and fur is stretched over this frame, protecting the warm animal mystery within.

Parisii begins to move again, following along after Fleurou, and Monsieur Charlou proceeds behind, off in his world with his cows, it seems, cut off from us.

We three stand for a moment looking back to the northwest, where the red has faded now into night. *"Regarde!"* says Rosalie. "La Vinzelles!" We see the four street lights of La Vinzelles like a diamond-shaped constellation in the vast black north mountain, merging now into the night sky beyond the Lot. Rosalie is carried away by its loveliness. She has never been there. "Oh, but I long to go, I long to go! Someday," she says.

How mysterious to think that Rosalie's rich and vibrant life, almost all her full and playful and passionate life, has been lived here within a radius of less than ten miles—since she was eighteen, here at Conques; and she has never been to La Vinzelles, which lures her with its starlight lamps.

She has been working since she was a tiny child helping her mother with the younger children. Rosalie, as the first of ten children has been since she was five or six helping to carry hot water from the cauldron in the hearth into the next room, where her mother was giving birth to the new baby, helping to mind the older ones, to feed them, instruct them, play with them, knit and clean clothes for them, and wash their clothes in water so cold sometimes she has to break the ice to do the laundry.

And as soon as she was able, she went out to work on farms roundabout. She'd go to rake up the hay here, at this farm, or to gather chestnuts there, at that one, or to help at the time of the killing of the pig at that one. Rosalie points. The owner of that farm was after her then, and he *still* is, Rosalie says, whispering. I tell him we are too old now, she says, laughing.

When she was eighteen and came to Conques to work in the Hôtel, she sent home money to help the family. (Just think of what she must have looked like then, says Jack, carried off in a rapture by the thought of the young Rosalie, rosy-cheeked and dewy-skinned, with her blue eyes and her thick, black, glowing hair, waiting on a table or carrying a breakfast tray into the room in the morning.) Most of her life, except for the few months in Paris when working in a hotel that belonged to an uncle, and except for her wedding journey with Charlou to Les Saintes Maries de la Mer in the Camargue (where the air, says Charlou, is very bad), she has spent hereabouts.

There stands La Vinzelles, sparkling in the night on her horizon. "Rosalie," I tell her, "Jack and I can take you there one day in our car."

"In the fall," she says. "After the *vendange*. There will be time then."

I try to describe their church, I try to tell her how the stone is white inside and wondrous, full of light, but the thing about it that is most curious is that the bell tower is not directly above the church; it is just to the side, up the mountain, built on a rock just above the church roof. There's a path, I try to tell her, and you go up that onto the rock above the church and you can look right into the tower at the huge iron bell itself and down onto the roof of the church, below the rock. (Jack couldn't quite make out that detail when, looking with his binoculars from the ridge above Bourrious, he first discovered La Vinzelles. He was trying to get a better look at the almost black Château of Selves, which is above La Vinzelles and to the west about a kilometer, when the tiny village clustered around below its church appeared in his view, and we decided to go there one day on our bikes.)

"And there's a beautiful statue of the Virgin Mary in a niche above a fountain by the cemetery," I tell her. "*Une Vierge Romane*" (a Romanesque Virgin), I say, "of painted wood. *Une belle Vierge Romane*." I say that because that is how Babet Fau described it when she told us about it. (We had not seen it on our first trip to La Vinzelles on our bikes.)

The Virgin at La Vinzelles, however, is standing, like somewhat later Gothic Virgins (and Virgins later still), with the Christ Child in her arms. But the look in her eyes, the look on her face, is that of the Romanesque Virgins seated in majesty—the *Sedes Sapientiae*, the Throne of Wisdom—holding the Christ child, the Word made flesh, in their laps—the look in the eyes of those Auvergnat Virgins of the twelfth century that we first saw when we were walking from Le Puy to Conques. These Romanesque figures, who are sometimes Black Virgins, hold out their large, long-fingered hands to protect the child whom they have borne, while in their eyes is a look of dazed grief and the knowing of all time, which penetrates the infinite tenderness, the love, they have for the Christ child, who they know will grow to be man crucified and die. The look in their eyes is the look of the knowledge of the miracle by which the child was conceived of God and born to grow to manhood, when he must die to be resurrected and taken unto the Father who is God, Who He is, and in Whom He is. It is the look of the Mother of God, who knows that the sword shall pierce her heart, for in His birth lies the destiny of His sacrifice. This look of tranced grief and tenderness disappears in time from the face of the young mother and reappears on that of the older mother holding the dead Christ on her lap in the pietàs of the fourteenth and fifteenth centuries in this region of central and southern France.

"*Regarde!*" says Rosalie. "*Le Pont Romain!*"

Far down below us we see the lovely old bridge spanning the Dourdou, its ancient red-sandstone Romanesque arches reflected in the water below.* It is illuminated gently, accidentally, by the streetlights of the *faubourg* and by the lights of the little inn, the Auberge du Pont Romain, built on the edge of the river.

---

*This old bridge with its "*dos d'âne*" (back of an ass), as Jean-Claude Fau says to describe the way it rises to a ridge about a third of the way across and descends then toward the far side, has, we are told, foundations of Roman construction and was part of the Roman road, which, it is suggested, turned at L'Estoulène to go south to Conques by the Porte de La Vinzelles and down to the bridge over the Dourdou and onward to Cahors, the ancient Divone. But Pont Romain does not, as Fau points out, mean Roman Bridge (in French *Romain* means Roman and *Roman* means Romanesque), nor is it a misspelling, as I had first thought, of *Roman* (Romanesque); rather, he says, it means Bridge of the Pilgrims, its name descending from the ancient word for pilgrim, *romieu* or *roumiou,* which we find so frequently preserved, he says, as, for example, at Fontromieu, in the place-names of this country around Conques and along the great pilgrim routes.

The old bridge had long fallen into ruin and the road as well, it is assumed, when Dadon at the end of the Dark Ages came to this wild *conque* to devote himself to God, but two hundred and some years later, early in the second millennium, it was here and rebuilt, we know, for it is mentioned in the *Book of Miracles,* in the eighth chapter of the fourth book.

This miracle was described by the anonymous monk of Conques who later in the eleventh century, after Bernard of Anger's death, wrote down further miracles that "by their merit simply could not be allowed to be lost to posterity or to remain unknown to the world beyond this corner of Aquitaine." It tells the story of Raymond, son of Bernard, the powerful lord of the Château of Montpezat. "Many of us had heard of this Raymond," the author says, "for he was renowned for the impiety of his acts, the nobility of his birth, and the ostentation of his pride." He had been sent by his parents to Cahors to the canonical school so that he might be attached to the College of Canons at the Cathedral of Saint Stephen. But Raymond "contracted the terrible and incurable malady of epilepsy, his seizures recurring at the time of every new moon." Hearing on all sides tales of the miraculous cures of Sainte Foy, Raymond came to Conques, and at her tomb he obtained by her benevolence the favor of a healing. After that he returned each year in gratitude to venerate the relics of Sainte Foy, his protector. "But his parents had developed an aversion to him. They could no longer place any hopes in the magnitude of his intelligence or in his abilities, and his brothers coveted his patrimony." They hated him with such abomination that together, his father and brothers, seized him and handed him over as hostage to the powerful Lord Gausbert of Gourdon de Castelnau de Montratier, with whom his father was at war. Lord Gausbert, who also saw Raymond with an irreconcilable hate, threw him into a dungeon. "It was the commencement of the holy time of Lent, which by the frugality of its observance leads to penitence and the washing away of sins," our author tells us. "But less salutary than that of hermits. Once a day he was fed a piece of moldy bread so hard that even soaked in water it was difficult to swallow."

His chains pressed cruelly against Raymond, for Lord Gausbert feared his extraordinary vigor and strength. He was bound with fetters and triple-locked chain as if he were a lion. Raymond was hardly able to move, and the chains that were wrapped round and round him were so heavy he could scarcely breathe. He prayed continually to Sainte Foy, invoking her name, begging her for his escape. This he did in all his waking moments, and when he could, he escaped from his afflictions briefly in sleep. So it was that on the night of Palm Sunday, "when the joy that filled the world with palms and flowers had hardly been able to penetrate into the miserable dungeon of poor Raymond," a young man, all resplendent, appeared to him and said, "Raymond, are you awake or are you sleeping?"

"Who are you, my lord?" he answered in his sleep.

"I am the proto-martyr Stephen, stoned to death. I have been sent to conduct you promptly to Sainte Foy."

"But how can we find her, the glorious virgin Fides?"

"Rise," said Saint Stephen. "This is no vain dream. Follow me and you will see her."

Then the sleeping prisoner crossed fields and moved through forests with the shining Stephen until they stood on the bridge over the Dourdou under Conques. Saint Stephen spoke, describing in detail the scene he would see in vision above him, identifying the glorious Fides with lines from the Song of Solomon as the dove, the undefiled one, the only one of her mother whom the daughter saw and blessed, the one who looketh fair in the morning, fair as the moon, clear as the sun and terrible as an army with banners.

When Raymond raised his head he saw the cloud as brilliant as fire on the summit of the mountain above; and in the midst of this cloud of light he saw the virgin Fides, radiating beauty and surrounded by a multitude of angels, to whom she spoke, asking them to sanctify the place below where her bones were guarded. He saw the angels all joyous to do her bidding, raising their right arms and shining with light and tracing the beloved sign of the cross over Conques. As the place received thus an abundance of holiness and grace, a thick vapor rose up from the Dourdou and covered the bridge and enveloped Raymond and rained on his clothes.

Coming to himself in his dungeon miles away in the country of Cahors, Raymond found that his clothes were wet with this rain water, he found that the chains that had so cruelly pressed against him had unrolled themselves. He was able to move. His feet were free. He was able to stand. He pushed against the door of his dungeon and its huge locks gave way without a sound. He crossed, run- ning, the jailers' room and hurried up the stairs and found the guards sound asleep. Finally he arrived at the upper apartments. There he paused, trying to figure out what to do. His chains had been much too heavy to even think of taking them to Sainte Foy. Then he saw a chessboard leaning against the wall. This he seized to take as a testimony of his escape. He went out, jumped from the high wall, not harming himself, and set off at a run.

But his feet were bare and the stones on the road were cutting into them painfully . . . and so it was that, at last, in time for the Easter Vigil, Raymond arrived at Conques, crossing over the bridge where he had stood in dream not a week earlier. He lay the chessboard ex-voto at the feet of Sainte Foy and fell on his knees before her and opened his heart in prayer. Then, having made the sign of the cross over his forehead and over his heart, Raymond recited publicly in detail the marvels accomplished by Sainte Foy in delivering him from the immense chains. Among the listeners in the assembly there was, by chance, Godefroi, the son of Lord Gausbert, come, he also, with an escort to make his devotions. He was seized with astonishment and asked how it could be possible that the captive could have been delivered from such chains. His astonishment redoubled at the sight of the chessboard, which had belonged to him.*

"All then recognizing the marvel of divine intervention made the basilica resound with their acclamations in honor of the power accorded to Sainte Foy by the Lord, who glorifies her merits by all sorts of prodigies."

Now as we move on toward Conques, the Pont Romain is hidden from our view. For a moment Rosalie sings, *"O Sainte Foy, nous mar-*

---

*This is, by the way, one of the earliest mentions of a chessboard in the literature of the West.

chons vers toi, O Sainte Foy." The melody moves like a fragrance through the night air and makes a lump come into my throat. It is the hymn we sing following the statue of Sainte Foy in procession on her festival day, when she is carried, enthroned, on her litter, by Charlou and three other men, who bear her from the Treasure, following the great processional cross (carried by Monsieur Louisou, Charlou's brother), the bishop, the archbishop, the prelates, and the monks carrying the censer; when we move across the cloister toward the East singing *"O Sainte Foy, nous marchons vers toi, O Sainte Foy . . ."* and in the pure light of day she seems more silvery and delicate and fragile and alone, borne along, a bit unevenly over the cobblestones behind the chevet of the church, so her lovely lantern earrings jiggle with their rubies and opals and trails of tiny pearls. Round toward the parvis before the western doors of the church we follow, singing then, *"Chantons, chantons, chantons Sainte Foy,"* and watched by the eyes of Christ in the great tympanum, we enter the Church of Sainte Foy, singing still, *"Chantons, chantons, chantons, Sainte Foy,"* as Rosalie now sings.

She leaves off and stops to examine the edge of the path. "It was right here. Yes, it was right here that the boys pushed Madame Benoit over. She was blindfolded."

That's what I understood Rosalie to say. "Some boys pushed Madame Benoit over? Blindfolded?"

Rosalie hears the horror in my voice and she begins to laugh. "A long time ago! Ahnnah! A long time ago when she was a girl. She wasn't hurt. She had blindfolded herself. She said she was going to walk as far as Espeyrac and back without seeing, like Guibert the Illuminé in the year that he was blind. The boys followed her and pushed her over here. Right here. They were jealous! Jealous! She wasn't hurt though."

I look down into the cherry trees and the walnut trees growing there. It is a good fifteen-foot drop. Maybe more. "But that's a long way to fall," I say. "That's about five meters, wouldn't you say?"

"She wasn't hurt," Rosalie says. "Oh, a few bruises and scratches, *sans doute,* but . . ."

"Another miracle of Sainte Foy," I say.

"*Ooouant,*" agrees Rosalie, matter of fact. (That's the closest I can get to the way people around here say *oui.* They may speak the old

Occitan language, but no one ever, so far as I know, says "oc" for
"yes" anymore. They say "*ooouant*" or "*oouehh*.")

As we continue, the path narrows and we go single file, downward. Above us in the night we can feel the mountain earth held
back by the stone-wall embankment, grown over with ivy and
blackberry bushes and grapevines. A towering rock rises up to the
right, and elderberry and hawthorn crowd the path. (An *infusion* of
hawthorn blossoms and leaves, gathered in May and dried in the
shade, is good for the heart, says Rosalie. And elderberry blossoms
gathered also in May and dried in the shade are good for the spring
cure, as well as for the conserving of apples. I remember seeing
Charlou come into their kitchen with a basket of elderberry blossoms—sprays of white quivering in their fragile loveliness. Suddenly one of those large bloodcurdling slimy brown *limaces,* slugs,
appeared among the blossoms, and to my vast admiration, Rosalie
plucked it off with her bare hands and dispatched it.) Below us
there are young ash trees, in a little grove, and we can hear sheep
startled beyond the trees in the night. Their hooves beat against the
earth as they run. "Bahhh!" says Rosalie. "Bahhhh!" No reply.

Just before the *capellette* the path widens and we emerge into the
light, starlight and Conques-light, where the path turns toward the
east to go down to the Porte de La Vinzelles; we stop a moment
below the steep slate-roofed tower of the *capellette,* where high up
behind protective bars, within a wooden altar niche, a statue of
the Virgin Mary also of wood stands with her child, who holds the
ball of the universe in His hand. The colors have long since faded,
so that she stands there gray as shadow in her perfect loveliness.
The statue was carved in the fifteenth or sixteenth century, and the
modeling is exquisite, the child voluptuous in His babyhood, the
young mother in her motherhood, serene with a touch of a smile
on her lips. I come here often and climb up the garden steps opposite to be able to see her better, and others too come here, bringing
bunches of flowers, which they leave in metal rings below the niche
to honor her, la Vierge Marie, and vases, too, of flowers they leave
sometimes, pushed inside the iron bars.

Once, in the eighteenth century, the historian the Abbé Servières
reports in his book *Conques: Ses Origines, Son Histoire* (Rodez, 1907),
a man climbing up the tower wall with the intention of doing some

harm to the statue or the relics contained in the altar fell and was blinded. And in the nineteenth century, three women down in the *faubourg,* looking up one afternoon, saw angels holding a golden monstrance hovering over the pointed roof of the *capellette.*

We stand looking out at the southern sky above the mountains opposite, where constellations glimmer like golden birds in the treetops.

"Look at the stars now. Ahnnah! Monsieur Jacques! *Regarde le Chemin.*" Rosalie means the Milky Way, which they call the Chemin de Saint Jacques, the Road to Saint James, or simply *"le Chemin."*

"La Capalette," Conques

I remember being here with Rosalie one August evening when the moon was more than half full, just at that point when the last of day was blending into the moonlight, and Rosalie began speaking of the stars. "Look how pale they are. You can hardly see them," she said, "yet there they are, there are the stars, it's *drôle,* they are always there, moving in circles, there is the moon, and here is the earth. They say the earth is round like a ball; it is everywhere the same. You go over that mountain, and the next, and the next"—she was gesturing—"and it is always the same, it's *drôle,* the stars, the moon, the sun, the earth. They say it is the same in Germany. Is it the same over there where you come from? Are the stars the same?"

"Yes, the same, the same stars," I said, filled with new wonder.

We continue on. Rosalie gives me her basket and opens the wooden door and steps into her magic garden for a moment to pick up another basket.

As we descend we see a dim light in the stone cowbarn that is built with its back against the thick old stone wall. Monsieur Charlou is bedding down Fleurou and Parisii for the night, and as we pass Jack nudges me with his elbow to remind me to admire Charlou's manure pile outside the barn under the old horse chestnut tree. Earlier today when we saw Louisou, Charlou's oldest brother, standing with his sheep in the field down near Goubert, standing straight with his staff, Jack said, "They are so elegant, they are so elegant in everything they do, all three of those brothers. Look how he stands there with his staff watching his sheep." And now speaking of Charlou, Jack says, "Every motion he makes in his work is elegant and perfect. Look at his cow-manure pile, how perfect he makes it. Every day he adds to it, but always it remains a perfect rectangular cube." As we pass, Jack claims he wants to send it to the Tate Gallery in London as a permanent installation because it is so perfect, so . . . (he finds the word)—minimal.

Back in Conques some of the baskets are left off in Rosalie's kitchen garden, where she washes leeks and carrots and turnips and potatoes, and so forth, in basins with a hose that comes from a spring in the hillside. The lettuces are left in the old *écurie,* the stable, and strawberries and asparagus go directly into the kitchen.

Jack goes on up the stairs back to our house to do a little work. Actually, he'll wash the dishes first. I know Rosalie suspects this to be so, but I go on pretending she doesn't know. I go in with her to get our milk and hang around her yet a little longer. Her legs are so weary I want to help. I ask if I can take the milk for her to Madame Castelbou and to the bakery. Sometimes we do this together. Rosalie laughs. She gives me the key for the door at the bakery. *"Portaille de laitch,"* milk carrier, she says, instructing me in the patois. *"Portaille de laitch,"* she says again sternly and then laughs when I try to mouth her mother tongue, it sounds so funny to her. She sends me off. This bottle for Madame Castelbou and this for the bakery. "Be careful not to drop them," she says.

I like doing this. Conques is quiet now, all the shutters are closed and everyone is asleep in their houses, it seems, except for us. On the far side of the Place du Château I open a wooden fence gate and cross a stone terrace to leave Madame Castelbou's milk right outside her door. Down at the bakery, next door to the bakery shop, I open a door with the key that Rosalie gave me, and I put their bottle of milk inside the door on a shelf to the right.

I go back to Rosalie's the long way, drawn by the church, by the need to be near it. Its thick walls seem to soften and to blend somehow into the night air, and the vast interior volume of the church wells up with the huge, mysterious, and shadowy Presence. Walking along past the stony length of it on the road halfway above, and stopping to look down on the scalloped schist-rock roofs of the radiating chapels, and on the oval roof of the *chevet* above them, and looking out at the great majestic volume of the church, I feel this immense and yet somehow humble, warming earth presence which is God filling the ancient church, swelling it somehow from silence into sound.

It is almost as if the church were breathing; and the sounds of the splashing of the Plô and the waterfall sounds of the Ouche down in the valley seem to penetrate through the walls and to be intermingling and coming from inside the church like whispers, like breaths, like prayers, like the echoes of chants going on and on in praise down through the ages, like bells ringing; so that beneath the hush of the Presence there is a kind of thronging silence calling up the memories of the lives that came to linger here in this hallowed place where centuries earlier Saint Fides lay entombed at first behind the altar of the Holy Jesus, with whose altar she afterward busied herself, using her girlish charms and wiles and tricks and jokes, and her great power, to obtain the gold that was needed to cover it from end to end; while she herself sat in majesty, crowned, and covered, too, with gold and gemstones, her hands raised, her head just so looking off into that light that long before, in the hour of her martyrdom, had come to comfort her and bring her great joy; and in those centuries of long pilgrimage, when she was not taken out in procession, she sat guarded by the iron grillwork that linked the columns of the choir with an iron webbing of spiraling scrolls interspersed with lozenges and flowers that formed a pattern of transcendent beauty and rose to barbed points with dragon heads and sharp tongues swooping down; so that from the irons of the prisoners she had miraculously freed, a transparent screen was made whereby the profane body might in no way enter, but the eyes, the mind, the spirit of the pilgrim could pass through from the material world into the sacred candlelight, into the aura of warm gold and many colored gemstones covering the body of this so feminine child, to touch the very bone heart of the holy shrine.

"Guibert, are you sleeping?"

"Yes, my lady, I am."

The streetlamps flicker in the windows of the church and seem to be the lights coming from the candles burning even now before the altar of Sainte Foy and the altar of the Virgin Mary in the vast stone quiet of the holy place.

When I return, Rosalie has lit the fire under her soup kettle, and she has put the plates and the soup bowls out on the table. The salad in a bowl is still over by the sink. Under the dim bar of fluorescent light in the ceiling, Rosalie is looking through a box of buttons and other sewing things for a coin she wants to show me, an ancient coin she found when she was digging up potatoes.

"Look!" she says, bringing it out. "Look! It is gold. It is very ancient. Look at the head!"

She gives it to me to hold.

The gold is warm. I try to see it better in the dim light. I wonder if I see the Grecian-like head, the curly hair, of Vercingetorix.

"It might be Gauloise," I say. "It might be the head of Vercingetorix."

"Ooouant," she says. "It is very ancient."

I am not at all sure of what it is. Rather, I am carried away by the feel of the old coin, by the thought of it up there in the earth of the potatoes in Rosalie's garden near where the Roman road passed. I don't disconnect this glimmering coin, difficult to see in the dim light above the table, from the feel of Rosalie's hands finding it in the black earth and the trails of little roots that must have come up with it.

When Charlou comes back I can see from the look in his eyes how tired he is. I start to leave. Rosalie brings the soup to the table and fills his bowl. He opens the drawer in the table and pulls out a loaf of bread. He makes the sign of the cross on the loaf with the Opinel knife he carries always in his pocket, and then, holding the bread against his chest, he slices it, cutting toward himself. He sits down, and sinking some bread into his soup, he begins to eat immediately.

"Bonne nuit, Monsieur Charlou," I say.

"*Bonne nuit,* Madame Ahnnah," he says. Often he simply calls me Ahnnah and he smiles at me and tells me that I am svelte. Charlou is very attractive to women, I have noticed, and I am no exception. I am pleased out of my skin by his compliments.

"*Buéne nuèch,*" I say in the patois, as Rosalie has taught me. "*À demos,*" see you tomorrow.

Rosalie begins to give me things—some strawberries, some parsley, two stalks of asparagus. We go out the kitchen door and she gets two eggs out of the coffer where she keeps them and pretends she is going to stuff them inside my blouse. Then she goes back for a bag for me to carry all these things and the eggs or I won't be able to get home with them and the bottle of milk as well. She apologizes that the eggs are no longer warm. When they are still warm, sometimes still hot, even, from the hens, she smoothes them across my eyelids and her own, for they are good for the eyes.

She comes down with me for a last check on Mr. Rabbit and his intended wives hopping and nibbling in their separate stall in the *écurie,* or stable. We stand a moment in the street outside her door. She points up at the house of the *forgeron,* at their bedroom window, all shuttered, and reminds me to be quiet, for—leaning her head to one side and putting her hands beneath it—she indicates that Monsieur is snoring.

When I come back to our house I hear the sound of Jack's brush swirling around in water upstairs in his studio. He is still working. I go up the other stairs in the *"petit appartement,"* as the Fabres call it, to my studio room above our kitchen for a few minutes.

The wooden cross is vanished now into the night above the black mountain mass. My room is stirring with soft leaf shadows moving in the dim light that comes from the streetlamp attached to the house, and from another streetlamp above, beyond the old walnut tree in the Quartier du Palais. There is a feeling of peace and mysterious life in this small room with the good wooden typing table Jack built for me in front of the southern window. (We've had to stand the bed against the windowless western wall of the room to make room for me to work.) My typewriter is closed. The antique crystal inkwell Jack gave me gleams in a pool of light. I can see my pens and pencils lying dormant beside it, and my grandfather's Chinese silver dragon-worked *feng shui* compass and sundial, my minutely carved ivory Eskimo husky dog, my rosary made of beads from the wood of a cedar of Lebanon (symbol of the Virgin "because of its beauty and the healing virtues attributed to its sap, and its height, which raises it over all the other trees, as the Virgin is exalted above all other women"). Madame Benoit brought the rosary to me specially from San Damiano, blessed by the Virgin, and it lies around the silver medallion of Conques and Sainte Foy with Prosper Mérimée's diagram of her church. These talismans I carry back and forth across the ocean with my manuscript and notebooks, dictionaries and other necessary books, and my fragrant round box from Pointe au Baril made of birch bark and sweet grass and porcupine quills, in which I keep paper clips.

I touch the papers and smooth the booklet Père André gave me earlier. Then I sit down at my table for a moment and pick up the pages I worked on last. They're thickening and they have reached the stage where they begin to feel good—rumpled and curled at the edges. They have been written in ink and then typed and then written over with ink. I cross out, compress, correct, add things, and think of more things and write them, and type it all up again, over and over, often thinking of something more as I type. By now these pages are dense with the gray words of my typewriter and the blue-black words in ink. They are ready to join the rest of my manuscript to await a final typing, and I am ready to go on. Always I read, hearing it all, either in my head or really out loud—in the unself-conscious trance of work I am not aware which, it is just that I hear it. I listen, all in the process of trying to bring it to life and to get it right and make it evoke what I envision.

Beyond my room the ear of Conques, the deep and ancient concha, is filled with silence soothed by the sounds of waters rushing, waters falling. I shut my eyes and put my forehead down on my typewriter and I think of Conques as the ear of Sainte Foy. I see her down in the night of the walled Treasure and I think of her ears, how large and clearly defined they are, the gold concha of her ear shaped like that of stone-and-earth Conques; I think of her earrings, which are gems hanging from her ears to light the way of pilgrims to Sainte Foy, to light the way of prayers to her ears, to her who listens that she might pray to the Lord for whoever prays for her intercession with Him; and Jesus hears her, and He reaches out to touch, to almost touch, the head of this young saint who prays so ardently; so one might say that entering into this age-old place of pilgrimage, which took its name from its shape—*ad instar conchae*—and praying here and reaching the ear of Sainte Foy, one reaches the ear of heaven. There are in heaven "golden vials filled with odours which are the prayers of the saints" (Revelation 5:8).

At Glanum we saw the stone slab of an ancient altar to Cybèle, and on either side ears were carved in the stone so that the goddess might hear. The ears of the Christ of our great tympanum are exceptionally large so that all the sorrows, the love, the turmoils, the hopes, and the fears in the hearts of humankind below might reach Him along with the prayers of Sainte Foy. And the fourth-century head of the Roman god-emperor, too, was made with ears larger than life so that, with its eyes on the beyond and its face purified of personal characteristics, it could be in time transformed into the head of Sainte Foy to wear the crown of her martyrdom and be graced by her lantern earrings—"veritable jewels of the most elegant form," Père André called them, these miniature lanterns with luminous oval garnets and moon-white opals set into the beaded goldwork, and minute pearls and garnets like tears falling from them, all glimmering faintly, as her eyes, even in the dark, give forth the radiance shining through them. She sits in majesty, stiffly, bearing on her person through the night jeweled images of ancient stories, of the gods and goddesses of the myths: Jupiter seated, his glowing upper body naked, holding Nike, the goddess of Victory, in the palm of his hand as if she were a doll; Apollo the healer, god of light and truth; Mars; Mercury; Ceres, goddess of the harvest and fecundity with her sheaves of grain; Diana; Minerva; Fortune, the goddess of abundance, carved in an emerald, her breasts gleaming as she holds in one hand sheaves of grain and in the other a cornucopia; a Nereid exulting as she rides on the back of Triton; the cow of Myron walking across an oval brown chalcedony with the luster of wax; another cow lying in the shade of a tree on purple amethyst; beautiful Isis, elegant Isis, standing with her sistrum on the face of a smooth black tourmaline; Ulysses as an old man walking home to Ithaca in the brown, white, and blue landscape of a ribboned agate; Hercules engraved in carnelian, the paws of the lion of Nemea fastened around his neck; Hygeia,

The earrings

goddess of health, giving food to the serpent of Aesculapius; panthers, a billy goat, satyrs and Mainads dancing; Aeneas carrying his old father, Anchises, on his shoulder and leading his little son Ascanius by the hand, fleeing the slaughter of burning Troy.

All these intaglios, engraved by masters of the glyptic art in ancient Greece and later in Rome, came down the course of the centuries, miraculously minute in their perfection, accumulating, often, magic powers to become at last the votive gifts of pilgrims to Sainte Foy. Here at Conques they were sown by the goldsmiths like flowers in a field upon her golden majesty, while ever, on the back of her throne, deep in the ovoid crystal carved in the time of Charlemagne, Jesus hangs on the cross, subsuming all within Him: "First, Midst, and Last, Converted One and Three . . ."

And she, looking out with this knowledge contained within her and shining through her, appears very much as she did in that time close to the turning of the first millennium when, after the celebrated healing of Guibert the Illuminé, she was much occupied going far and near all over the province, gathering gold and gemstones for her own statue as well as for the great altar of the Holy Savior.

She looks much as she did on that night when, as she sat in majesty in her church, well guarded, with a lantern ever lit beside her, she went off to ask Bernard, the abbot of Beaulieu, to bring his golden doves to her at Conques. Her throne, she felt, could not be complete without his golden doves—so wonderfully fashioned these doves were, all gold, and inlaid with precious gemstones, as Bernard of Angers tells us in the sixteenth chapter of the first *Book of Miracles.*

Sainte Foy, he writes, went off to visit Bernard, the abbot of Beaulieu, by night and appeared to him in dream, as was her way, this young saint of the most radiant beauty, still a child, not yet quite adolescent. And though she spoke to the good abbot clearly in her pure celestial voice, asking that he bring his golden doves to her at Conques, still, when he awoke in the morning, he brushed off the memory of her request, telling himself it was but a dream.

The following night she went off a second time and appeared to him again in dream, saying, "Good abbot, my father, I am Sainte Foy, I ask you most graciously, please, to bring your golden doves to Conques and offer them to me ex-voto. I need them, you see, to complete the summit of my throne."

And a second time, on rising in the morning there in his abbey on the banks of the Dordogne, two or three long days' journey from Conques, Bernard, the good abbot of Beaulieu, said to himself as he looked at his golden doves, "It was only a dream."

But when she appeared to him a third time, he recognized the fact that the request came from heaven. In the morning he held his golden doves in his hands. So wonderful they were, the jewels in their eyes catching the light so enchantingly. Surely, he thought, the saint would be content with an equal weight in gold.

So he set off on a pilgrimage to Conques taking with him not his golden doves but gold, gold that weighed as much as, or more than, his golden doves. This gold he offered to Sainte Foy most solemnly and he rested three days and nights at the abbey of Conques and made his devotions.

On the night of his return to his abbey at Beaulieu, however, she appeared to him once again in dream. This time Sainte Foy spoke to him in a fierce and urgent manner. It was his golden *doves* she wanted, she declared; not all the gold in his possession would satisfy her: She must have his doves!

So fierce was she that his dream awoke him in the night. Then, though weary from his long journey, he deemed it wise that he set off again as soon as daylight came, to go once more on pilgrimage to Conques. This time he took with him his golden doves, and when he arrived he offered them most humbly for the summit of her throne. He set them there as she had wished, telling one and all the story of how Sainte Foy had come to ask for them in dream.

There the golden doves remained for many a year to grace the memories of those who came on pilgrimage to Sainte Foy, as Bernard of Angers noted, commenting that they completed graciously the decoration of her throne. There they remained, and when they disappeared nobody now alive knows.

But when you stand still in front of Sainte Foy for a period of time, her statue—which, by the presence of her relic and by the mysteries of art through the centuries, leads one beyond the material world into the realm of the spirit—seems, owing to the tricks of one's own body's blood and nerve and brain movements, to be aware of the life breathing in the world around her. Her eyes appear to move ever so slightly, as if in her tranced inspiration of the Light which is the Lord she is nevertheless conscious, as she always has been, of the here and now, of the ones who are near, praying, yearning, needing help and comfort, and of the ones who are in other ways interested in the details of her statue. Her hands, too, holding the tiny vases, appear to move while yet she holds them absolutely still.

And occasionally a smile appears on her lips, a smile that is not so much a smile as the look of trying not to smile—the antique smile, Jack calls it. At these moments, I am fond of imagining, something about her Père André is delighting her; or perhaps in the vast mysterious reserves of that memory she recalls her guardian of old, the warrior-monk Gimon; and then, one by one, the people and the stories of her many *joca* drift into her consciousness, and she cannot keep from smiling; she cannot keep from smiling, either, when she remembers the trouble and effort the good abbot of Beaulieu had to go to before, reluctantly, he brought his golden doves to her.

In her stillness, too, she, her face like the mask of a Celtic deity, knows perfectly well who came to abscond with her doves, and how they were punished by the Lord for this sacrilege.

"Her I call La Puissante [the Powerful]," Père André said to me one day, waving his white-robed arm in the direction of the majesty of Sainte Foy. "And her La Gracieuse [the Gracious, the Grace-full]," Père André said, indicating the lovely statuette of Sainte Foy with her oval face and her high forehead and her long, flowing hair, standing with eyes downcast, holding her grill and her palm, the statue in silver and gilded silver made at Villefranche de Rouergue in 1495. It gives off like a perfume the sweet essence of grace, of modesty and peace.

Ahh, Père André, what gifts he has given me—the gifts of his richly spiritual, loving, intelligence, the gift of his faith, and of his closeness through years to Sainte Foy.

During the long winter season, when there are only a few visitors to the Treasure, and Père André has time to himself, he sits in his office next to the entrance, reading, writing, taking care of correspondence, working on whatever comes to his attention, or on whatever he thinks needs to be said. He annotates books and articles on Conques and the Treasure, at times with wonderfully acerbic and sometimes eccentric comments, in his beautiful clear hand,

in the book margins or between the lines. He writes about Sainte
Foy with the deepest care and love, explaining her, illuminating her
and her message.

He has a wonderful vocabulary and a marvelous command of
language. He wants to write a book about Conques during the Revolution, but I don't know if he has begun it or whether it is still in
the form of notes and ideas. There are times, he told me, when for
long periods he cannot write at all, not even a letter. His huge intelligence does not escape torment. He keeps a journal, but not in
his office. His journal he writes at night in his room before he
sleeps, I believe, but whether he does this during his painful periods of depression, I do not know.

(Nor will I ever know, for on his death, his journals will be
burned. Ricou, Charlou's brother, will say to me with tears in his
eyes, "He is with the angels now.")

Sitting here in the night, I do not think of that near future when
Père André will be with the angels and we will cry for him gone
close to Sainte Foy. Rather, I think of him so alive and ample in his
white monk's robe just the other day down in the Treasure, saying,
"Regard the splendor! Look at the wonder of what she has gathered
around her. And kept with her through the centuries, through wars
and revolutions, not to mention the temptations of private greed.

"The richness of it all!" he said. "Not a month passes that I don't
discover something new I have never seen before."

(This is true for all of us who devote ourselves to Sainte Foy. One
fall when Jean Sègalat went to Venice and returned after ten days,
he said, "Tell me, Anne, what did you discover while I was gone that
you had never seen before." I took him into the church and showed
him the face of Sainte Foy I had found in late October when the sun
is low and the church fills with its soft light. I had found a face of
Sainte Foy looking out from her prison in the fourteenth-century
mural on the wall of the sacristy—so touching, it moved me to
tears. "Very good, Anne," said my professor.)

"Come, look at the reliquary of the arm of Saint George," Père
André said. This Saint George whose arm bone is preserved within
a thirteenth-century arm reliquary of silver and gilded-silver, is not
Saint George who killed the dragon but he who, as a boy, was a student in the abbey school and became then a monk of Conques until

he was elevated to be the bishop of Lodève in 877. There he is buried in the cathedral.

"Look!" said Père André. "Tell me what you see." The silver sleeve is smooth outside an inner, filigreed, gem-sewn sleeve tight around the wrist. The hand is raised in the blessing (or the sign of the Word). Low down on the sleeve, beneath a jeweled rectangular door which once could be opened to reveal the relic within, we see a very small figure of Christ in gold nailed with three nails to His cross. Above His cross flies a haloed eagle. "Regard the halo of the eagle," commanded Père André.

"The halo has a cross," he said. "The eagle represents the soul of Jesus Christ." He spoke softly, awed and moved. "I never saw that before today."

We looked at the minute image of the soul of Jesus Christ flying upward from His cross at the moment of His death; and filled with sad joy, we drifted along past shining reliquaries, past the smiling face of Jesus sitting on the lap of Mary, His raised right hand representing the inspired and inspiring Word, the Holy Wisdom, which we receive as the sign of blessing. We moved on until we stopped before the reliquary of Pepin.

"As a work of art it is sublime," Père André said as we gazed at the front of the rectangular reliquary in the form of a church or a house where, beneath the filigreed roof with the images of the sun and moon in circles of gold repoussé surrounded by pearls and sapphires, and between the tall figures of John and of Mary, Jesus hangs on His cross so touchingly, His body almost filling the space of His cross. His nailed hands, His naked arms are lifted as if in praise of God His Father, even in His pain; and His head, which we usually see fallen forward in the hour of His death, is here tilted slightly to the side as He, still living, His halo gleaming, looks out and down from His large eyes with an expression of such sorrow and compassion that one cannot look upon His face without being stirred. "Forgive them, Father, they know not what they do," He said. To the good thief He said, "Today thou shalt be with me in Paradise," and with these words He formed a crucible of hope for the generations of believers to follow Him in time: Like the good thief, they, too, might come to be with Him in Paradise.

Now the town bells ring twelve, and then slowly, twelve again. Midnight is come. Formerly it was the proper hour of matins, and the monks filed into the church to chant the psalms and prayers of the hour.

Père André sleeps in his room above the cloister close as ever to the chapel of the Treasure. *Caretaker of this radiance,* he signed himself in English, wondering if we could say that in English. Ahh, Père André, caretaker of this radiance. I think of this radiance there somehow in his mind, even as he sleeps, warm and gold, a soft, round, interior light.

Wasn't it that, this radiance, that the people of Conques struggled and contrived to keep during the Revolution—not the gold and the gemstones the soldiers sent by the Directoire were after. No, the riches belonged to no one. It was for the relics from the age of Christ Himself and the centuries that followed, and the art that they inspired to contain them a thousand, nine hundred, eight hundred, five hundred years ago, for these rich yet humble reliquaries and the bits of wood and cloth and flesh and hair and bones that they contain, in particular the bones of Sainte Foy and the radiant voice of God speaking mysteriously through her reliquary statue, their palladium—this is the radiance they risked their lives to save on the eve of the hour when all this would otherwise have been lost to the world.

So I sit here in the dark at my typing table, looking out into the night with the wings of my mind hovering over my book of Sainte Foy. Even though it is still only partway to where it will be, and even though I have many times despaired of being able to make it as good as it must be, still it has already brought so much to me as I work to bring it to life and inform it, absorbing knowledge, which in turn is absorbing me and leading me toward Christ the Word.

.   .   .

A year ago in the fall as we slept in our bedroom under the roof in the "*grand appartement*" above Jack's studio, I dreamed the roof was gone and I could see the night heavens and all the stars in that part of the sky, the southwestern sky, where I would have been looking, asleep in my bed on my back. I could see the stars, and then suddenly from either side, all around, all the stars swooped toward one another, curving, looping, with luminous tails like comets, like falling stars in their swiftness, while I lay there in bed stunned, breathless. And then the stars formed a cross, which stayed in the sky as if for me. The cross was outlined in bright stars, and within it was studded with stars in a lovely pattern, and it seemed somehow fragile and delicate, not terrifying at all but sweet and feminine and beautiful, as if to say, Look, see how pretty I am; and I knew somehow in my dream that the stars in the form of the cross were like Sainte Foy, they were herself turned into stars in the cross of stars.

My dream seemed so tender and dear to me, so glorious, that I was afraid I might cry if I spoke of it. I wanted to tell it to Jack but I didn't think I could. I didn't even think that I could write it down for several days, I just kept it there in my mind, in the lump in my throat. Then I wrote it.

That evening at supper Jack talked about the cross. What a perfect symbol, he said, and he spoke of the eloquence of its forms and of the spaces it creates. He was talking about Christianity, about what a mysterious religion it is. He loves it when we sing in church during mass, "*Il est grand le mystère de la foi,*" of the faith. Sometimes he says this almost crying when he sees something anew, like Jesus holding Mary His mother when she—her soul—becomes in His arms a little child again at the moment of her death. "What other religion has such mystery?" he asked. I told him my dream through my tears and he said it was like a vision.

I thought of how when I first saw Sainte Foy, the top gone from my head, I seemed to see through the walls of what we ordinarily call reality her perfect body and soul, preserved as radiance in the space of her statue, and the angels who stood round her; so in my dream, the roof gone from the house, as I lay there stilled in my sleep, an infinitesimal being, I witnessed the stars in the heaven move in a way defying all natural laws to show me a cross, within

which seemed to be Sainte Foy, whose colors were given to heaven, LITTLE
revealing the light which is ever present and yet beyond in her who SAINT
knew the face of Christ outside of time in the hour of her martyrdom, manifesting herself in the here and now of my mind by the
will of God: "God is marvelous in His saints."

A small figure of Sainte Foy, not more than eight inches high, appears on the reverse face of the great processional cross in silver
made at Villefranche de Rouergue in 1503, eight years after the
statuette Père André calls La Gracieuse. In style she resembles the
graceful girl Foy, holding her grill and her palm, wearing her robe,
but there is a halo round her head on the cross, her eyes are closed,
and she is more sensually rapturous than the earlier statuette, as she
occupies on the reverse face of the bejeweled glowing cross the
same position that the crucified Christ occupies on the front. But
this cross is not like the cross of my dream.

Later I saw that the cross in my dream was like the cross on the
reliquary of Pepin, "that radiant splendor," where Jesus stands
somehow, His feet splayed, suspended in the confines of His most
elegant cross, which is defined by tiny pearls and green jade-stones
set, each one, in minute globes of gold, the whole itself contained
by double rows of exquisite gold pearling all glowing like the stars
of my dream, like the stars of my dream, which moved as won-
drously as seraphim, all luminescent with folded wings, soaring in
the night to form a jeweled cross filled with the soft radiance that
seemed to be Sainte Foy somehow revealed for me, mysteriously
there in the starry cross in the heavens, saying, "Don't be afraid.
See! See how pretty I am! See what I can do!"

Endnote

As a writer, Hannah was often called a perfectionist, and that used to drive her to distraction. She felt sometimes that it was a comment on the length of time it took her to produce a body of work rather than on the work itself. *Little Saint* took an especially long time for a number of reasons. Hannah had to educate herself for this volume, relearning French and chasing down and translating obscure sources. The more she learned, the bigger the book got. It grew from one book with nine chapters to three books. Too, Hannah was dealing with the ongoing life of a village. The story deepened as the people of Conques came to trust and love her and share their stories with her. She changed the names of some of the villagers but not others.

At the time of her death, Hannah was very close to finishing this first book. She had planned to pull out some of the more scholarly material from the body of the work and fashion the information into informal notes to appear at the back of the book. There was a section, too, that she had wanted to add right before the ending.

I met Hannah in 1983 at New York University when she was teaching a writing workshop. While she and Jack were in Conques, I stayed in their apartment on Barrow Street. I also began typing on the computer the manuscript for *Little Saint* and notes for the two later books.

(The idea of translating her work onto a disk was almost miraculous to Hannah.)

After her death, her husband, Jack Wesley, and I sat down and read the manuscript from beginning to end. Our concern was that the book wouldn't feel complete. But we agreed that it did. We sent *Little Saint* as promised to Sam Vaughan at Random House, and he agreed with us. We all knew that if anything was missing, we couldn't fix that. The only thing we would be able to do was check for unintended repetition, and Jack would be able to clarify details and questions about Conques.

To edit *Little Saint,* we three sat down together for days with the manuscript after it had been through a first edit and then copy-edited and went through it page by page. There were some lively arguments, but all the changes made were by unanimous consent. For much of a week, we immersed ourselves in Conques, hearing Hannah's voice, feeling her passion for Sainte Foy and the villagers, remembering her generous spirit, missing her.

Sam Vaughan deserves a great deal of thanks for his guardianship of the *Little Saint* book, and his patience. Like Gimon, he's keeping the candle lit for Sainte Foy. Like Hannah, he's a Protestant and a "stranger to saints," too. He points out the interest, dedication, and commitment of Random House people, including: Deborah Aiges, Virginia Avery, Kimberly Burns, Andy Carpenter, Amy Edelman, Karen Jones, Carole Lowenstein, Eric Major, Timothy Mennel, Tim Mooney, Stacy Rockwood, Kathy Rosenbloom, Carol Schneider, Olga Tarnowski Seham, Joseph Sora, Sheryl Stebbins, and the specialists in Mary Bahr's rights department, including Sabrina Hicks, Tracy Howell, Tracy Pattison, Linda Pennell, and Lainie Rutkow.

This may not be the book that Hannah ultimately wanted it to be, but, like the tympanum at Conques, one must look at the work "in time, with time." *Little Saint* is a beautiful, complete, unfinished work.

—*Sarah Glasscock*

HANNAH GREEN, wrote Robert McG. Thomas of *The New York Times* in her obituary, was "an acclaimed author who wrote one slender novel of . . . delicately distilled perfection." She died in 1996, six months after her "classic work," *The Dead of the House,* originally published by Doubleday in 1972, was reissued in paperback form by Books & Company/Turtle Point Press.

Married to the artist John Wesley, Ms. Green was born in Glendale, Ohio; studied with Wallace Stegner and Vladimir Nabokov; and taught at Stanford, Columbia, and New York universities.

Her work was published in *The New Yorker.* She was also the author of one book for children.

SARAH GLASSCOCK is the author of the novel *Anna L.M.N.O.* and worked closely with Hannah Green.

Hannah on the road to Conques

ABOUT THE TYPE

This book was set in Galliard, a typeface designed by Matthew
Carter for the Merganthaler Linotype Company in 1978.
Galliard is based on the sixteenth-century typefaces of Robert
Granjon.